THE PRU-BACHE MURDER

THE PRU-BACHE MURDER

THE FAST LIFE AND GRISLY DEATH OF A MILLIONAIRE STOCKBROKER

JEFFREY TAYLOR

HarperCollinsPublishers

Photographs follow page 152.

The Cat in the Hat passages courtesy of Dr. Seuss Enterprises, L.P., © 1957 Dr. Seuss Enterprises, L.P., renewed 1985.

HarperCollins books may be purchased for educational, business, or sales promotional use. For information please write: Special Markets Department, HarperCollins Publishers, Inc., 10 East 53rd Street, New York, NY 10022.

FIRST EDITION

Designed by R. Caitlin Daniels

Library of Congress Cataloging-in-Publication Data

Taylor, Jeffrey
    The Pru-Bache murder : the fast life and grisly death of a millionaire stockbroker / Jeffrey Taylor. — 1st ed.
        p. cm.
    Includes index.
    ISBN 0-06-017970-8
    1. Prozumenshikov, Michael, 1953–1992. 2. Murder—Minnesota—Minneapolis—Case studies. 3. Stockbrokers—Malpractice—Minnesota—Minneapolis—Case studies. 4. Prudential-Bache Securities, Inc.—Case studies. I. Title.
HV6534.M66P768 1994
364.1'523'09776579—dc20   93-48656

94 95 96 97 98 ❖/RRD 10 9 8 7 6 5 4 3 2 1

ACKNOWLEDGMENTS

I am very grateful to my editors at HarperCollins, Larry Ashmead and Eamon Dolan, for their vision, skill, and enthusiasm. Thanks also to my agent, Ed Novak, who got me started and encouraged me along the way with his storyteller's sensibility and business savvy.

S. J. Taylor, my first reader, gave selflessly for my benefit, offering indispensable guidance and inspiration from beginning to end. Beth Hagen, Tim Converse, and Joe Grace were stalwarts down the stretch. Larry Taylor, my father, was a staunch spiritual advocate and good friend on many difficult days. Heartfelt thanks, one and all, for your patience and support.

I am indebted to Sergei Tikhanen, my guide during a reporting trip to Russia—may he always find a cafe open and amply stocked—and no less indebted to four fine research assistants, Angela Bolton, Arthur Kane, David Unze, and Garrett Weber.

Many thanks to my bosses at the *Wall Street Journal*, Glynn Mapes and Doug Sease, for their forbearance. Thanks to Jane Berentson of the *Journal*'s page-one staff, who edited the article on which this book is based. Thanks to *Journal* reporter Richard Gibson, my collaborator on that article. Thanks to Tim Schellhardt, Chicago bureau chief of the *Journal,* for timely suggestions and moral support. Thanks to John Koten, former Chicago bureau chief, for letting me write the book.

And special thanks to the many of Michael Prozumenshikov's colleagues, clients, and acquaintances who spared time to share their diverse memories of this complicated, driven man.

This living hand, now warm and capable
Of earnest grasping, would, if it were cold
And in the icy silence of the tomb,
So haunt thy days and chill thy dreaming nights
That thou would wish thine own heart dry of blood,
So in my veins red life might stream again,
And thou be conscience-calm'd. See, here it is—
I hold it towards you.

—John Keats, untitled fragment

I know two Michaels, and they are completely different people. They act
different, they talk different, they look different.

—Mark Goldburt, Russian immigrant

PROLOGUE

It was probably a deer that someone had poached and gutted.

There were hundreds of animals about, foraging for what little greenery was left on trees and shrubs above the foot-deep snow. During the latter months of the long Minnesota winter, so many of them starved to death that most people saw no harm in shooting one out of season and gutting it where it fell.

Yes, Jack Turner decided, looking down at the patches of crimson-stained snow at his feet, it had to be deer blood.

But the gate was off its hinges, and that was vandalism.

Someone had barreled through it in a car, or maybe a truck. It was Turner's duty as public works supervisor for Marine-on-St. Croix, a riverside village forty-five miles east of Minneapolis, to report the damage.

The pale January sun had sunk below the line of oak and pine trees to the west, and the temperature, already below ten degrees, was plunging. It would be a nuisance to have a sheriff's deputy out this late in the day. And Turner, a short man wearing a jacket and wire-rimmed glasses, had left his insulated coveralls at home.

Nevertheless, he hopped into the driver's seat of his blue Ford pickup, turned it around, and headed off toward the nearest phone. Ice and gravel crunched and popped under the Ford's wheels as it rolled along a rust-colored road at the eastern edge of an open meadow. The field served as a composting and waste water treatment facility for the village, and it was Turner's responsibility to maintain it.

He eased down the sloping road as it curved left and descended to meet state Route 95. As he waited to make the right turn, Turner glanced at the old steel gate, leaning against a wooden post to his left. One end remained chained and padlocked to the post; the hinges at the other end had been shattered.

It was five minutes to the town's only service station—Standard—where Turner used the pay phone to call the Washington County sheriff's office. He had it in his mind to drive home and change into a heavier coat, but as he climbed into his pickup he saw the green-and-white Washington County squad car cruise by. So Turner followed it to the compost site, humming along with the song on his truck radio, which he kept tuned to a rock-and-roll oldies station.

The deputy, a big man with a blond mustache, introduced himself as Rob Daniels. Together, the two of them inspected the compost-site gate, as Daniels jotted a few notes on a small pad. Then Turner led the deputy up the hill on foot. He had plowed this gravel road the day before to clear away the new snow, and somebody must have been up there since then.

There were three irregularly shaped blood stains, one much larger than the others, and a spot where someone had urinated in the snow. Boot prints led back and forth from the gravel to where the stains lay, about ten feet from a tall pile of tree branches and brush. The snow around the red spots had been flattened.

It certainly looked like someone had cleaned a deer here, Daniels agreed. But there weren't any deer tracks nearby. And where were the guts?

The two men crunched around the brush pile, looking for the entrails. They found none.

Wrestling his way up onto the pile, the deputy came across a big piece of a clear plastic tarp that appeared to have blood frozen to it. He pointed it out to Turner. Then the two men followed a set of prints that led fifty yards to the tree line at the western edge of the field. They found nothing there.

By now the sun had set, and a brutally cold wind was whipping across the clearing. Inside his boots, Turner's feet had gone numb.

Maybe the poacher had thrown the entrails onto the brush pile and they had fallen down inside, Daniels said finally. He would file a report and let the day-shift sergeant decide whether to have another deputy stop by tomorrow.

In any case, it was no good prowling around in the dark.

The morning brought little relief from the cold snap, the winter's worst so far. Yet by 10:30, bundled up in his coveralls and a stocking cap, Turner was back at the compost site to repair the gate.

Still curious about the blood stains, he first guided the truck to the top of the hill. The sound of the engine rousted a few black crows from the top of the brush pile. Otherwise, everything looked the same.

Now, as the crows circled overhead, Turner drove back down the hill to examine the gate. It had once been painted bright red, but years of harsh winters and glaring summer sun had faded the color. There were six horizontal bars spaced over intervals of about eight inches. Each bar was solid steel, an inch in diameter. Whatever hit the gate had dented three of the bars, leaving traces of copper paint.

A new gate would be expensive, and the dents weren't so bad that this one had to be replaced, Turner concluded. A new set of hinges was all he needed. He climbed into the truck, drove to the hardware store in the nearby town of Scandia, and, less than an hour later, was back with the parts.

Even working with gloves, the repairs were easy. It took only twenty minutes to install the new hinges and reattach the gate; the hardest part was dragging the heavy thing across the gravel. But Turner's mind wasn't on the work.

For one thing, he told himself, the field above wasn't visible from the highway. Whoever rammed the gate had to have known what was up there.

Another puzzle: Anybody could see that crashing into a metal gate would bang up the front end of a vehicle. Who would do that just to go poaching?

Turner considered the persistence of the crows. Natural scavengers, they gathered only when they smelled something to eat.

Why were they on the brush pile? What was it they were after?

There had to be something up there. And Turner decided he was going to find out what.

The maintenance man's right index finger stabbed the buttons of the pay phone. There was ringing on the line, then a female voice—the sheriff's office dispatcher. Turner started talking, much too fast.

"This is Jack Turner from the city of Marine," he heard himself saying. "I had a deputy out here yesterday, up at the compost site on Route 95. There was . . . we thought . . . "

"Slow down," the dispatcher said firmly. "Start again."

"I think I found something up at the compost site," Turner stammered. "The sheriff better get back up here . . . right away."

Turner had trotted up the ice-caked gravel road in his heavy work boots, leaving the truck parked by the gate. He moved fast, his breath coming out in steaming gasps.

The snow crunched under his feet as he approached the big pile of brush. He could see discarded Christmas trees among the limbs and branches. The pile was tall, much taller than he was.

He circled it twice, peering through the gaps between the branches. Nothing.

He paced back and forth along the northern edge of the pile, where most of the boot prints were. He spotted an indentation down close to the ground and knelt for a better look.

Then he saw it: A dark green garbage bag, tucked way back among the dried leaves and evergreen boughs. At dusk, it would have been all but invisible.

It occurred to Turner that he hauled most of this brush up here and piled it himself. He damn sure hadn't left any trash bag in the heap.

But what was in the bag? It was too far back to reach with his hands. Picking up a long stick, Turner was surprised to find himself trembling as he began to poke at it.

He tugged down on the bag, but it was snagged on something. He thrust his arm forward with the weight of his body behind it and jerked at the shiny plastic until, finally, it tore free. The lip of the bag came sliding down.

Jack Turner felt the hair on his forearms rise. As he bounced to his feet, a momentary vertigo came over him and a rushing sound was in his ears. He wheeled around, half expecting to find someone behind him holding an axe.

No one was there. He was alone on the frozen field. Tiny flecks of snow, borne aloft by the wind, stung his reddened cheeks. His one impulse, he remembered, was to run—to get the hell out of there.

Now, as if from far away, Turner heard the voice of the sheriff's office dispatcher. Her tone was becoming impatient.

"What is it?" she demanded. "What have you found?"

"I'm not sure," Turner managed to say.

But he was sure. It was a piece of a human body. And it looked like a recent kill.

PART 1
THE STORYTELLER

CHAPTER 1

Michael Prozumershikov placed his hand over the phone receiver and gave his sales assistant three seconds of undivided attention. A stockbroker by profession, he was used to handling two or three calls at once, and he had become deft at making even heavy hitters feel good about holding for him. "I have something here you might like. Let me just check it," he might say, or, "I have a call from the back office to confirm the trade," before jumping on the phone with some other client.

On this day, January 28, 1991, his computer screen showed nothing especially interesting, but now his assistant was motioning for his attention. "Michael," she said, "it's John Petcoff."

Normally this was good news, but today Prozumenshikov wasn't so sure. Petcoff was one of his most adventurous clients, a man who seemed to welcome the risks of speculation. It was easy for a broker to make money handling trades for such an aggressive investor; the sheer volume of the transactions more than made up for the break he gave his client on commissions. Moreover, Prozumenshikov enjoyed Petcoff's homespun manner, which belied his status as one of the most successful venture capitalists in the neighboring state of Wisconsin.

Taking his hand off the receiver, Prozumenshikov apologized to the client on the other end and promised to call back later. Then he punched the button next to the flashing light. "John," he said. "How are you?"

Petcoff's hard work, business sense, and guts, Prozumenshikov knew, had made him a wealthy man. A second generation Bulgarian-Croatian born into a big, poor family, Petcoff had parlayed ownership of a single gasoline service station into a network of stations throughout Milwaukee and its suburbs. Booming population growth had turned many of the stations into prime commercial property, which Petcoff now leased to retailers and fast-food chains.

Petcoff had specialized in buying close-out merchandise from tire and battery manufacturers. Then he moved the surplus goods by declaring himself, in screaming newspaper ads, "Tire and Battery King" of Milwaukee. This, to Prozumenshikov, displayed a streak of intuitive genius: Just by calling himself "the king," Petcoff became the king. The stockbroker had used this simple but potent formula himself, many times over.

Now Petcoff belonged to a circle of nouveau-riche businessmen who lived and worked in the northern cities of Milwaukee and its more affluent neighbor to the west, Minneapolis. At sixty-two, the Milwaukee man showed no sign of slowing his pace: He was developing hotels and buying up undervalued goods, anything from diamonds at an estate sale to geraniums from a failing nursery.

For the past four years, Prozumenshikov and his blue-chip client had carried on a close, if disembodied, professional relationship. It wasn't unusual for them to talk on the phone five times a day. And if Prozumenshikov respected Petcoff's achievements, the feeling was mutual.

The Wisconsin businessman had always identified with his stockbroker's dynamic rise from humble roots. Prozumenshikov, he knew, was a Russian immigrant who had been working as a janitor only a few years earlier. A dentist in his native city of Leningrad, Prozumenshikov knew little English when he arrived in the United States and nothing at all about American finance. Now, at age thirty-seven, he was a senior vice president at "Rock Solid, Market Wise" Prudential-Bache Securities, Inc., working at a showplace branch office that catered to the residents of Minneapolis's most exclusive suburbs.

In his first full year at Pru-Bache, Prozumenshikov had vaulted into the ranks of its Chairman's Council—the firm's top ninety stockbrokers nationally. Before Pru-Bache, he had distinguished himself at Minnesota offices of Wall Street powerhouses Drexel Burnham Lambert and Merrill Lynch, Pierce, Fenner & Smith. It fascinated Petcoff that this expatriated Russian, raised socialist, had so quickly mastered the intricacies of capitalism. Prozumenshikov's career had coincided with the greatest bull market in Wall Street's history, a happy accident that helped him reap material rewards beyond the wildest fantasies of his youth.

Michael was affable, hard-working, and optimistic—traits Petcoff admired. Petcoff knew a good salesman when he talked to one, and Prozumenshikov was as natural and effective at selling as anyone he had ever met. Earthy and direct, Prozumenshikov used his thick Russian accent as an asset, a point of interest for his American clients. He spoke quickly and energetically, spinning scenarios of financial opportunity that appealed even to seasoned business people. Lately, he had snared as clients Scott Studwell and Tommy Kramer, retired stars of the Minnesota Vikings football franchise. This coup impressed Petcoff, an avid football fan who had played for his college team.

Prozumenshikov was particularly skilled at sizing up companies whose stock prices were artificially low, perhaps because their industries had fallen out of favor on Wall Street. He was also well-versed in playing the market in new issues of stock, in which growing companies dole out equity in their businesses in exchange for capital to develop products. And Prozumenshikov had taught Petcoff to do profitable trades, pairing shares of stock he owned with corresponding stock-options contracts.

Over the years, Petcoff had rewarded the broker with hundreds of thousands of dollars in commissions. But in Petcoff's mind, what was more important was that he had put his trust in Prozumenshikov.

Some other brokers were aware of Prozumenshikov's relationship with the Milwaukee businessman, if only because of the tales Michael told about it. One story went like this: Early in his career, Prozumenshikov had called Petcoff without introduction and pitched a stock to him. After doing a few trades, Petcoff was sufficiently taken with the young broker and he invited him to his home in Wisconsin. Prozumenshikov found the house nestled in a wooded compound surrounded by rifle-toting guards and German shepherds. Petcoff led Prozumenshikov downstairs to a basement recreation room. There he showed the broker a pool table, its legs hollowed out and filled with cash. "Play your cards right," Petcoff had supposedly said, "and some of this can be yours."

It was a terrific yarn, one that easily held a client's interest while Prozumenshikov made a sale. It also engendered a certain awe among those of his colleagues with whom he chose to share it.

But it wasn't true. Petcoff had no guards, no house in the woods and no pool table, hollow-legged or otherwise. And Prozumenshikov had never met Petcoff in person.

Not that he hadn't tried. He had repeatedly offered to fly to Milwaukee or pay Petcoff's way to Minneapolis, but his client had declined. In Petcoff's business life, each contact had its proper station, and a stockbroker's place was at arm's length, over the phone.

Before the stock market crash of 1987, Petcoff had never suffered a major loss trading with Prozumenshikov. And the crash, he understood, wasn't his broker's fault. For other people, losing $600,000 in a single day would have been a crushing blow. But Petcoff could afford it. He knew the risks, and it wasn't in his nature to despair. Prozumenshikov, for his part, had been as charming and supportive as ever: "Don't worry, John, don't worry," he had said in his broken English. "We make it back."

Something about Prozumenshikov's guileless manner preempted and deflected anger. Whatever the broker talked about—whether he was praising some fledgling company's stock or insisting that he was best qualified to manage money Petcoff kept at other brokerage firms—his conviction seemed absolute.

Lately, though, Petcoff had been feeling suspicious. Past incidents that once seemed trivial had begun to take on more sinister overtones. On one occasion, Prozumenshikov had asked for an address in another state in order to process a purchase of securities that weren't approved in Wisconsin. Petcoff gave him the address, but felt uneasy about it.

Next came the snafu with Petcoff's account records. Just after Prozumenshikov had taken his latest job at Pru-Bache, Petcoff's trade confirmations had arrived bearing another broker's name. This, Prozumenshikov had said, was because of a mistake at Pru-Bache. Later, Petcoff learned that Wisconsin securities regulators had been holding up Prozumenshikov's credentials while they investigated complaints investors had filed against him. The complaints were dismissed later, but the event had contributed to Petcoff's disenchantment.

Meanwhile, Petcoff's trading losses became more frequent, and they no longer seemed tied to market aberrations. The previous September, a $30,000 loss on stock options recommended by Prozumenshikov had particularly galled Petcoff.

Recently, business publications had run a number of articles about problems in the corporate hierarchy of Pru-Bache, and this publicity hadn't enhanced Petcoff's confidence. In the years to come, the firm would become the target of the biggest fraud investigation ever mounted by federal and state securities regulators. In 1993, it would agree to pay at least $371 million to settle charges that it defrauded investors by mass-marketing risky investments throughout the 1980s.

For his part, John Petcoff had begun to wonder whether anyone at the firm was watching his own Pru-Bache stockbroker—providing guidance or counseling restraint. True, Prozumenshikov encouraged aggressiveness; that had always been part of what Petcoff liked about him. And, certainly, the Milwaukee man wasn't afraid of risk, provided that it was balanced against reasonable expectation of reward. Yet, strangely, while trading with Prozumenshikov, Petcoff's own trading strategies had become reckless—much more so than in the accounts he maintained at other securities firms.

This unnerved him. The Tire and Battery King had known a few compulsive gamblers in his time, and he didn't like what he was beginning to see in himself.

Today, in Petcoff's mind, the gray that shaded his relations with Prozumenshikov had sharpened to black and white. This time he was sure the broker had willfully disregarded his instructions. And for what? To make a buck, he told himself.

"Michael," he said now, "did you get those shares back? The Reebok and the Glaxo?"

For some time, Petcoff had been holding one thousand shares each of Reebok International, Ltd., the athletic shoe manufacturer, and Glaxo Holdings PLC, a British pharmaceutical company. The two companies had suffered through hard times, losing market share to competitors. Since Petcoff bought the shares, the stock prices had plunged.

Still, Petcoff had resisted Prozumenshikov's urgings to sell the stocks, because he believed things would turn around. Sure enough, innovation at the two companies had improved their prospects.

Glaxo had recently developed new drugs to treat nausea in chemotherapy patients, migraine headaches and rashes such as eczema and psoriasis. And Reebok had won back business from archrival Nike Inc., by unveiling a secret weapon: The Pump, an athletic shoe with a built-in air bladder and a gadget that inflated it for a custom fit. Retailing for more than $100 a pair, the shoes had become the rage on basketball courts throughout the United States—so popular that in some cities youngsters were stealing them from one another at gunpoint.

In a strategy designed to maximize Petcoff's return on the Reebok and Glaxo shares, he and Prozumenshikov had sold stock options that entitled other investors to buy the stocks from Petcoff on a preassigned settlement day. The options could be reversed if it seemed likely—as it now did—that the stock prices of Reebok and Glaxo would rise. And two weeks ago, Petcoff had told his broker to reverse the trades.

But Prozumenshikov had failed to do so. Against Petcoff's will, the stocks were bought out from underneath him. And he thought he knew why: Selling the stocks would infuse Petcoff's account with cash. Prozumenshikov could then use the money to buy something else for his client. And Michael would earn a commission on the new trade at Petcoff's expense. He believed Michael had intentionally failed to protect his stocks.

Now Petcoff unleashed a furious tirade against Prozumenshikov. He was disappointed and angry, he said, and he expected Prozumenshikov to correct the trade immediately. "Michael," he said slowly and sternly, "you can't do this. You can't just trade other people's accounts."

Prozumenshikov didn't try to defend himself. He had learned, in years of dealing with customers, that it often was best simply to promise a correction. "I misunderstood you," he told his client. "Don't worry, John, I correct it. Watch the next statement." But even in the face of Petcoff's anger, Prozumenshikov couldn't resist adding a plug for another stock he'd been researching. To Petcoff's astonishment, he started a whole new pitch. Then he attached a moral, one that angered Petcoff even more: "You should never look back, John. You've got to go forward."

Petcoff was having none of it. Until Prozumenshikov got the trade reversed, he said, he wasn't interested in any more stock ideas. "You can't do this kind of thing," he repeated before slamming down the phone. "People just won't sit still for it."

Most clients who got to know Michael Prozumenshikov on the telephone were shocked when they later met him face to face. For many of them, his high-pitched voice, thick accent, and unbridled intensity conjured up a vision of a lean, severe Soviet man, perhaps with black hair and piercing blue eyes.

In person, he looked more like an oversized choir boy. His face was round and youngish, dominated by large brown eyes and a pug nose. His most striking feature was a thick mop of red hair that drew sharp contrast to his pale skin. Once a fireplug of a young man with broad shoulders and a neck like a bull, he now sported a frame filled out by the good life. An even six feet tall, he was an imposing presence, stocky and powerfully built.

Prozumenshikov favored conservative business suits and ties, but he immediately shed his suit jacket when he arrived at work each morning. Occasionally, he would roll up his shirt sleeves to reveal a jagged scar. This, he once told a colleague, was from a teenage knife fight in Russia. Growing up in Leningrad was rough, he explained, but declined to elaborate.

From Prozumenshikov's right wrist dangled a bracelet of twenty-four-carat gold, and on his left he wore a Rolex wristwatch. On one plump finger, a large diamond glittered in a golden setting. The broker was something of a fixture in local jewelry shops, where he frequently traded up to more expensive watches or bought some new bauble for his Russian-born wife, Ellen. He drove a Mercedes-Benz sedan, which he studiously avoided parking outdoors. Ellen drove a Volvo.

In all things, Prozumenshikov's tastes ran to the ostentatious— gaudy, some of his colleagues thought. To their way of thinking, the Russian stockbroker was ambitious but unsophisticated, displaying an obsession for status symbols—the best cars, the most expensive restaurants, Montblanc pens and other costly trinkets. From the outside, his personality appeared to run no deeper than that. Almost no one knew Prozumenshikov well enough to understand what drove him.

Such appetites weren't typical of the five thousand or so expatriated Soviet Jews living in greater Minneapolis. Most of them had come to the United States under the Helsinki Accords of 1975, in which the Soviet Union liberalized emigration policies in exchange for recognition of its territorial gains in Europe. Not all were Russian like Prozumenshikov— some were from Ukraine, Belarus, and other formerly independent countries annexed by the USSR. Many chose Minneapolis because they had distant relatives there. Between 1880 and 1920, thousands of Jews fleeing violent anti-Semitism in Russia and Ukraine had settled in Minnesota.

In this close-knit community of Soviet immigrants, discretion was the watchword. Tremendous diversity within the community did little to diminish the common bond. One frequently invoked saying in Russian, translated loosely, meant: "Don't take your garbage out of the house." The adage had special significance when applied broadly: While Soviet immigrants might quarrel among themselves, to outsiders they tended to present a unified front.

Prozumenshikov was an exception. Ugly confrontations with some of his Russian clients had made him wary of the community as a whole. He was convinced that fellow immigrants were jealous of his success. He had transformed himself, he told colleagues, and climbed so far so fast that it rankled those whose limitations stymied similar progress. Ellen Prozumenshikov, who seemed to many Russians to feel a stronger bond to the community than her husband, nevertheless agreed about the jealousy: "People are good to you when you're down, but when you jump over they don't like it," she said later.

So Prozumenshikov had distanced himself from much of the Russian community. Not long ago, he had put the finishing touches on his dream house. It was a world apart from the tangle of low-rise apartment buildings where many immigrants made their first American homes, a working-class suburban neighborhood some of them jokingly called the "slobodka," or Russian ghetto. And farther still from Leningrad, where most newlyweds shared cramped flats with their parents. On the rare occasions that Prozumenshikov discussed his past with colleagues, his voice took on a bitter tone: "Now if you can imagine," he would say, gesturing for emphasis, "you and your whole family would have to live in two small rooms."

Prozumenshikov's new house was huge, white and ultra-modern, nestled in a suburban enclave that had once been a forest. Crisp vertical and horizontal lines and big plate-glass windows gave it the appearance of a colossal Malibu beach house. If it looked out of place at the end of a lane of neocolonial Midwestern homes, Prozumenshikov didn't seem to mind. With an architect's help, he had worked out many of the details himself. The front door led through an alcove into the living room, where a fireplace of black marble soared to a cathedral ceiling. In the center of the living room stood a low, black-leather sofa and a glass coffee table barely six inches off the ground. Prozumenshikov had built the house for Ellen, but she called it a monument to his extraordinary achievements.

From this palace in the woods, it was a fifteen-minute drive along country roads to the Pru-Bache office in Wayzata, the epicenter of Minnesota affluence. The office occupied the ground floor of a three-story building of red brick and black granite. It commanded a sweeping view of Minnetonka, a large natural lake to the south. In the language of the Sioux tribes that once inhabited central Minnesota, Minnetonka meant "big water." It was the legendary home of Waziya, Sioux god of the

North, a giant who blew cold winds from his mouth. The giant had given his name, slightly altered, to Wayzata, which occupied the northern shore of the lake.

To Native Americans, Lake Minnetonka had been sacred, but the twentieth century had seen it transformed into a playground for Minnesota's corporate elite. Wayzata's expensive shops bore such names as "Points North" and "Posh," while the local grocery store called itself "Country Club Market." Nearby, sprawling mansions lined the shores of the lake. Many of the heirs and executives of Minneapolis's biggest companies—Pillsbury, General Mills, Honeywell, Northwest Airlines, 3M, and others—made their homes in Wayzata and its neighboring suburbs. These communities were well-represented on *Fortune* magazine's list of the four hundred wealthiest Americans—it was, in fact, the closest the upper Midwest came to gentry.

Prozumenshikov was utterly unintimidated by Lake Minnetonka's inbred society. At one time or another, he had succeeded in selling stocks to many of his wealthy neighbors.

Like professional sports teams, stockbrokerage firms such as Pru-Bache were always looking for new talent: established brokers with big client lists who could boost their firms' commission earnings. Pru-Bache had hired Prozumenshikov from Drexel Burnham Lambert in 1989, when Drexel—debt-ridden and villified by the federal investigation of its junk-bond king, Michael Milken—dismantled its entire national stockbrokerage operation, including its Minneapolis office.

At Prudential-Bache, Prozumenshikov's hiring had coincided with a period of profound corporate soul-searching. Eight years earlier, the Prudential Insurance Company of America, the nation's biggest insurance concern, had created Pru-Bache by acquiring the Bache Halsey Stuart Shields brokerage firm. Prudential spent $385 million for Bache and, in the years that followed, plowed more than $1 billion into its new national brokerage outfit. The man hired to preside over Pru-Bache, a free thinker named George Ball, had embarked on an expensive hiring program—luring analysts, investment bankers, and big-producing stockbrokers such as Michael Prozumenshikov.

But by January 1991, Prudential had yet to see much return on its investment. Ball, the Pru-Bache chairman—a man known for quirky, rambling memos, including one comparing his daughter's acne with troubles in investment banking—had presided over a series of multimillion-dollar losses and would soon resign. The tense climate trickled down even to such regional outposts as the Wayzata branch.

Now Prozumenshikov peered out the window of his office at Lake Minnetonka, which on this cold January day was frozen solid. If the quarrel with Petcoff that morning had upset him, people who spoke to him later couldn't tell. Like researching stocks and developing a strong sales pitch, absorbing a client's anger was a skill that every broker had to learn, Prozumenshikov once explained to a young colleague. And the Russian-born stockbroker knew how to take the heat. The dispute over the Reebok and Glaxo stock, though serious, would pass.

What bothered Prozumenshikov more was Petcoff's insistence on continuing to do business with other brokers. The more Prozumenshikov lobbied for exclusivity, the more firmly Petcoff resisted. After their long relationship, this recalcitrance felt like betrayal to Michael. He had worked hard to bring Petcoff good investment ideas. Other wealthy clients had turned over the bulk of their money to him. Why couldn't Petcoff do the same? Why didn't John trust him?

Later that afternoon, Prozumenshikov received a call from a fellow immigrant named Alex Bernstein. Bernstein, once a stockbroker for a rival firm in Minneapolis, had helped Prozumenshikov get started in the business. Alex had left Minnesota two years earlier for Washington, D.C., to take a job with U.S. Sprint, the long-distance phone company. Since then, the two men had drifted apart.

Earlier, though, in 1985—the first full year of Prozumenshikov's career as a stockbroker—they had talked at least once a week. Bernstein had given Prozumenshikov pointers on prospecting for clients. They traded stock ideas and compared notes on production: who was making more in commissions, who had signed up the best-known clients. They compared notes about doing business with fellow Russians—many of whom, Michael asserted, took market losses as a personal affront.

Bernstein's departure from the brokerage business had been gradual. While still working as a broker, he had founded an import-export company with one of his clients. The firm had negotiated joint ventures with entrepreneurs in Russia and eastern Europe, including one venture that produced compact discs. Later Bernstein gave up both the import-export firm and his job as a broker, taking his new position at U.S. Sprint, where he negotiated Soviet ventures for the company.

Today, however, Bernstein was phoning Michael to ask for help. He had just been through a divorce, he told Prozumenshikov. The stress of the breakup had cost him his job at Sprint. He had moved back to Minnesota and was living with his parents while he looked for work. "What should I do?" he asked in Russian. "Are there any openings at your firm?"

Although he was asking, the truth was that Bernstein was far from sure that he actually wanted to return to the pressurized profession of selling stocks. An intellectual with an introspective cast, he had tired of the hard-sell tactics of the 1980s-era brokerage industry. The interests of stockbrokers, he had come to believe, were in basic conflict with the investing goals of their clients. He vividly remembered nights when he had left work disgusted, convinced that he had prostituted himself to make a sale.

Nor, if the truth were told, was Alex particularly fond of Michael Prozumenshikov. In only his second full year in the brokerage business, Michael's income had surpassed Bernstein's for good. After that, it seemed to Bernstein, Prozumenshikov had called him mainly to gloat.

For his part, Prozumenshikov was openly shocked by Bernstein's predicament. Once he had admired "the Barracuda," as Alex had been known in the local brokerage industry. And Prozumenshikov had been so impressed by Bernstein's import-export ventures that he was trying to co-opt the idea himself. Now here was his former colleague, out of a job.

Prozumenshikov quickly pushed aside any feelings of sympathy for his old mentor. One Russian broker at Prudential was enough, he told Bernstein. There weren't any openings at all at the firm. Had Bernstein ever considered selling cars? Prozumenshikov had a friend who was a former Mercedes salesman and might be able to help.

Bernstein was offended. "I'm not interested," he said. "I'm not going to become a *car* salesman."

Then perhaps, Prozumenshikov mused, he might be able to help Alex by asking whether any of his former colleagues at Drexel Burnham Lambert knew of a firm that was hiring. If Alex would give him a few days to make some calls, Prozumenshikov would see what he could do.

For the rest of the afternoon, Prozumenshikov remained in high spirits. He hadn't seen fit to tell Bernstein, but the downtown Minneapolis branch of another Wall Street firm, Shearson Lehman Hutton, had been wooing him for months. To persuade him to leave Pru-Bache, the manager of the Shearson office was now dangling a package of incentives that could make him $800,000 richer.

He was also looking forward to his upcoming trip to California. The company-sponsored junket, a perquisite for his production at Pru-Bache, began in four days. There would be dinners, drinks, an expensive resort in Santa Barbara. And Prozumenshikov wasn't shy about running up big bills on the company tab.

Early in Michael's career, Ellen Prozumenshikov had been obliged to beg her husband to take vacations; he worried that his absence gave other brokers an opportunity to make inroads with his clients. At Prudential, however, he felt more secure. He was the star of the office, and nobody dared to encroach on his territory.

Nothing could be more to Prozumenshikov's liking than an all-expense-paid vacation at the center of the corporate fold.

And why not? Didn't he deserve it?

CHAPTER 2

The Blake School stands on a hill in the Minneapolis suburb of Hopkins, a venerable red brick building surrounded by sweeping lawn and tall oak trees. Arguably the finest preparatory school in Minnesota, Blake accepts students aged five through eighteen, educates and grooms them, then ushers them on to expensive private colleges and the Ivy League.

It was a source of great pleasure to Ellen Prozumenshikov that her nine-year-old son, Daniel, was a student at Blake. She knew people who wanted to enroll their children but couldn't afford it—friends who listened enviously when she or Michael spoke about the quality of the curriculum, the individual tutelage each student received. Blake's tuition wasn't cheap, but she and her husband intended to provide Daniel and their younger son, Ariel, with the finest schooling available.

Ellen waited as her elder son climbed into the Volvo, fresh from his supplemental after-school training in Judaism. She was a graceful woman—about five feet five, with a pleasant, round face and a contagious smile. Her short brunette hair fell around her face, framing it, and her dark eyes sparkled with intelligence. When she spoke English, her Russian accent was fainter than her husband's—at times almost imperceptible.

A dental hygienist, Ellen had declined to give up her job even after Michael's career took off. She liked the work, the daily contact with people, and the Prozumenshikovs could still use the money. As much as Michael made, he managed to spend more. In fact, the opulent lifestyle on which Michael insisted had placed the couple deeply in debt. There was little cash available, for instance, to chip away at more than $150,000 in credit-card balances accruing thousands of dollars in interest every month.

As Ellen weaved through the after-work traffic, she used the Volvo's cellular phone to call Michael.

"I picked up Danny," she told her husband. "I'm on my way home."

"Okay," he said. "I'm going to be wrapping up in about fifteen minutes, and I'll be home too."

Ellen glanced over at her son. He was rangy and thin, with dark hair, more like her than his stocky father. He was shy around strangers but irrepressible at home, full of energy, spunk, and fun. Unlike his father as a child, he didn't seem especially interested in athletics. It pleased Ellen that he liked books and was academically inclined. At this age, Daniel Prozumenshikov was very much his mother's son. He sometimes pressed his small face close to hers as he spoke to her, as if he were about to give her a kiss. She would hold him before her and bestow one of her special smiles, without pulling her face away.

By now it was 6 P.M., and the worst part of the rush hour was over. Michael's drive home from the Prudential-Bache office in Wayzata was short. Perhaps his car would already be in the garage when she and Daniel arrived.

More than two hours later, Ellen's husband still wasn't home. This was unusual. When he had to miss dinner, Michael always called to let her know. Yet the food stood on the table, now cold, where she had left it after she and the boys finished eating. Ellen had phoned Michael's direct line at the office, but no one answered.

Ellen Prozumenshikov's husband was a workaholic. In the six years since he had landed his first job as a stockbroker, he had worked twelve-hour days, five days a week, through colds, flu, and many business holidays. For the first couple of years he had also worked weekends, when he could reach prospective clients at home. He usually ate lunch at his desk.

Lately, the unfolding Persian Gulf War against Iraq had roiled financial markets, increasing the stress of her husband's job. Trying to anticipate how the conflict would move stock prices—and helping clients position themselves to capitalize on the inevitable ground invasion of Kuwait, when it came—had taken a toll on him. He knew only one way to respond to the pressure. He worked until he was ready to drop.

He was no doubt with some client even now, in an unexpected business meeting outside the office. Ellen was sure Michael would call home soon.

At precisely 8:45, he did. This fact stuck in Ellen's mind because she had been waiting for the call, and she noted the time when the phone rang. Michael said he was sorry that he hadn't phoned earlier. He was meeting with a client and needed a favor. "I'm not in the office," he said. "I don't have any phone numbers. Can you give me Stuart Kloner's number?"

Stuart Kloner was Michael's client, business partner, and one of his best friends. A heavyset, mustached chain-smoker who had once worked in a luxury car dealership, Kloner met Prozumenshikov when he sold the Russian broker his 1986 Mercedes-Benz sedan. Now they were partners in a venture called PAK Trading: "P" for Prozumenshikov and "K" for Kloner. The "A" was Michael Armajani, a globe-trotting salesman of heavy machinery and farm equipment, who made a business of finding foreign buyers for goods produced by American companies. Together, they were trying to market products to the rapidly changing Soviet Union—items including American medical supplies and condoms. So far, they hadn't had much luck with it.

That Prozumenshikov hadn't bothered to memorize Kloner's home phone number testified to the huge volume of telephone calls he placed each day. It also betrayed a defining trait of Michael's personality: Although he and Ellen socialized with other couples, he had few close friends of his own. The people he called friends were mainly business associates, with whom he shared little of what was in his heart.

Dutifully, Ellen looked up Kloner's phone number and read it to her husband over the phone. He thanked her, and then, in a grave tone, said something that struck her as odd: "Don't worry," he said, "I'll be home soon." Of course she wouldn't worry, now that he had called.

It was only later that Ellen remembered another peculiarity of the conversation: Her husband had been speaking Russian. Michael considered it rude to speak his native language in front of American clients—even to his wife. Engaging in conversations a customer couldn't understand detracted from the atmosphere of trust that was so vital to the broker-client relationship.

If he was speaking Russian in the presence of a client, his companion was probably from the Soviet Union. And these days, only a handful of Michael's fellow immigrants remained on his client list. Ever since that terrible business with the lawsuit, Michael had gone out of his way to avoid doing business with the Russians.

* * *

Right away, Jim Tallen suspected that something was wrong.

A veteran stockbroker who managed Prudential's Wayzata branch, Tallen had supervised Michael Prozumenshikov for nearly two years. Prozumenshikov was a rarity in the business, and not just because he was an immigrant. He was entirely self-motivated, a workhorse who seemed to need neither the carrot nor the stick to produce nearly $1 million a year in commissions on securities trades. Pru-Bache had recruited him eagerly, offering him an up-front bonus and a big percentage of the commissions he brought into the firm. His selling skills were, on one level, a boon for Tallen himself, whose own compensation varied according to his staff's sales performance.

Still, supervising the Russian broker had proved to be a challenge. His single-minded determination made him a good salesman, but sometimes it ruffled feathers. Michael resented being told no. And he encouraged many of his clients to trade aggressively, in some cases exceeding generally accepted norms for account activity. Tallen had fielded phone calls from clients unhappy about Prozumenshikov's handling of their accounts; at least one of these clients eventually filed a formal complaint. Recently, the Pru-Bache manager had deemed it necessary to terminate the firm's relationship with one of Prozumenshikov's customers, a fast-talking financier whom Tallen found unsavory.

Tallen was used to Prozumenshikov's quirks, which included relentless drive, a vivid imagination, and an occasionally hot temper. But the tale Michael had to tell on this night was bizarre, even for the man the Minneapolis brokerage community had taken to calling "The Mad Russian."

"Jim," Prozumenshikov began without so much as saying hello, "I need you to do something. I have a customer who was supposed to pick up $200,000 at the office earlier today, and they couldn't get there. Can you bring $200,000 to Ellen?"

Michael rambled on, sounding agitated. Hadn't Tallen's father given him $200,000 to buy a new boat? Michael needed the money right away because his client had to leave town that night. Just this one time, he said, he needed a favor.

Tallen was flabbergasted. Pru-Bache had strict rules stipulating how money was to be paid out to clients. Brokers were required to formally

request any payment, specifying the reason for the request. It was delivered as a check, never cash. Moreover, neither Tallen nor any other Prudential manager would ever deliver money anyplace late at night. And
Tallen's father, a retired butcher, didn't have $200,000.

Prozumenshikov knew all this as well as Tallen did. Even if Tallen
had the money on hand—and he didn't—Michael couldn't possibly be
serious. Maybe he was in some kind of trouble. As Tallen probed for
more details, the conversation began to resemble a game of Twenty
Questions.

"Are you free to talk?" Tallen asked.

"Yes," Michael said in a tense tone that seemed to imply the contrary.

"Are you with the customer at this time?"

"Yes."

"Can you tell me who it is?"

"No."

"Are you going to be home soon?"

"Yes."

"Can I call Ellen? Is it all right if I speak with her?"

"That's fine."

Prozumenshikov rattled off the digits of his home telephone number.
Then he blurted: "But didn't you say this morning that your father just
gave you $200,000?"

"Michael," Tallen said, "I never said anything like that to you."

"I must have made a mistake," Michael muttered. Abruptly, the line
went dead.

That night, Stuart Kloner arrived home late. There were messages
waiting from his friend Michael Prozumenshikov, each to the same
effect: "Very important. Call me or I'll call you." Michael had left his
home phone number, and he had last called only a few minutes earlier.

Kloner liked talking to Prozumenshikov, whom he regarded as a
kind of latter-day Horatio Alger. Seeing the world through Michael's
appreciative perception was like seeing it for the first time. On that first
day, Kloner remembered, Michael's eyes had widened as he ran his hand
over the sleek hood of a showroom Mercedes, like a boy fingering a
brightly wrapped present. Indeed, Prozumenshikov so prized the magnif-

icent automobile that Stuart seemed to stand tall in Michael's estimation by his association with it.

Since then, Kloner had learned a few things about his enthusiastic friend. Stuart had traveled, at Prozumenshikov's behest, to Russia in an unsuccessful try at selling U.S.–made surgical products to Russian hospitals. The trip had been difficult—Kloner spent several miserable nights in a decrepit hotel with no heat or soap—but it lent him a new understanding of who Michael was, and what he had overcome. Now Kloner and his wife were frequent dinner guests at the Prozumenshikovs' home. The families shared partial season tickets to the Minnesota Orchestra.

Kloner picked up the phone and dialed Prozumenshikov's number. It was Ellen who answered.

"Michael called me," Kloner said. "I just stepped in."

"He is not home," Ellen Prozumenshikov said. "I know he was trying to reach you, but he couldn't get ahold of you. Didn't he leave you his number where he is?"

"No. He left your number."

This seemed to worry Ellen. As she began to describe the evening's strange events, Kloner could see that she had good reason for concern.

Michael had phoned home several times asking for phone numbers. He said he was with a client, but he wouldn't tell Ellen who—or where he was. Then Jim Tallen called, and Tallen's account of his conversation with Michael had been no comfort at all.

By the time Kloner hung up the phone with Ellen, he was as baffled as she was. When Michael called back, Stuart would try to figure out what was going on.

But Michael Prozumenshikov did not call his friend again that night.

Ellen Prozumenshikov had just put the children to bed when Michael phoned her for the last time. His voice was calm and even.

Ellen had been married to the intense young man she met in Leningrad since she was eighteen. He was a doting husband and father. The legacy of their sixteen-year marriage was ceaseless change—more adjustments than most people make in a lifetime. Michael, she believed, was the most optimistic person she had ever met. His indefatigable hope had cut a swath through the turbulence of time, a bridge from the spiritual repression of Russia to a better life.

Now, again, she tried asking Michael where he was. It was clear that he couldn't tell her.

He told his wife not to worry, as he had done each time he spoke to her on this wintry Monday night. He told her that he loved her, and then he said goodbye.

CHAPTER 3

Michael Prozumenshikov stood before his assembled classmates reciting from the script he had prepared. The news from America was grim, he told them. Hundreds of workers had lost their jobs after striking for better wages and medical care. No other jobs were available, and now they were likely to starve. It was another example of America's exploitation of working people, most of whom would be delighted to live under a socialist system.

A few of the students in Prozumenshikov's class listened attentively while others rolled their eyes at one another or gazed out the window. This was a game they all played together, under the supervision of their political instructor at the First Leningrad Medical Institute. Some, such as Prozumenshikov, were better at it than others.

Prozumenshikov was a member of the Komsomol, Russia's Communist youth league, with a position of some responsibility: He was the student officer who reported to his class on politics and world events. This entailed reading several Russian newspapers, including the young Communists' version of *Pravda* and a daily Leningrad paper, and recounting with a Marxist-Leninist spin the news from the West to his classmates.

It was the spring of 1971, and in Leningrad, as in other Russian cities, long-suppressed debate over the place of Jews in Soviet society had burst into the open. Never allowed to advance freely in their careers, Soviet Jews who demonstrated a commitment to Communism were treated better than those who didn't. Yet ever since the death of Joseph Stalin, it had been difficult for the regime to gag dissent. Some Soviet Jews had even demanded the right to emigrate.

The eighteen-year-old Prozumenshikov, though Jewish, took no such antagonistic stands. He was nearing the end of his first year in dental school, and he meant to get a good job when he graduated. Like many others, he was simply working within the official channels to try to get ahead.

Consistently, Prozumenshikov placed higher on his annual ideological exams than on his math or science tests. "Very good in policy and politics," read the political instructor's evaluation of his 1971 exam. "Knows Marxist-Leninist theory well."

Outside the classroom, however, Prozumenshikov's Marxist loyalties wavered. The members of his predominantly Jewish circle of friends talked about the aggressive anti-Semitism of the Soviet state: its support of Arab countries hostile to Israel, its use of Jews as scapegoats for "economic crimes," and other domestic problems.

Only a few years after the last of Prozumenshikov's classroom reports on capitalist abuses, his political instructor would be surprised to learn that this once-promising pupil had applied for permission to leave Russia.

For while Prozumenshikov might defend Soviet socialism in public, the truth was that it was suffocating him. He was tired of the nervousness in people's eyes, the restless shuffle past store shelves all but devoid of goods. He wanted something better for himself than a lifetime of waiting in line.

As for doctoring news for the Komsomol, well, that game was easy. Telling stories had always been his special gift. Prozumenshikov didn't know it at the time, but the routine of mouthing ideology he didn't believe was good practice for his future career as a stockbroker.

The first three decades of Michael Prozumenshikov's life were an exercise in hard labor for meager rewards. Adversity was the Russian birthright, in no city more than in Leningrad and among no ethnic group more than Soviet Jews. The all-consuming drive that would later amaze Prozumenshikov's American friends and colleagues was a result of childhood deprivation that most of them could never comprehend.

Prozumenshikov was born in 1953, the only child of working people. His father, Joseph, was a supervisor at the Red Viborzhitz steel factory in an industrial district of North Leningrad. His mother, Ida, was a music teacher at an orphanage. One of Michael's earliest memories was of his father, a burly but gentle man, returning home from the factory at the end of each day to sit down to a plain supper, with only the walls of the family's little bedroom separating them from the smells and sounds of the many others who shared their apartment.

In Leningrad housing was scarce, especially since the end of World War II. The city had few private apartments and virtually no single-family homes, so it was common for several families to share one large flat. Michael grew up in such an apartment, a rambling, six-bedroom affair with long hallways and high ceilings. It occupied the top floor of a five-story building in the Petrograd district, one of Leningrad's oldest neighborhoods.

The flat had once belonged to a wealthy doctor, who filled it with antiques and silver and lived there with his family and a staff of servants. After the Bolshevik revolution of 1917, looters had carried off most of the valuables, and the new common law of property forced the doctor to share his home with two dozen people until he died.

In 1957, when the Prozumenshikovs moved in, thirty-one people were living there, one family in each of the six bedrooms and two more couples in cordoned-off common rooms. The space was allocated by the Soviet state—nine square meters per person. Everyone in Michael's flat used a single bathroom and prepared their meals in the same small kitchen. There was no hot water, and the cold water that ran out of the taps looked like tea. Until he was seventeen, Michael would sleep in the same bedroom as his parents.

The flat was situated on Kuybusheva Avenue, a bustling commercial thoroughfare filled with trucks, tiny Russian-made automobiles, and electric trolleys. A butcher shop occupied the ground floor of the apart-ment building, and young Michael's first sight as he left for school in the morning was usually a long line of people waiting to buy a cut of meat.

The women in Michael's flat tended to serve as surrogate mothers for one another's children. Maria Rezchikova, a grandmotherly woman who sometimes watched Michael when his mother was out, thought of him as a good boy who was a little too domineering. For instance, he always insisted on being the commander when he and his best friend, Sergei—the child of another family living in Michael's common flat—played war, a favorite childhood game. "So full of life he is," she would say of Michael to the others who shared the apartment.

The Prozumenshikovs were the only Jews living in the apartment, but they made no display of their Judaism. There was only one syna-gogue in the city, and KGB informants were always among those present at services. Michael's father could be sure that any attempt to exercise his religious heritage would be reported to his superiors at the factory. If the Soviet state's hostility to religion seemed especially pernicious—at its most basic level, an attempt to stamp out one of the few sources of warmth and companionship available to people—it was nonetheless effective in Michael's case. Years later, he would tell colleagues that his life in Russia had turned him into an atheist.

Seared into the memories of Michael's parents was the horrific Nazi siege of Leningrad, during which the German army surrounded the city for more than two years, periodically shelling it and allowing no supplies to enter. For Leningrad's 165,000 Jews, there was another fear: that the German army would occupy the city and they, too, would be carried away to the rumored horrors of Auschwitz or Treblinka. By the end of the siege, each Leningrad resident was receiving a daily ration of only one piece of bread, and there was no coal or wood to heat homes during the winter that marked the end of the war. More than six hundred thousand of Leningrad's three million inhabitants starved or froze to death. Prozumenshikov's parents had been young and strong enough to survive the siege.

As a child born ten years after the war, Michael Prozumenshikov lived with its legacy. He visited the memorial to the siege victims—a giant statue of Mother Russia, weeping as she gazes down on rows of anonymous mass graves. People had died too quickly to bury them individually, and Michael couldn't be sure in which of the graves his dead relatives lay.

The city of Prozumenshikov's youth nevertheless retained a kind of dilapidated grandeur, but now the classically beautiful buildings erected by Peter the Great were lumped together with cheaply constructed Soviet housing projects. Decades of pollution and neglect had stained and corroded the palaces and cathedrals in central Leningrad. Older sections of the city, such as Michael's neighborhood, were falling apart.

Politically, Russia was disintegrating as well. Nikita Krushchev, the new first secretary of the Communist Party, had instigated political reforms that had the unintended side effect of spawning social unrest throughout the Soviet Union. People began to demand more individual freedoms. The Communist Party soon dumped Krushchev and replaced him with Leonid Brezhnev, a hard-liner who spent the next decade trying to halt the process Krushchev started.

As yet, young Michael Prozumenshikov had no dreams of leaving Russia. He continued playing his childhood games, defending Leningrad with toy infantrymen against imagined German attacks, and spinning intricate fantasies for Sergei.

In school, Michael studied diligently and showed an aptitude for language and literature, but his grades in math and science were barely above average. He was excellent at sports and from the age of ten stronger than most of the children in his class. Coaches selected him as a candidate for the hammer throw, a track-and-field event popular in Russia.

As he grew older, Michael came to realize that he was better off than many of the other students at his school. His family could afford vegetables, bread, and even meat, when such groceries were available. The children of Communist Party members ate best of all—enjoying luxuries such as sausages, cheese, and sweets—and their families lived in private flats. Confronted with these discrepancies of privilege, Michael was determined to become part of the favored rank.

Another lesson sprang from the hooliganism rampant in the streets of Leningrad, which hadn't yet hardened into the organized crime widespread in today's Russia. Gangs of young ruffians made life tough for outsiders in all districts of the city. But Michael knew how to handle himself with his fists, and he was always ready if someone was foolish enough to start a fight. His wife said later that Prozumenshikov's childhood endowed him with "the personality of a fighter."

He was raised to achieve, and, although he displayed little talent for science, he planned to become a doctor or a dentist. Michael used athletics, hard work, and pragmatism born of the tough Leningrad streets to get ahead. He was strong enough as a teenager to compete with adults in sports. The Leningrad chapter of the national sports organization called "Spartak"—after the Roman slave-athlete Spartacus—took an interest in him. It was to sponsor him as long as he lived in Russia.

When he was seventeen, Michael applied to the dental school of the First Leningrad Medical Institute. It was the best medical university in the city, and he was accepted despite his mediocre performance on entrance exams. He received the equivalent of three Cs and a B on the four tests. Entrance requirements tended to be more lenient for athletes, and Spartak wanted Michael to stay in Leningrad so he could compete on the Leningrad athletic team.

More good news came only a few months later: Michael's family had finally received clearance to move into a private flat in a new building, a reward for Joseph Prozumenshikov's years of service at the factory. For Michael, this meant hot water for baths, more privacy, and a view out a sixth-story window, though all he could see were multistory concrete buildings like his own, rising above the tops of the birch trees below.

Dental school turned out to be a slog. Instructors in his chemistry and physics classes heaped on a heavy load of work that seemed, to Michael, to have little relevance to his goal of becoming a practicing dentist. Many of his fellow students were the children of doctors or scientists; their families already belonged to the Soviet intellectual class. Michael was forged in the role of the outsider, trying to force his way in, and would continue to think of himself that way in the future.

In college, Prozumenshikov faced an entirely new worry: his politics. In elementary and high schools, teachers had prattled about the Soviet state's compassion for common people and painted the West—the United States in particular—as ruthless and exploitative. Yet at the time, Prozumenshikov's interest in such political propaganda hadn't seemed very important.

At the medical institute, however, there was pressure to conform, carefully orchestrated and more sinister. What he said appeared to matter a great deal to people he had never met. Older students would approach him and ask what he thought about this or that political event—the U.S. war in Vietnam, for example. These students seemed friendly, but Prozumenshikov couldn't be sure what their motives were. A political instructor assigned readings and gave tests in Marxism and Russia's revolutionary history. Even Michael's literature professor required him to express political views.

Michael learned to spout pro-Soviet slogans, and he became adept at identifying Marxist themes in virtually any book, painting, or piece of music. In one of the early essays he wrote while at the institute, Prozumenshikov demonstrated his facile ability to recite the standard Communist line. Writing about Mikhail Sholohkov's "Virgin Land Upturned," Prozumenshikov equated the newly upturned earth in farmers' fields with the social upheaval of the 1917 Russian revolution.

But at the same time, Michael intentionally kept his casual conversations shallow, limiting his contacts with students he didn't know well to discussions of sports. There were few people he trusted enough to tell them what he really thought, so he said as little as possible. And, at a time when Jewish membership in the Communist Party and its offshoot organizations was dwindling rapidly, he joined the Komsomol.

Many of Prozumenshikov's friends were also Jewish, but not all of them. The stocky young man could often be seen—in the hallway outside his classroom or outdoors on the slate-gray courtyard of the institute—talking and laughing with a certain upperclassman. This was Anatoly Bobrov, a tall, lanky fellow with an affable grin and a wart beside his prominent nose. Bobrov was an athlete like Prozumenshikov, who played basketball on both the medical institute and Leningrad teams.

A popular student, Bobrov always seemed to be on his way to a party. Unlike Michael, who worked hard for everything he earned, Bobrov was known to be brilliant but undisciplined. Prozumenshikov was flattered by the interest Bobrov took in him, and he envied the ease with which Bobrov excelled at his schoolwork. On a scale of one to five, the elder student's exam scores were all fives, although he never seemed to spend any time in the library.

For his part, Bobrov admired Prozumenshikov's athletic achievements. Michael was, by far, the best hammer thrower at the institute and one of the best in Leningrad. Bobrov read about his sporting exploits in the newspapers, and the two often swapped stories about their competitions. At one meet, Prozumenshikov set a Leningrad record for the hammer throw, and later he won the Soviet Master of Sports medal.

After talking with Michael a few times, Bobrov decided that he liked him, although he found the younger student a little stiff. He enjoyed trying to penetrate the barrier of Prozumenshikov's self-imposed reserve, jibing him about some uncharacteristically weak throw in a track-and-field competition or cheerfully exhorting him to abandon his schoolwork and come out to a party.

Prozumenshikov always declined these invitations. Though he became animated when talking about sports—his face would light up when he named the famous athletes he competed against—he didn't talk easily about his family background, and he deflected questions about his own feelings and opinions.

He often seemed tense, especially when exams loomed. It struck Bobrov as odd that Prozumenshikov whipped himself into a paroxysm of anxiety about his tests, studying straight through the night and showing up for classes with sunken, red-rimmed eyes. Michael was a B student during his first year, but his work soon slipped to the C level. It was Bobrov's opinion that Prozumenshikov's obsessive work ethic hurt, rather than helped, his performance. Once when Bobrov asked him why he tortured himself so, Michael shared a moment of rare intimacy: He was miserable unless he was working, he said. He was terrified that he would fail and be forced to become a laborer.

During Prozumenshikov's third year at the institute—Bobrov's last year—Soviet authorities barred Michael from attending an international competition in Poland because he was Jewish. The decision seemed to drive Prozumenshikov further into his shell. He still stopped to talk to Bobrov from time to time, but the elder student got the feeling that Michael had begun to perceive differences between himself and non-Jews like Bobrov. The upperclassman regarded Prozumenshikov's mostly Jewish social circle as separatist; he suspected that Michael thought the parties thrown by Bobrov and his hard-drinking friends were beneath him. Later, Bobrov heard from another classmate that Prozumenshikov wanted to leave Russia.

Bobrov graduated from dental school near the top of his class and got a sought-after job at a dental clinic on Nevsky Prospect, the grand boulevard where Leningrad's elite lived and worked. He would hear little of Prozumenshikov until two years later, when he learned through the grapevine that Michael had made a mistake during a dental internship that caused a patient to become gravely ill from a tooth infection. There was a great deal of gossip about the gaffe among alumni of the institute; Bobrov was genuinely sorry, because he remembered Prozumenshikov fondly.

On the bus he rode to dental school, Michael met Ellen Rubashkin, a student three years younger than he. Ellen was quiet, polite, and very pretty—well-liked by Michael's parents. Within a few months, she and Michael were inseparable.

The two of them began planning a future together—one outside the boundaries of Russia. Other countries were pressing the Soviet Union to relax emigration restrictions for its Jewish citizens, and a 1972 visit to Moscow by U.S. President Richard Nixon had helped to persuade the Communist government to let some people go.

The state began selectively approving visas for Jews to leave the USSR for Israel. To emigrate, a Soviet citizen needed a formal invitation from someone living abroad. Yet even fulfilling this requirement didn't guarantee the right to leave. Soviet authorities invoked various excuses and restrictions to keep some people in the country. Anything from a stint in the army to allegedly inflammatory political activities could be used as an excuse to deny an exit visa. Charitable organizations in the West helped Jews who wanted to leave by loaning them money and making travel and lodging arrangements.

In 1974, Ellen's elder brother, Boris Rubashkin, succeeded in obtaining permission to leave Russia. His first stop was in Italy, where Israel had established a way station for Soviet expatriates. There Rubashkin, a psychiatrist, received word that a Jewish organization in Minneapolis was offering to sponsor émigrés who wanted to settle in Minnesota. Later that year, Rubashkin moved to Minneapolis—one of the first of thousands of Soviets who would settle in the northern American city over the next two decades.

Boris Rubashkin's long-distance accounts of life in the United States quickly terminated Michael Prozumenshikov's tenuous loyalty to Communist Russia. Through Ellen, Michael began to hear fantastic stories about life in the West—streets lined with dozens of amply-stocked restaurants and grocery stores offering a riot of consumer goods unknown in Russia.

Before, Michael had only suspected that what the Soviet state told him about the West was a myth. Now he knew it. The betrayal of his society was complete—it had all been a lie, right from the start. This realization left an indelible stamp on Prozumenshikov's personality. For the rest of his life, he would be suspicious of authority figures and spurn rules as unfair obstacles to his own success.

In the short term, he continued to work hard and tried to get a decent job. He sequestered himself for weeks to prepare for his graduating exams in 1975, and the work paid off. He did well on nearly every topic, and the institute approved him for graduation, declaring that he had achieved a good working knowledge of the principles of dentistry. Prozumenshikov's performance was weakest on the physical aspects of dentistry—drilling, making false teeth, and the like—a shortcoming that would cause big problems later in the United States.

It was difficult for all but the very best dental students to get jobs in Leningrad. Most lower-rank students like Prozumenshikov were shipped out for assignments in ghastly places like Siberia and Kazakhstan. On June 30, 1975, the day that he graduated from dental school, Prozumenshikov signed an oath pledging that he would travel wherever society needed his skills.

Even as he signed the oath, however, he was doing everything he could to remain in Leningrad. The First Leningrad Institute had once awarded Prozumenshikov twenty rubles, a small fortune at the time, for placing high in a track-and-field meet, and now Michael turned to athletic organizations for another kind of succor. He wanted help avoiding a forced move to the Soviet hinterlands.

A. V. Petrov, the Leningrad director of Spartak, wrote a letter on his behalf, asking that the institute employ Prozumenshikov in Leningrad because the organization wanted him to remain a member of the Leningrad athletic team. The local office of the Council of Physical Culture and Sport made a similar appeal. Prozumenshikov's marriage to Ellen Rubashkin the previous March—they had married young, he twenty-one and she eighteen—also helped.

The lobbying worked. That summer of 1975, the institute awarded Michael an internship at a clinic in the city, although there were better qualified candidates available. And even the error he made diagnosing a patient's toothache, which led to the patient's being hospitalized, didn't keep the clinic from offering him a permanent job after the three-month internship. If Michael had any doubts about leaving Russia, this mistake may have helped to dispel them. His former classmates' gossip about the flawed diagnosis deeply wounded his pride.

Two years later, Michael and Ellen Prozumenshikov received permission to leave Russia. They decided to go immediately and join Ellen's brother in Minneapolis, although Ellen had finished only four of her five years at the institute.

To Michael, brimming with hope and anxiety as he prepared to vault into the unknown, it seemed that he was about to shed his Russian identity completely. He would cast off the stigma of his working-class roots and mediocre academic performance in the anonymity of a society that rewarded hard work and perseverance. All that would remain of Mikhail Josef Prozumenshikov of Leningrad were the recollections of the friends and relatives he left behind—and a few documents tucked away in dusty record rooms. In time, he believed, the memories would fade and the documents would be discarded, leaving only the new reality of Michael Joseph Prozumenshikov, United States citizen.

He was wrong. He could learn a new language and customs, climb the corporate ladder at a powerful financial institution, build a castle and fill it with expensive toys, reinvent himself a dozen times. But Michael Prozumenshikov would never escape his Russian heritage.

Russia had been the genesis of his intellect and his character. And Russia would be the death of him.

CHAPTER 4

Valery Gilevich was outside the operating room scrubbing his hands when a nurse told him that a Russian man had been admitted to the hospital. Traffic accident, she said. Did Val want to run upstairs and visit the new arrival?

Gilevich, five feet eight and wiry, his black hair and mustache just beginning to gray, dried his hands and stepped into the doctors' lounge for a cigarette. As a physician, he was acutely aware of the dangers of smoking, but he ignored them.

In Leningrad Gilevich had been a cardiologist, but his Soviet medical training wasn't recognized here in the United States. He had started at the Minneapolis Metropolitan Medical Center as a nursing assistant, a job far beneath his competence. Bored after two years of drudgery, he had cornered the chief of the medical staff and successfully petitioned to be promoted to surgical assistant.

But by now—1978—Gilevich was stuck. He couldn't win accreditation as a doctor without intensive retraining and testing. He had failed the battery of U.S. medical exams once, and he wasn't willing to spend years preparing to take them again. His salary supported his family comfortably; by Russian standards, he was making a lot of money.

Stubbing out the butt, Gilevich decided to go upstairs and see the new Russian patient, who was said to be suffering from a back injury. Visiting hours were over, and the man might be lonely.

But when he walked into the hospital room, Gilevich could see that his countryman was in fine spirits. A big man with wavy red hair, he was sitting upright in bed, reading by lamplight. When Gilevich spoke in Russian, the man looked up, flashing a smile. He extended his hand and introduced himself by his Russian nickname—Misha Prozumenshikov, rather than the formal Mikhail.

Prozumenshikov asked Gilevich to have a seat. He was a dentist, he said, working as a janitor while he prepared to take the U.S. dental exams. He had been in the country only a few months. He had come with his wife, Ellen Rubashkin of the Leningrad Rubashkins.

It turned out the two men had a lot in common. They had both studied at the First Leningrad Medical Institute, and both had been assisted in immigrating by the same man, Michael's brother-in-law, Boris Rubashkin. The Rubashkins, in fact, were close friends of Val's parents. Prozumenshikov and Gilevich plunged into the intimacy of their shared past. They discussed common acquaintances—teachers at the institute, students who had gone on to distinguished careers. After a while, inevitably, the talk shifted to life in the United States.

Prozumenshikov was clearly in a hurry to succeed. His dream, he said, was to open his own dental practice where he would be the boss. When Gilevich suggested that the U.S. dental exams might prove more difficult than Michael expected, Prozumenshikov bristled. Somewhat testily, he pointed out that Boris Rubashkin had managed to get through his medical exams. He was confident, he said, that he would pass the tests.

Gilevich gazed out the window of the upper-story hospital room, where he could see the lights of Minneapolis glittering in the darkness. Then he looked back at Michael Prozumenshikov.

For such an ambitious and determined man, Val mused, forced hospitalization so soon after arriving in America ought to be depressing. But Prozumenshikov seemed happy about his situation. Far from worrying about getting back on his feet, he appeared to regard the episode as an opportunity.

"I'm earning money to be lying here in bed," Prozumenshikov crowed, more than once. He explained that he had bought incidental insurance that covered his hospital bills and paid him cash each day. Then he ticked off his likely hospital expenses and estimated the total he expected to collect by the end of his stay. Gilevich, Prozumenshikov strongly advised, would do well to acquire similar insurance. The advice sounded like a sales pitch: You too can grow rich by being blindsided at a traffic light.

Despite his ordeal, however, Prozumenshikov looked healthy to Gilevich. His face bore no severe cuts or bruises, and he seemed able to move without discomfort despite his complaints of back pain.

Gilevich had been working at the hospital long enough to recognize the pattern. He suspected that this man wasn't badly hurt, that Prozumenshikov was exaggerating the injury in order to collect on his insurance. The game wasn't new; it seemed to be an American tradition. What was odd—and therefore interesting to Val, who was more amused than shocked by life's little oddities—was how quickly Prozumenshikov had figured it all out.

When Prozumenshikov said he was planning to sue, Gilevich was sure he had guessed right, and he was struck by the remorseless candor with which Michael described his plans. He didn't ask, but Gilevich wondered who had told Prozumenshikov about personal injury lawsuits.

Before Val left to return to his routine on the overnight shift, he and Prozumenshikov exchanged pleasantries and agreed to get their families together for dinner sometime. Privately, Gilevich was ambivalent about the idea. Prozumenshikov was cordial enough, but he seemed overly intense and, on some level, cold. Val was sure that he and Michael would never become close friends.

Michael and Ellen Prozumenshikov had arrived in Minnesota during the winter of 1977 and spent their first weeks at Boris Rubashkin's suburban home. The transition to life in greater Minneapolis, a city as cold as Leningrad but without its well-planned public transportation system, wasn't easy.

But for recently arrived Russian émigrés, there was compensation. The welcoming ritual included help from friends or relatives in learning the area, arranging transportation, and getting enrolled in English classes—plus a party, which Boris threw to help Michael and Ellen meet other immigrants. Most of these people were new to the United States, but some, like Boris, had been in the country for a few years. Despite the initial hardships of the new city, all of them were delighted to have escaped the Soviet Union.

Among those at Rubashkin's party were Rafail and Zina Shirl. Zina was a beautician who seemed to know everyone in the Russian community and acted as a kind of one-woman Welcome Wagon for new arrivals from the USSR. Born Ukrainian, she had been among the first Soviet citizens to win the right to leave in the 1970s, and she took pride in describing herself as one of the original Soviet "refuseniks." When Richard Nixon visited Moscow in 1972, Senator Hubert Humphrey of

Minnesota had given the president a list of refuseniks to discuss with Leonid Brezhnev. Zina's name was on the list.

Welcoming parties like the one where Prozumenshikov met the Shirls would pay unforseen dividends. When he became a stockbroker, Michael would enlist many of the people he met at these gatherings as his clients. And he would turn to socially connected immigrants like Zina Shirl for introductions to others in Russian and Ukrainian enclaves throughout the United States.

But in those early days, Prozumenshikov devoted his energy to becoming a dentist. While Michael studied for his dental exams, Ellen worked as a dental hygienist to support them. They lived in a series of small apartments, mostly in the working-class suburbs immediately west of Minneapolis.

They found that Ellen's income didn't pay their expenses, so Michael took whatever work he could find—at first, a job mopping floors at a hospital. Later, he washed dishes at a nursing home, labored in a metal scrapyard, and cleaned apartments when other tenants moved out of his apartment building.

Even when he thought a job was beneath him, he worked at it almost slavishly. At the hospital where he was a custodian, he left his floors spotless, and he seemed personally offended when other janitors slacked off. "This is unforgivable," he told his boss years later, when the overnight staff failed to clean a brokerage office to his satisfaction. "These people should be fired."

Michael had studied English in Russia, and it was improving quickly with practice. He completed a two-month English course at the University of Minnesota, and while he wasn't yet fluent, he could communicate fairly well.

Learning American dentistry wasn't as easy. To win accreditation, Michael had to pass written exams on science and dentistry, then demonstrate a mastery of practical skills such as drilling, making dentures, and filling cavities. Each of the tests was long and difficult; most people who managed to pass them on the first try were recent graduates of good U.S. dental schools.

Boris Rubashkin and Michael's dentist convinced him that preparing for the tests would take months or, more likely, years. It was futile, Michael understood, to try any of them before he was ready. He studied on his own, poring over textbooks and giving himself sample tests from exam-prep handbooks.

Because Michael worked in the evening, he and Ellen tended to socialize late at night. They became good friends with another couple from Leningrad whom they met at a party, Mark Goldburt and his wife, Stella.

Goldburt was a tall man with a florid face and a goatee. He joked, he argued passionately, he waved his arms to emphasize his points. He seemed to love making Michael laugh. Seven years Michael's elder, he offered his friend warmth and support, and Prozumenshikov reciprocated with gratitude. To Michael, an only child, Goldburt was like the elder brother he never had.

In Mark Goldburt's memory, now darkened by the regrets of a soured friendship and the greater tragedy that followed, those happy early years reside as a series of idyllic images, a simple life full of long days and limitless possibilities. The Goldburts and the Prozumenshikovs got together nearly every night, most often at the Goldburts' home, enjoying dessert and coffee or sipping vodka. It wasn't unusual for Michael and Ellen to go home quite late.

Unlike Prozumenshikov, Goldburt had found it easy to market his professional skills in the United States. An engineer, he got a good job within a month after immigrating and eight months later, he and his wife bought their first house.

The ease of Mark's acclimation seemed to bother Michael. Hadn't he himself been in the United States longer, and wasn't his English better than Mark's? He occasionally felt obliged to point out that Goldburt had been required to pass no series of tests before going to work, as if to remind himself and his friend why he was having more trouble. Once, he shocked Mark by deriding engineering as an second-tier profession, far easier to learn than dentistry.

At first, though, these tantrums were rare. Michael was full of ambition and confidence, and Mark Goldburt was an encouraging one-man audience for his dreams. Over dinner, they discussed where Michael should open his dental practice and where he and Ellen would eventually buy a house.

The Goldburts had rented their first American apartment in the suburb of St. Louis Park in a building filled with other recent immigrants, and they had quickly made a lot of friends. For reasons Michael never explained to Mark, the Prozumenshikovs chose to live apart from the Russian neighborhood, in a different suburb. This, it seemed to Mark, had isolated Michael and Ellen from potential friends. By introducing them to other Russians, the gregarious Goldburts drew the Prozumenshikovs into an active social life, which Mark could tell was more important to Ellen than to Michael.

When the time came for Michael to take his first dental exams, the results were good. Despite his less-than-perfect English, he succeeded in passing both of the preliminary written tests. Encouraged, he decided to try one of the practical tests: a so-called bench exam designed to evaluate his clinical skills on plastic models without actually working on a patient.

The bench test found him wanting. Michael had learned his craft in the technologically backward Soviet Union, where dentists worked with antiquated machinery and inferior raw materials. And unlike the written exams—a concrete answer for every question—the bench test was subjective. The examiners who hovered over Michael as he did his lab work had broad latitude to find fault. They failed him, recommending that he enroll in dental school to polish his skills.

Prozumenshikov was disappointed, but he bounced back quickly. He had always been at his best when confronting adversity; it seemed to make him stronger, like a boxer who sneers after his opponent lands a solid blow.

He now sought advice from his own dentist, who told him about a special program for immigrants at the University of Manitoba in Winnipeg, Canada. There Michael could work in a modern laboratory and get a dental degree, which his dentist thought would help to sway the judges the next time he tackled the bench test.

By now Ellen was pregnant and money was tight, but the young couple decided he should go to Winnipeg anyway. So he left in September 1981 to begin the two-year program. It was as hard a time as Michael and Ellen would ever face.

The money he had won from the successful settlement of his personal-injury suit had long since been spent. Michael was so poor that he had to fill his suitcases with food to take back with him after one of his occasional visits. To save money on these trips, he flew standby on a commercial shipping airline rather than a passenger plane. Both he and

Ellen were lonely during his long absences, and as the pregnancy progressed it became increasingly difficult for Ellen to cope on her own.

While Michael was away, Ellen met another couple from Leningrad, Julia and Zachary Persitz. Julia had recently given birth to her first child, a son, Daniel Persitz. and she gave Ellen valuable tips on childbirth and infancy. When Ellen's son was born, Michael couldn't afford to be there. It was Julia who provided the crucial support for Ellen, coaching her before childbirth and helping out afterward. Ellen decided to name the boy Daniel, the same name Julia and Zack had chosen for their child.

It was Julia who accompanied Ellen for the baby's first visit to the pediatrician. The two women exchanged phone calls about cholic, diaper rash, and sleepless nights. And when Ellen returned to work—only six weeks after giving birth—she often spent her lunch hour at Julia's house.

Like Mark Goldburt, Zack Persitz had landed on his feet in the new world. The Persitzes lived in their own house in a middle-class suburban neighborhood, and Zachary, an engineer like Goldburt, was working as a dam inspector for the state. Julia, a professional violinist, played in a local chamber orchestra and gave private lessons at her house.

Julia and Zack first met Michael during one of his visits home, and it was clear from the start that Zack and Michael didn't share many interests. Zack was quiet and sensitive, a sometime sculptor and poet who liked talking about art; Michael, it seemed to the Persitzes, was mainly interested in money. Though he had very little of it at the time, talking about wealth and wealthy people "did something for him," Julia says. His eyes, she noticed, actually sparkled when he described the goods he planned to buy.

Zack thought this was silly. But Julia liked Ellen, and for his wife's sake Zack tried to get along with Michael. They often passed time together by talking politics. For most Russian immigrants, the liberal rhetoric of the U.S. Democratic party stirred up disturbing memories of Russian socialism, and Zack and Michael were no exceptions. Both registered as Republicans, and they would take turns criticizing U.S. democrats and Russian socialists, in no particular order. The two men didn't always agree. Yet they seldom quarreled, because Zachary, when confronted by some strident challenge to his views, simply fell silent and glared.

Ellen had always been strong-willed, and while Michael was in Canada she found the inner fortitude to carry on. Only occasionally, in

private moments, would she confide to Julia of her frustration that
Michael wasn't yet established as a dentist. "I was a little bit lost," she
would say later. By the winter of 1981, four years after arriving in the
new world, the Prozumenshikovs seemed no closer to achieving their
mutual goals. With Michael still studying in Canada, Ellen moved into a
humble two-bedroom apartment in an industrial area of St. Louis Park.

The reprieve from Ellen's isolation came unexpectedly. The following summer, apparently before his training was scheduled to end,
Michael suddenly returned to Minneapolis. When Mark Goldburt asked
why, Michael was evasive. Goldburt's dentist, the same man who had
suggested that Michael enroll at the Canadian school, told Mark that
Michael had been caught cheating on one of his exams. Goldburt didn't
know whether to believe this story, but he decided not to ask Michael
about it.

In any case, Michael was still planning to take his qualifying exami-
nations. He pinned his narrowing hopes of passing the remaining tests on
advice from a dentist at Ellen's office who had heard that testing standards were more lenient in other states—particularly Washington and
California. To prepare for the tests Michael practiced at night in Ellen's
office, using the equipment to drill and fill cavities in false teeth. Mark
Goldburt couldn't help admiring his friend's perseverance despite seemingly endless setbacks. "He did a lot of things," Goldburt says. "He tried
so many different ways to achieve his goal."

Prozumenshikov borrowed $2,000 from a local businessman to fly
to the West Coast for his bench exams, but, again, he failed them. He
returned home deeply in debt, with menial labor as his only immediate
alternative, finally forced to confront the reality that he would never
become a dentist in the United States.

To Goldburt, Michael blurted convoluted explanations for his failure. The state dental boards, he said, had free-ranging authority to reject
candidates for their own reasons. He implied that he had been singled
out for rejection because he was Russian. These excuses made Mark
uncomfortable. "You don't have to talk about this," Goldburt would say.
"It doesn't make any difference." It seemed to him that his proud young
friend scarcely heard his reassuring words; the growing financial dis-
crepancy between Michael and his peers was obviously torturing him.

It wasn't long before Michael admitted to Goldburt that he had given
up on dentistry. But he chose to cast the decision in a peculiar light: He

now seemed to think that being a dentist wasn't good enough for him. He showed Goldburt a trade journal that listed the average starting salary for new dentists at about $40,000 a year. "He says this wasn't what he was dreaming of," Goldburt said. Privately, Mark suspected, Michael may have still harbored hopes of becoming a dentist, but in the short term he knew he had to earn some real money.

Michael had first heard about the stock market from a friend in Canada, but it was Goldburt who, during one of Michael's visits home, had told him about the mechanics of buying stocks. As Prozumenshikov and Goldburt took a walk after dinner one evening, Michael asked whether his friend ever invested in the stock market. Yes, Goldburt said, he had. What's more, he had made money at it.

Owning stock, Mark said, was the same as owning a small piece of a corporation. Like many first-time investors, he had started by buying stock in the company where he worked—Norston Communications, whose business was installing telephone equipment for other corporations. After a year at Norston, Goldburt was eligible to buy its stock for a markdown from the regular price. If he wanted to, he could have sold the shares for a small profit the day after he bought them. But Goldburt's boss had advised him to hold the stock. And the suggestion paid off. A year later, when he finally decided to sell, his $500 stake in Norston was worth $1,700.

Michael's reaction to this account was both surprising and personally gratifying; Goldburt had never seen his friend so impressed. Since that day, Michael had asked Mark a dozen times to repeat the details of the Norston investment—the purchase price, the sale price, the period Mark had held the shares, Goldburt's reasons for selling. With less success, Goldburt had since bought shares in other publicly traded companies from a stockbroker, and Prozumenshikov also grilled him about these transactions. Michael was particularly interested in what the stockbroker did and how much he charged for his services.

At last, Michael told Goldburt what he planned to do. He would make his way in the world by investing in stocks.

The stock market fascinated Prozumenshikov because, to him, it represented the essence of capitalism—a concept of participation in business utterly foreign to his experience in the Soviet Union. He had started with dentistry because it was what he knew, but if he could make a good life for himself and his family by doing something this uniquely Western, so much the better.

As he had so many times before, Michael leaped into his new dream feet first. He started by reading everything he could lay his hands on. Each day he devoured the *Wall Street Journal* and the business pages of the *Minneapolis Star Tribune*. He read *Barron's Investors' Weekly* and subscribed to the *Value Line Investment Survey*, a stock-picking service.

Each week *Value Line* mailed him reports prepared by its team of researchers. Ellen watched, amazed, as Michael spent hours hunched over the reports, studying financial tables about companies that made everything from shirts to cupcakes and doing calculations in a notebook. These reports acquainted Michael with the language of business. In casual conversation, he began to talk about corporate earnings, market share, profit margins, dividends. He also learned to look, as *Value Line* did, for undervalued stocks by comparing a company's stock price with its earnings and deciding whether people would want to buy more or fewer of its products in the future.

Michael was no less fascinated by the capitalist institution of personal credit. In his spare time, he applied for dozens of credit cards. And while some banks turned him down because of his paltry income, many others were happy to fork over their cards.

He wasn't choosy. He opened credit lines with any company that would have him, regardless of the interest rate it charged. During one dinner party at his apartment, he showed his guests two dozen cards, issued by banks based all over the country. To Mark Goldburt, who was conservative in financial matters, it seemed that Michael treated the credit cards like play money. He took cash advances to begin speculating in stocks, unimpressed by the fact that he would have to earn an 18 percent profit simply to break even.

At first, Michael did his trading through a broker at a local office of Prudential-Bache Securities, with whom Zack Persitz had invested some money. Prozumenshikov dabbled primarily in penny stocks: the cheap shares of small companies, many of them based in Minnesota. But he hounded his broker for details about more expensive investments and the risks associated with each, including the blue-chip stocks of big corporations, government and corporate bonds, mutual funds, stock options, even commodities.

He continued working at odd jobs, but he became more and more obsessed with the market. He was inordinately pleased with himself when he made even a small amount of money investing in stocks. To his friends, it was as if a door had opened and Michael had entered a new world; it was hard to get him to talk about anything else.

At the time there was only one Soviet-born stockbroker working in Minneapolis, and it didn't take Michael long to find him. When Alex Bernstein, a native of Odessa in southern Ukraine, hosted a seminar on investing for Soviet immigrants, Michael was among the twenty or so people who attended. Michael called him soon afterward, and Bernstein had no trouble remembering the heavyset red-headed man who peppered him with questions throughout the session.

Michael opened an account at Bernstein's firm, Engler-Budd, Inc.— one of the many local brokerage companies based in downtown Minneapolis—and transferred his money over from Prudential-Bache. He began buying stocks through Bernstein, who was full of enthusiastic recommendations.

These stock picks didn't always work out. One of the first stocks Michael bought from Alex was Continental Airlines, which Bernstein regarded as an undervalued gem. Within a few weeks, however, Continental entered bankruptcy proceedings and its stock price plummeted. Michael called Alex every day to quiz him about the losses he was suffering and Continental's prospects for emerging from bankruptcy.

At one point, Michael showed up at Bernstein's office to complain about Continental. Alex had learned to expect emotional reactions when his Russian-born clients lost money, so he girded himself for an angry outburst of some kind. But Prozumenshikov didn't appear to lose his temper. He spoke slowly and evenly, so that when the insult finally spilled out, it was all the more chilling: "Bastards like you," Michael said, a faint smile playing around his lips, "deserve to be hanged."

Yet the bad experience with Continental did nothing to diminish Prozumenshikov's interest in the market or, apparently, his faith in Alex Bernstein. Other Bernstein recommendations fared better than Continental, and, over time, Michael's account moved into the black. Michael told Mark Goldburt he was making more in the market than he paid in credit-card interest and was becoming a sophisticated investor. And the more Prozumenshikov learned about stocks, the better he understood that he had made his foray at an exciting time.

It was 1983, early in the Reagan presidency, and life had returned to the listless U.S. stock market. Since 1979, the Dow Jones Industrial Average of thirty major U.S. companies had risen almost five hundred points. Investors were flocking from bonds and real estate into stocks, and the financial press was now bandying about the possibility of a sustained bull market on Wall Street.

Looking to build on his modest trading success, Prozumenshikov decided that it was time to increase his stock-buying clout. He invited a dozen couples to his apartment in St. Louis Park, served drinks and pastries, and then, with his fellow immigrants perched on every available chair in the cramped living room, Michael rose to speak.

The stock market, he said in Russian, was about to enter a period of unprecedented growth. He had read an article in the *Star Tribune* in which leading market observers predicted that the Dow Jones Industrial Average—and here he departed from Russian to use the English phrase—would rise from 1100 to 1700 over the next three years. This was an incredible opportunity, Michael said forcefully, for those of his friends who were bold enough to reach out and take it. He was experienced in investing, he said. He knew how to choose stocks both profitably and prudently. He was starting an investment club, and he was inviting everyone in the room to join it.

Mark Goldburt, wedged into the corner of a narrow sofa with a drink in his hand, was impressed. He had no idea Michael could be so articulate and persuasive. Goldburt looked at the faces around him, and he saw that Michael was making a good impression.

"Of course it's possible we could lose money by trading individual stocks," Prozumenshikov went on. "But the market is going to go up, and if we go with different stocks we minimize the risk. I have some good trading ideas. If you invest, I'll manage the money, but you will keep the profits."

Here, Michael paused. Throughout the room, a half-dozen conversations started at once. A few of Michael's guests had dabbled in the stock market, and some of these people began talking excitedly to those seated next to them. After a moment, someone spoke out above the din.

"Well, it sounds okay Michael," the man said, "but how much money are we talking about? A thousand dollars? Two thousand? And how much will you put in?"

Prozumenshikov seemed incredulous. "Come on!" he said. "You are all engineers . . . professionals. You have permanent jobs and good salaries. You're going to invest only a couple thousand bucks? I'm just cleaning offices, and I'm going to invest ten thousand dollars. You can't make money unless you invest money."

This produced a ripple of a different kind. Michael's tone was decidedly condescending. Most of the people in the room were older than he was, and they didn't like a younger man talking down to them. "Wait a second, Mike," a gray-haired man said slowly. "If you want to invest ten thousand dollars, it's your business. But why do I have to invest my ten thousand dollars with you? And what kind of proof do I have that you are professional and that I won't lose my money?"

"I know how to do this," Michael said impatiently. "The market will go up. It's a very good deal."

Goldburt could see that Michael was losing the room. The truth was that he himself was shocked by Michael's tone; it revealed a side of his friend's personality that he hadn't seen before. The patter had sounded reasonable at first, but he was no longer sure what Michael's motives were.

Goldburt had no way of knowing that his concerns were well-founded, that over the next few years Michael's business dealings with his fellow Russians would produce little but pain and anger on both sides. "Looking back," Goldburt would say later, "this party was the very beginning of the great change in Michael. But it took a long time and I didn't see it right away."

In the end, everyone went home angry, and no one agreed to invest any money. The meeting had been unpleasant and embarrassing. Michael and Mark didn't speak of it afterward.

One day, Prozumenshikov invited Alex Bernstein to his apartment. To Bernstein the man seemed frustrated, almost desperate. Michael told Alex that he had been unable to pass his dental exams, and now he didn't know what to do. Trading stocks was fun, but it didn't produce enough money to live on. After seven years in the United States, his earnings as a custodian were only $63.75 a week. Prozumenshikov asked Bernstein whether there was a future for him as a stockbroker.

Bernstein wasn't thrilled about the idea of competing with another Soviet-born broker for the Russian community's savings. But he couldn't ignore a fellow immigrant's plaintive appeal. Reluctantly, he described the training and credentials required to become a broker. He suggested that Michael begin by reading a book on the subject that he had found useful, called *How to Buy Stocks*. Alex told Michael how he had broken into the business. He had talked his way into a job with the brokerage firm Smith Barney Harris Upham in 1980. There he had impressed his bosses with his aggressive pursuit of clients; he had opened 160 customer accounts in a few months. Be aggressive, Alex urged Prozumenshikov. Sell yourself.

Prozumenshikov took Bernstein's advice. He began calling and visiting local brokerage firms, promising big sales to any firm that took a chance on him. In September 1984, he secured a job offer from a small brokerage firm called Keenan & Clarey, Inc., where brokers were provided with desks but had to pay their own phone bills. The catch: He couldn't start work until after he passed a securities exam, and the company wouldn't pay him to study or to take the test.

Michael enrolled in a two-month securities course, then took the exam. Compared with the dental tests he had endured in the past, the brokerage test administered by the National Association of Securities Dealers was easy. He passed it, and joined the staff at Keenan & Clarey.

Not long after starting work at the tiny firm, Michael and Ellen Prozumenshikov drove with another couple to Lake Calhoun—one of the many small natural lakes that dotted greater Minneapolis—before going out for dinner. It was a pleasant place, where a sidewalk ran along the shore of the lake, separated from the water's surface by the occasional patch of oak and elm trees. There, the Prozumenshikovs walked and talked with their friends, the Brezmans, who were also from Leningrad.

The men strolled in front of the women, each pair absorbed in their own conversation. Prozumenshikov was discussing his plans for the future. As a stockbroker, he predicted, his energy and persistence would finally be rewarded and he would realize his dreams. The big house, the expensive car, the best schools for their children.

Michael Brezman, a lanky man who stood a full five inches taller than Prozumenshikov, lifted his gaze from the path at his feet and peered down at his heavyset friend. He didn't seem to understand.

"Why, Michael?" he asked. "Why must you have all these things?"

His companion paused for a moment, as the shadow of a bad memory appeared to cross his face. Finally he spoke, spitting out each word with grim determination.

"Because," Michael Prozumenshikov said, "I have eaten enough shit."

CHAPTER 5

Wall Street's biggest retail brokerage firms, which earn profits by paying people in their branch offices to peddle stocks and bonds, are fond of dignifying these brokers with such titles as "financial consultant" and "account executive." Even so, others within their own firms—the proprietary traders and investment bankers—tend to disdain retail stockbrokers as mere salespersons.

Standards vary throughout the industry, but many brokerage managers will confess that there are, more or less, three traits that make or break a stockbroker. Intelligence isn't one of them. An operative IQ is necessary, but a quick mind won't compensate for a lack of these three vital qualities. The first of them, skill at selling, can be taught. The second, a strong work ethic, can't.

The third trait is probably the most important. Call it self-esteem or ego, it amounts to an unshakable belief in one's personal superiority, accompanied by an intense desire to prove it every day. Swaggering is common among the best stock salespersons. They regard themselves as the elite of their profession and often look down on those who sell less than they do.

This posturing protects a broker from the psychologically bruising routine of selling. No rebuff is too rude when someone phones offering unsolicited investing advice, no rejection too abrupt or profane. Day after day, as they phone strangers trying to sell their stock ideas, brokers are constantly hearing nasty things about themselves. Over time, the abuse tends to wear down an insecure or introspective personality.

"This business beats you up so bad that if you have low self-esteem you internalize it," says John Kelly, a sales manager for Merrill Lynch, Pierce, Fenner & Smith, the nation's biggest brokerage firm. "Once you internalize it, it eats up your gut and you start thinking it's your fault.

People with high self-esteem let it bounce off. They'll just say: 'It's too bad. That guy's not going to have a chance to work with me.'"

In Michael Prozumenshikov's case, the question of self-esteem was complicated. He thought highly of himself, and he expected to succeed. Yet he carried a measure of shame about the poverty of the country from which he came.

Prozumenshikov wanted to be the best. For him, that meant being rich. American affluence thrilled him, tantalized him, offered itself up as his life's mission. In Russia there had been nothing worthwhile to buy, even if he had money. In America, if he were rich, he could buy any-thing. And in the starkly material milieu of the brokerage industry, Prozumenshikov's values were a perfect fit.

Merrill Lynch, besides employing more brokers than any other firm, also controls more customer assets—about $400 billion at the time. It is a formidable if somewhat bloated institution that is among the leaders in virtually all areas of securities sales, trading, and corporate finance. Its lavish New York headquarters boasts the largest and most expensive trading floors on Wall Street. Across the country, many of its branch offices are similarly posh. In the mid-1980s, Merrill maintained one branch of its Minnesota operation in a skyscraper high above Minneapo-lis and another in the rich suburb of Wayzata. And into these hallowed halls strode an improbable figure—an unpolished Russian immigrant named Michael Prozumenshikov.

When Michael phoned him for the first time, Dennis Kellner, the manager of Merrill's Wayzata office, had an opening for a stockbroker. But salespersons from small firms like Keenan & Clarey were a dime a dozen, and they were flooding Kellner with calls about the job. Kellner, a veteran sales manager with an eye for talent and a no-bullshit personal style, wrote off most of these people after one or two conversations— phone patter weak or halting, not enthusiastic enough about themselves. But there was something different about Prozumenshikov.

The Russian accent, first of all, was intriguing. It was accompanied by complete ease on the telephone. And Michael told Kellner he was working more than one job at once, as a janitor by night and securities salesman by day. That spoke of strong personal drive. Interested, Kellner scheduled an appointment to meet Michael in person.

During the interview, Prozumenshikov talked about his native coun-try and the obstacles its economic system posed for ambitious young people. He told Kellner about his athletic exploits in Russia. He said the Russian community in the United States, an ethnic group that worked hard and saved money, was a pool of potential investors into which only a Russian broker could tap. "One thing was obvious," Kellner says. "This was a guy who needed to succeed—a guy who had been success- ful in obtaining some goals while in Russia, but had to give that up and really had a burning need to regain what he had lost."

Over the next couple of weeks, Michael bombarded Kellner with follow-up phone calls. Had Dennis made a decision? Could Michael come to work at Merrill? Kellner put him off, but was impressed by his persistence.

True, Kellner told himself, the Russian broker was raw. But he appeared to be loaded with potential. What's more, he would be cheap to hire. Because he wasn't yet established in the business, Merrill wouldn't have to pay an up-front bonus to get him. Kellner decided it was time for Michael to meet Dean Hutton, manager of the Minneapolis branch of Merrill Lynch.

Hutton, a ruddy, barrel-chested man who combed his brown hair flat across his head, embodied the conservative Merrill Lynch tradition. He wore well-cut suits and enjoyed power lunches. He rubbed elbows with the cream of corporate Minneapolis—Carl Pohlad, the millionaire owner of the Minnesota Twins, was a golfing buddy. He had strong opinions on most financial matters and was frequently quoted in the local newspa- pers. He reviled rock-and-roll brokerage outfits like the one being assembled in Minneapolis by Michael Milken's junk-bond house, Drexel Burnham Lambert; these firms were always trying to lure away his top- producing stockbrokers.

As Michael Prozumenshikov settled into a leather chair in Hutton's twenty-seventh-floor office and began talking about himself, Hutton could see that Michael's vibrant personality contradicted all that he thought he knew about Russia. As Hutton saw it, "The Russian personal- ity is long suffering, silent. Just look at the music that comes out of Rus- sia, the sadness, the grief. Dark and gloomy, that's Russia." They sat there, the well-heeled brokerage manager and the stereotype-busting Russian immigrant—and Hutton decided he liked what he saw.

Prozumenshikov was hardly typical of the Merrill Lynch financial consultant. Still, if Kellner's hunch could be trusted, the accent would be an asset with clients rather than a liability. Moreover, it was obvious that

Prozumenshikov would work hard, and effort was worth a lot. This man, in fact, looked as hungry as anyone Hutton had ever met.

He himself wouldn't actually offer Prozumenshikov the coveted job at the nation's premiere brokerage firm; because Michael would work in Wayzata, it was Kellner's role to do that. But Hutton, Kellner's boss, decided to put his stamp of approval on the hiring.

From the beginning, Dennis Kellner was astounded by Michael Prozumenshikov's work habits. At his desk by 6:30 A.M., he would quickly read the *Wall Street Journal* and the business section of the *Minneapolis Star Tribune*. By 7:30, before the New York Stock Exchange opened, he had scanned the computer for new stock offerings, stocks that had traded actively the previous day, and for available cash to spend in his customer accounts. He would then begin calling clients and potential clients. Unlike some brokers who, as Kellner knew, would use any excuse to avoid picking up the phone, Prozumenshikov called people all day long. He was always the last to leave at night. During the eighteen months he spent at Merrill Lynch, he wouldn't take so much as a day of vacation time. "Nobody worked harder than Michael," Kellner says.

From Prozumenshikov's own point of view, he had landed in nirvana. The Merrill Lynch name conferred respect he had never enjoyed at lowly Keenan & Clarey. Merrill's office offered a view of Lake Minnetonka and the mansions that surrounded it. Everywhere Michael looked, conspicuous wealth was on display—fine clothes and art objects in the shop windows, the Mercedeses, BMWs, and Volvos parked outside the shops. In local restaurants, Michael overheard teenagers quarreling with their parents about whether they would take the Honda or the Porsche to college.

Ensconced in his tidy office, he developed the habit, which would last for years, of keeping photos on his desk of the things he wanted to own. At Merrill, these were images of a white Mercedes and a lakeshore mansion he particularly admired. To motivate himself, he stared at the photos as he phoned prospective clients.

As he had promised he would, Michael mined the Russian community for clients, delivering a pitch to any fellow Soviet with savings or an inheritance and pledging big returns in the American stock market. He often approached potential clients at parties or after services at Temple Israel, his synagogue in Minneapolis. Though inexperienced, Prozumenshikov even then was extremely persuasive. He capitalized on his fellow immigrants' suspicion of outsiders and traded on the trust their common ancestry conferred. In the Russian community, word quickly spread that Prozumenshikov understood the stock market and spoke the common language.

He focused his efforts among concentrations of Soviet immigrants in the near west suburbs of Minneapolis, closed communities that formed a kind of Little Odessa in Minnesota. But he also solicited their relatives and friends around the country. When these people became his clients, they often handed over their life savings or their children's college money. "I told him: 'I don't want to play games. I don't care if it makes only seven percent or eight percent,'" says Shuli Panich, a Ukrainian immigrant living in Columbus, Ohio. "Trust me, trust me," Prozumenshikov said.

Mark Goldburt immediately opened an account at Merrill Lynch, but he wanted to do more to help. Pushing out of his mind the ugly memory of Michael's aborted "investment club" meeting, Goldburt decided to throw a party to try to drum up business for Michael.

Goldburt invited forty people to his suburban home, so many that they spilled out of his living room into the kitchen and the hall. "We have a new Russian broker in the house," he told his guests. "We will drink a little bit, we will talk a little bit, and then Mike will explain what he can do for us."

At the time, tax-free individual retirement accounts, or IRAs, were very popular. Most people at the party had heard of IRAs or had opened them through their banks. Now Goldburt exhorted his friends to move their money to Merrill Lynch. "What difference does it make for you to open this IRA with Mike or with some bank?" he said. "Why give business to some bank when you can help your friend?"

Michael stood up and explained the mechanics of IRAs. He also noted that the Dow Jones Industrial Average was climbing, and recommended a few stocks that Merrill's research department liked at the time. "If you want to invest in stocks," he said, "I can help you." Mark noted that Michael was good at simplifying financial matters in his native language. "All these special terms, you know, he could explain them in plain Russian," Goldburt says. "It was very important."

The party went more smoothly than the disastrous investment club meeting; by the end of the night, Michael had opened twenty-eight customer accounts. He called Mark at work the next day to thank him. "He said he's so happy, and I'm real good friend," Goldburt says.

During this period, many immigrants close to Mark Goldburt noticed that Prozumenshikov seemed to become more interested in making friends. He made a special effort, for instance, to befriend Mark Tsypin, a fellow Leningrad native who invested $15,000 at Merrill Lynch after Goldburt's party. Despite this, Tsypin never really understood what Goldburt saw in Prozumenshikov. "He was—I don't know if you have same expression in English—a 'cold fish,'" Tsypin says. "He was friendly to some degree, but never allowed anybody to become his close, close friend."

Not content to enlist only Russians as clients, Prozumenshikov worked tirelessly to sell stocks to others as well. He added to his client list by "cold calling" prospects whose names he got from lists of known stock-market investors, internal corporate directories, or just out of the phone book.

Most brokers hated cold calling—or, as some call it, "smiling and dialing"—which amounted to phoning people they had never met and touting this or that stock: "I hear great things about RJR Nabisco," or, "Have you considered investing in chemical stocks?" Here too, Prozumenshikov was different; he actually seemed to enjoy it.

Even with his limited command of English, he wasn't afraid to phone total strangers. He routinely worked weekends, when he could reach prospects at home. Another of his favorite methods was waiting until 5 P.M. to call a businessman at his office; by that time the secretary would be gone and the man was likely to pick up the phone himself. "Other brokers would say, 'Gee, I couldn't call that guy. He's the chairman of General Motors.' But it didn't bother Michael," a colleague says.

Prozumenshikov's sales tactics, in fact, commonly extended to stretching the truth. One Minneapolis businessman whose father had loaned Prozumenshikov money while Michael was in dental school remembers rebuffing the broker when he called to offer stocks. The businessman later learned that in a pitch to another prospect, Prozumenshikov had identified him as a client.

His pitch when cold calling was simple and direct. Whereas many brokers scripted their pitches carefully and changed them frequently, Michael settled on an approach he liked. He wouldn't change more than a few words of it during his next six years in the business. "Hello," he would say. "This is Michael Prozumenshikov of the investment firm Merrill Lynch," or, as Michael pronounced it, "May-rrill Leench."

"I'm calling," he would continue, "because I'd appreciate the opportunity to make more money for you." It was an offer that few people could flatly refuse. "Very seldom did anyone just hang up on him," a colleague says.

He loved spinning scenarios about the companies whose stocks he chose to recommend, and he always had a story to tell when a prospect seemed receptive. Intuitively, Michael closed sales hard. He didn't hesitate to tell someone already active in the stock market that his portfolio was larded with losers. "Why do you own that stock?" he would query the prospect skeptically. "That's not doing anything for you."

Michael asked Mark Goldburt, who had taken a job at the Control Data Corporation, for a copy of his company's internal corporate directory so he could cold call Control Data's 46,000 employees. Reluctantly, Mark turned over the directory. He finally balked when Michael asked for permission to use Goldburt's name when calling the founder of the company. "That was the first time that I said no," Goldburt says. "I just started my work with Control Data and I didn't want to lose my job the next day."

At first Michael hawked stocks that were recommended by Merrill's first-rate research department, which was based in New York. On his desk sat a speaker called a squawk box, through which analysts in New York communicated with brokers throughout the country—telling them about changes in Merrill's stock recommendations and about interesting new issues of stock that Merrill's investment bankers were underwriting.

But as time passed, Michael began to rely more on his own research and on tips from his clients. He showed a preference for cheap, speculative stocks, although he also sometimes traded the expensive shares of big blue-chip companies. "Initially, it's hard to get people to buy eighty-dollar-a-share stocks or even twenty-dollar stocks," Dennis Kellner says. "It's easier to get people interested in an eight-dollar stock."

Prozumenshikov had read an article in a local newspaper praising the management and products of the Minnesota-based Tonka Corporation, the toy company, and now he sold shares in Tonka to a number of his Russian clients. "I purchased twelve hundred dollars worth of Tonka stock," says Michael Brezman, another Leningrad native who invested money with Prozumenshikov after Mark Goldburt's party. "It climbed like four dollars a share, from forty-five dollars to forty-nine dollars. I sold it right away, and I made a little bit. I was satisfied."

Prozumenshikov went out of his way to put the best face on the stocks he recommended. To him, the glass was always half-full. A luke-warm recommendation seldom made a sale, and a broker received a commission only if he could get the client to buy. Therefore, if Prozumenshikov liked a stock at all, he loved it, even if circumstances called for something less than unqualified endorsement. Like Merrill Lynch in its television ads, Michael was truly "bullish on America." No broker with a balanced point of view could compete.

"Clients are looking for someone who is forceful, who is convincing and has strong opinions," Dean Hutton says. "And that's the way Michael was. He was absolutely sure of everything."

One of the clients Michael had signed up using Goldburt's Control Data directory was John Beskar, an engineer for the company and a sometime investor. "He called me and came on very forcefully, with super stories of how much money he made for people," Beskar says. "He claimed he could double my money in a couple of months. It sounded like he had so much money it was coming out his ears."

Many of the stocks Michael picked during his early days at Merrill Lynch did well for his clients. In the bull market of the mid-1980s, when stocks rose month after month on a strong economy and waves of buy-outs, mergers, and acquisitions, it didn't require a lot of market savvy for an aggressive stockbroker to look like a hero. His first Russian clients made profits, and referrals were plentiful after that.

Prozumenshikov always asked his clients to refer him to their friends and relatives. His dream was to fill his client list with rich people—big investors who weren't afraid to actively trade stocks worth huge sums of money. But at the beginning he didn't care how much a client invested; no account was too small for him.

When he made a sale, he told Goldburt, he felt an exhilaration like nothing he could name, a wave of wonder and excitement that he, a Russian, was becoming a successful capitalist. Whereas his colleagues at Merrill Lynch might question whether making money truly made them happy, Michael never did. It gave him a deep, visceral thrill. He was, he decided, a born salesman.

Michael grossed $200,000 in commissions during his first full year at Merrill Lynch, taking for himself about $75,000 of that total. Such numbers, unheard of for a rookie stockbroker, were an indication that his long-term production potential was virtually unlimited. In all his years in the business, Dean Hutton had known only one other rookie to match Prozumenshikov's sales totals.

Michael's relationship with Alex Bernstein, the other Russian broker in town, became intensely competitive. They called each other's Russian clients, urging them to defect. "That's the kind of rat race we live in as brokers," Bernstein says. Prozumenshikov knew Alex counted George Pillsbury of the prominent Minnesota baking family among his clients. Bombastically, Michael informed Bernstein that he would soon land the titans of industry himself.

Of the two men, Prozumenshikov proved to be the bigger producer. After 1985, his commissions would consistently be higher than Bernstein's, and Michael would phone Alex frequently to rub it in. "He'd call me and say, 'I got new account, hundreds of thousands of dollars. How much do you have?' And God forbid I should have more than him at any time," Bernstein says. "If he had more, he would gloat."

In the local offices of Merrill Lynch, Prozumenshikov's exploits inspired both admiration and envy. Some brokers—those whose own unqualified success gave them no reason to be jealous—got a kick out of him. After all, how many successful Russian stockbrokers were there?

Other colleagues, though, sniffed at his raw aggression, snidely suggesting that his overbearing sales approach might be better suited to the used-car business. Behind Prozumenshikov's back, one wag gave him a nickname: "The Mad Russian." For the rest of Michael's life, the derisive title would define him in the brokerage industry, both in Minneapolis and among his top bosses in New York.

And although Prozumenshikov was smooth on the telephone, his office manner left something to be desired. He had little time for idle conversation—an office was for working, he said—and some of his colleagues resented him for it. He looked down on anyone he saw as less bright or aggressive than he. A devoted family man, he never went out drinking with other brokers. He developed a reputation for being arrogant, when pathologically driven was probably nearer to the mark.

Prozumenshikov was simply stunned that everybody didn't work as hard as he did. "He didn't understand that people would rather take a long lunch than make a few extra phone calls," says his former boss, Dennis Kellner. "They have this wonderful opportunity to make all this money, and they're not working thirteen hours a day to do it. Well, why not? He didn't understand it."

At the office Christmas party that year he was stiff, although everyone liked his wife, Ellen. "Michael was on stage even at the Christmas party," Dean Hutton says. "Very definite, very focused, always wanting to talk about business. He never let his hair down. I don't remember ever seeing him laugh."

One day, a man named Clement Seifert walked unintroduced into the branch and was directed to Michael's office. Seifert was sixty-one, just retired from his forty-four-year career as a carpenter, and was looking to convert his IRA account into more profitable investments. A World War II Navy veteran, Seifert had served on a destroyer escort involved in antisubmarine warfare in the Atlantic. His face, wrinkled, lined, and pallid, was topped by a head of pure white hair; his voice was a slow rumble, deepened by years of chain-smoking True menthols.

Seifert wasn't against playing the market a bit, but he cautioned Michael that he didn't want to risk losing his savings, which was all the money he had. Michael smiled and assured Seifert that his money was safe at Merrill Lynch, the most respected of all brokerage firms. At that moment, Seifert hadn't the slightest premonition of the anguish Prozumenshikov's tactics were to put him through during the next four years.

Many of Michael's clients asked about mutual funds, which are pools of stock chosen and managed by experts. At first, Prozumenshikov had been eager to sell them. But he quickly figured out that money invested in mutual funds, while it might fulfill a client's investing goals of stable growth, was inert; it didn't trade, and it didn't generate commissions for him. If a client owned mutual funds when he or she came to Merrill, Michael often tried to talk the person into selling them. Supremely confident of his own stock-picking abilities, he promised clients they would earn better returns by letting him pick the stocks. This way, he also made more money himself.

Seifert believed Michael when the broker told him the mutual funds he had been holding for years weren't suitable. "These are no good," Prozumenshikov said. "You can do better than this." Michael sold the funds for about $25,000, which the broker then used to trade stocks that he liked. Letting Michael sell the mutual funds was a mistake; despite Michael's supposed misgivings, they would actually perform quite well over the next few years.

Because Seifert couldn't always be reached, he gave Prozumen-shikov verbal permission occasionally to buy or sell a stock without call-ing him first. And Michael didn't hesitate to do so. On one occasion, he annoyed Seifert by abruptly selling stocks in the General Motors and Maytag corporations that had been in Seifert's family for years. But in the bull market of 1985, Clem's account was earning profits almost regardless of the stocks Prozumenshikov chose. Michael is the profes-sional, Seifert told his wife. He must know best.

Dennis Kellner, Prozumenshikov's boss, wasn't so sure. A grave man whose witticisms were mainly of the dry variety, Kellner took to heart Merrill Lynch's image as a conservative haven for its investors' money. And in this cautious attitude, Kellner was typical of his firm. Many firms paid lip service to maintaining integrity in customer accounts; Merrill had an institutional commitment to doing it. The firm had even been known to crack down on its big-producing stockbrokers.

Kellner couldn't quibble with Prozumenshikov's work ethic, but he had begun to notice problems with the Russian broker's hard-selling style. There was a fine line between salesmanship and unscrupulous con-duct, and Michael, Kellner believed, was testing it. The first signs of trouble were the huge commissions Michael generated from what was still a relatively small pool of customer assets.

It wasn't unusual for a broker to overhaul a client's portfolio when the client first came to Merrill Lynch, selling stocks the broker saw as underachievers and buying shares in companies with more potential. Because the firm charged a fee for most trades, this process usually brought in thousands of dollars in commissions for the broker and the firm. After the initial overhaul was complete, though, things were sup-posed to settle down. For most investors, it was more appropriate to hold stocks for months or years than to trade them actively.

Most new brokers at Merrill Lynch generated annual commissions worth about 1.5 percent of the total assets their clients invested at the firm. After the first year, the pace of trading was expected to slow; in the second year, brokers usually earned commissions worth only a fraction of a percent of their clients' assets.

Michael, by contrast, brought in commissions worth a whopping 5 percent of assets during his first year and continued to generate far more than the norm in his second year. He once told another broker that it was his habit to do $2,000 worth of stock transactions every morning, whether market conditions justified them or not. Merrill had computer programs that culled trading records and spit out warnings when a broker's trading became too active; to Dennis Kellner's dismay, Michael was lighting up the warning system like a pinball machine.

The activity in Clem Seifert's portfolio was typical of how Prozumenshikov worked some of his accounts. According to federal regulators, in a stable stock portfolio worth $200,000 or less, more than one trade a month is probably too much activity. During ten months in 1985, Michael executed ninety-four transactions in Seifert's $70,000 account. The next year, Prozumenshikov would rack up 129 transactions in the account—a breathtaking total, especially for retirement savings.

From Kellner's point of view, this kind of trading was dangerously close to churning, the process of executing stock trades against a customer's best interest simply to generate commissions. Churning is illegal under federal securities laws and can cost a firm thousands of dollars in restitution and fines. And under the law, churning, like statutory rape, doesn't have to be committed involuntarily. Trading activity can reach a volume that regulators call statutory churning, at which it doesn't matter whether the client authorized the trades.

Merrill Lynch was in the habit of automatically mailing out letters to clients whose accounts were unusually active, asking whether they were happy with their broker's investing strategy. Most of Michael's Russian clients didn't write back. When Kellner called these clients at home, the answer was always the same: Yes, we like Michael. He's doing a fine job. Kellner got the feeling that Russian clients trusted Prozumenshikov, a fellow immigrant, far more than they trusted his American boss. "They were very close-mouthed," Kellner says, "and I wasn't part of their group."

Michael himself wasn't above using his Russianness to obfuscate. "He knew a lot more than he was willing to let on," Kellner says. "If he was caught at something, he would blame it on lack of knowledge and his Russian background, when in reality he knew exactly what he was doing."

Now Kellner and Dean Hutton began to confront Michael about the activity in his accounts. Michael defended himself by telling his bosses that most of the stock trades were "unsolicited" orders, meaning that buying a particular stock had been the customer's idea rather than his own. "He could talk you out of anything," Hutton says. "You'd start off convinced that he was dead wrong. After ten minutes of conversation you'd bear witness for him, convinced that he knew exactly what he was doing."

Kellner also noticed, however, that Michael was in the dubious habit of guaranteeing to clients that a company's stock would rise to a particular price. If a stock price didn't reflect the strength of a company's earnings, Michael would recommend the stock to a client by calmly predicting that the share price would, say, double within six months. Although he based such projections on actual numbers—the company's existing price-to-earnings ratio, adjusted to account for some favorable recent earnings report—it wasn't certain, or even very likely, that the stock would perform as he expected. Kellner had never heard any other broker so brazenly guarantee his own musings.

Also troubling to Kellner was the fact that Prozumenshikov apparently didn't manage his personal finances any better than his stock-price predictions. It was office policy to open brokers' incoming mail routinely in case it contained complaints from their clients. Occasionally, bills arrived at Merrill from Michael's many credit-card lenders demanding delinquent payments. The debt Michael was carrying—already tens of thousands of dollars—amazed his bosses. This young stockbroker, making serious money for the first time in his life, was managing to spend more than he earned. "He didn't have the foggiest notion, a clue about such things as fiduciary responsibility," Dean Hutton says. "I think Michael spent more money than most of us ever see."

The fact was that Michael was in a huge hurry to accumulate the trappings of material success. "When someone asked Michael what kind of car he wanted, he'd say a Mercedes," a colleague says. "He'd say it like the question was ridiculous: What other kind of car would anyone want?" While still living in his two-bedroom apartment in working-class St. Louis Park, he often looked longingly out the window of the Merrill Lynch office at the mansions lining the shore of Lake Minnetonka.

When the time came to buy his first home, he had to settle for less. After a three-month search, he and Ellen chose a house in Plymouth, a suburb near Wayzata. One afternoon, he took Kellner to see it. It was an attractive three-bedroom, split-level home in a quiet, tree-filled subdivision, and Kellner thought it was a fine choice.

But Prozumenshikov seemed dissatisfied. "He didn't think it was good enough for him," Kellner says. "He was talking about how he was going to get a better one." Yet with his credit-card debt and short history of substantial employment, Prozumenshikov had trouble qualifying to buy even a modest home. Kellner helped to close the deal by writing a letter praising Prozumenshikov's work habits and skills as a salesman.

At most brokerage firms, there is an ongoing tension between the pressure to produce commissions and the desire to maintain integrity in customer accounts. Some disgruntled former investors would go so far as to suggest that the brokerage industry's stated goal of safeguarding its clients' financial interests is fatally compromised by an insatiable thirst for profits. Too often, when profits and ethics collide, the bottom line prevails.

Although some of his habits distressed his bosses, Michael's big production nevertheless "gave him a kind of hero status" at the firm, Dean Hutton says. "The funny thing about our business is that if you produce a lot of numbers, people overlook how you do it. As much as I hate to admit it, we stroked Michael a lot. You say, 'God, great job Michael.' Then you look at his books and say, 'I wonder what he's doing here. I wonder whether we have a problem.'"

Dennis Kellner was becoming convinced that, as far as Michael was concerned, Merrill did have a problem. In his second year in the business, Prozumenshikov's earnings were astounding: He was on a pace to gross $500,000 in commissions. And the more sophisticated Prozumenshikov became, the more he seemed to cut corners.

One of his later tactics was asking what percentage rate a potential client was earning on a bank savings account. Upon hearing the earnings totaled a paltry five or six percent, Michael would exclaim, "It's foolish to leave money in a bank account in a booming market. I can guarantee you at least two more percent." Guaranteeing returns in a stock market known for its unpredictability wasn't allowed at Merrill, regardless of Michael's ability to deliver on his promises.

Another of his methods was telling clients that he had bought this or that stock for his relatives. "He would say, 'Hey, I recommend you buy this stock because I bought it for my son,' or 'I bought this for my grandmother,'" Michael Brezman says. As Michael used this line again and again, Brezman wryly noted that his broker's relatives couldn't possibly have enough money to buy all the stocks Michael said they did.

Michael even loaded up some of his clients' individual retirement accounts with speculative stocks. He sold investors on these purchases by pointing out that any profits they earned in their IRAs weren't taxable. What he often neglected to mention was that losses in IRAs can't be claimed as income-tax deductions, as they can in regular accounts. Many of his clients learned this only later, when preparing their tax returns.

Perhaps the biggest problem Dennis Kellner saw in Michael's style was how highly leveraged his clients' accounts were. Investors can use what are called "margin" accounts to trade with money they don't have. Margin accounts work like cash advances on credit cards: Buying on margin means borrowing money from the brokerage firm to buy stock, using existing shares as collateral.

If the price of the leveraged stock rises, the client earns a profit—minus, of course, the interest rate the firm is charging to loan the money. If the stock price falls, the investor must pay the firm cash—called a "margin call"—to maintain the value of the shares being used as collateral, or else some of the stock will be forcibly sold at a loss. A sharp decline in the stock price, as might occur during a stock-market crash, can inflict devastating losses on clients with big margin accounts—losses far greater than they would have suffered if they had stuck to investing their own money.

Prozumenshikov persuaded dozens of his clients to open margin accounts, to expand their buying power, and, not coincidentally, to build the pool of assets he could use to trade and earn commissions. Several other brokers in the Wayzata office controlled more customer assets than Michael; only one, whose assets were vastly greater than Michael's, had more money in margin accounts than he did.

Kellner painstakingly tried to explain the dangers of margin trading to Michael. "Margin," he would say, "is a two-edged sword. It works great going up, but the markets go down too, and when that happens you can get caught." Kellner talked in specifics, sketching numbers on a pad to show Michael the painful losses some of his margin clients would suffer if the price of a single stock fell sharply. Prozumenshikov didn't seem to care. "The client wants to do this," he insisted. "He understands the risk."

Prozumenshikov had actually been quite forceful in talking some of his clients into trading on margin. To Clem Seifert, for instance, "he said it would be foolish for me not to trade on margin because I could make more money," Seifert says. "He also said if I died nobody could collect the margin debt."

During Michael's time at Merrill, the heavy margin trading in his accounts was uneventful. Some of his clients did well enough in the stock market to offset the interest they were paying to trade on margin; others didn't. Only later would Michael's fondness for leveraged stock trading wreak its most terrible consequences.

Meanwhile, a few of Michael's clients were starting to gripe about losses in their accounts. John Beskar, the Control Data employee, had deposited all the stock he owned at Merrill Lynch when he opened his account with Prozumenshikov. Then he had borrowed about $10,000 from Merrill to trade other stocks on margin.

On some of the shares Beskar made a little money, but more often he lost it; an investment Michael recommended in Mobil Oil Corporation did especially poorly. In spring 1986, Beskar closed his account and terminated his relationship with Prozumenshikov. By that time, he had accumulated a debt of about $1,200; he couldn't reclaim his remaining stocks until he paid it.

This infuriated Beskar, and he filed a complaint against Michael with the Minnesota Commerce Department, alleging that the Russian broker made false claims and acted against Beskar's best interest. "Stockbrokers," Beskar says, "are parasites. The public would be better off if they didn't exist."

Michael, for his part, had experienced an epiphany of sorts: In the great gray divide between a stockbroker's responsibility to disclose risk and a client's obligation to clearly communicate his investing goals, brokers had made enough money to buy a factory full of new Mercedes-Benz sedans. And despite the supposedly stringent safeguards built into securities laws to protect investors, Prozumenshikov saw plenty of room to maneuver.

By Dean Hutton's reckoning, the fact that many of Michael's clients were Russian gave him greater latitude to deceive them. "The folks he was dealing with were not well-schooled in ways of this economy," Hutton says. "A light bulb went on. Michael realized he had an opportunity, and he took advantage of a lot of people."

Now only Dennis Kellner stood in his way. And Michael was growing impatient with Kellner's prattling about rules and financial prudence. He was chafing under the stewardly Merrill Lynch tradition; his bosses, he decided, were stifling fuddy-duddies who didn't appreciate his hard work. A year and a half after joining Merrill, Prozumenshikov was no longer happy there.

More than once, Michael lost his temper and screamed at Kellner, but these episodes only seemed to strengthen Kellner's resolve. Kellner was turning up the heat, demanding that Michael change his approach to the business. "We were telling him that there were things we were not going to tolerate, things he could not do," Kellner says. Prozumenshikov, convinced that his worth to Merrill far outweighed any liability, complained to Dean Hutton about the pressure he was getting. "Please," he said, "just get Dennis off my back."

Hutton knew better. "Michael," Hutton said, "I can't get Dennis off your back. He's your boss. He's been in business a lot longer than you have, and I think you better listen to him." Athough Prozumenshikov didn't know it, Kellner was doing him a favor.

Despite the problems he was having with Dennis Kellner, Michael's huge production of commissions was drawing attention from other firms in Minneapolis. Self-employed consultants called headhunters took it upon themselves to monitor the production of stockbrokers in the area and tell rival firms about hot new prospects. One firm that got interested in Michael this way was Drexel Burnham Lambert, which was trying to build a national brokerage network that could challenge Merrill Lynch.

Soon Prozumenshikov was receiving monetary offers to jump ship. Called "waffles" in the Minneapolis brokerage community, these offers usually included an up-front cash bonus and a big percentage of gross commissions. Michael made a point of bringing up each offer with Dean Hutton. "I keep hearing these offers," he would say. "I'm wondering if I should be listening to them." In Hutton's view, Michael was exploring Merrill's commitment to him—and trying to figure out whether anyone above Dennis Kellner's level was distressed about his active trading and heavy use of margin accounts.

Even if Michael were a trouble-free employee, which he wasn't, Dean Hutton saw no percentage in forbidding him to speak with other firms. Hutton liked successful brokers who listened to the offers and then decided to stay with number one. So he reminded Michael of the advantages Merrill offered to a stockbroker—its sterling reputation and strong research and investment-banking capabilities. Then, as he always did in these situations, he pointed out the flaws in the offers Michael was receiving. First, he said, you have to pay taxes on any cash bonus you receive. Second, if you leave Merrill, half of your clients will probably opt to stay here. Still, Hutton said, "When you get an offer that dazzles you, come and tell me and I'll be honest and tell you if it's a good one."

One day in July 1986, while Dennis Kellner was on vacation, Michael showed up unannounced at Dean Hutton's office. His face was flushed and he seemed excited. Hutton showed him in and closed the door. Then, somewhat breathlessly, Michael told Hutton about his latest offer from Drexel.

The deal, he said, included a signing bonus of about $100,000—two-thirds of which would take the form of a loan so Prozumenshikov didn't have to pay taxes on it until later. Drexel was also offering Michael a huge 50 percent cut of the gross commissions he brought in during his first year at the firm. Lastly, Michael told Hutton, he was offered the title of vice president at Drexel. The title was just a nicety, really. Everyone understood that Prozumenshikov was a salesman, albeit a supercharged one.

In some ways, Dean Hutton regretted what he was about to do. Michael was a hard worker and a big producer, one of the most fearless salesmen he had ever known. Soon, Hutton was sure, Michael's commission earnings would catapult him into the top ranks at any brokerage firm in the country.

Yet Hutton realized that Prozumenshikov was never going to work out at Merrill Lynch. His heavy margin trading on behalf of small investors and retirees was a disaster waiting to happen. The Russian broker, Hutton decided, had a compulsion about money, a craving for wealth that was compelling him to do business in an irresponsible way. Furthermore, Dennis Kellner was uneasy about Michael's habits, and Hutton respected Kellner's judgment. "Dennis and I both knew that he was not going to be reined in," Hutton says. "He was not going to work like we wanted him to, like Merrill Lynch wants its people to work."

Now Hutton paused and looked straight into Michael's eyes. "Michael," he said simply, "I think you'd better take their offer."

And that, as they say, was that.

CHAPTER 6

In his fortieth-floor office at the Minneapolis headquarters of Drexel Burnham Lambert, Bill Krebs proudly displayed the symbols of his management philosophy: a piranha in an aquarium and a sign on the wall that read, "Fire! Aim! Ready!"

Brash, bright, and volatile, Krebs was boss and unquestioned guru of Drexel's Minneapolis operation. His hair was silver but his face bore no wrinkles, and behind steel-rimmed glasses his eyes gleamed with barely contained intensity. One running joke had it that Krebs's heels set off sparks when he paced the sidewalks of downtown Minneapolis. He often started his day by pumping up on coffee and leading some of his salesmen through a session of yoga.

In his high-octane approach to the brokerage business, Krebs was a Mazerati to Dean Hutton's Cadillac. That was the way his superiors at Drexel wanted him, for they had charged their man in the corporate mecca of Minneapolis with wresting market share from brokerage leaders like Dean Hutton's Merrill Lynch. Krebs had opened Drexel's Minneapolis branch himself in 1984 and had quickly alienated competing brokerage managers by going on a hiring binge. The king of the big-money recruiters, he delighted in using cash bonuses to lure away top guns from rival firms. To find the best young talent, he used headhunters; one of the most reliable of these scouts was a former agent for the Central Intelligence Agency, to whom Krebs spoke only by phone.

Krebs had hired 125 people, many of them top-producing stockbrokers at rival firms in Minneapolis. "I created a twenty-million-dollar business in three years, and unfortunately you don't do that unless you step on some people's toes," Krebs says. "The toes I stepped on were the branch managers' in town." His aim was to build the Minneapolis office into one of Drexel's top retail branches. And although, by the time he fell from grace, he wouldn't attain that lofty goal, the cast of colorful overachievers he assembled would make Minneapolis famous throughout the Drexel retail system.

There was John Noonan, a burly born-again Christian and former Xerox salesman, whose intensity during a pitch to sell Krebs photocopiers had inspired the Drexel boss to offer him a job on the spot; Rick London, a laid-back, long-haired, cerebral stockbroker with a flair for picking stocks; Steve Lindell, an innovator who worked with a team of brokers who brought in huge commissions by marketing short-term investments to big financial institutions; Dan Bubalo, Krebs's assistant manager, whom Krebs suspected of gunning for his job; and, most recently, Michael Prozumenshikov, the Mad Russian. "These people who I hired were the top producers in town," Krebs says. "Brokerage firms have one or two of these people in their offices, and I had them all together."

Drexel had put plenty of money at Krebs's disposal, and his job of draining talent from other firms was further simplified by what competing brokerage managers had taken to calling "the Drexel mystique." The mystique, of course, emanated from Drexel's Beverly Hills branch, where Michael Milken was using high-yield bonds to restructure corporate America.

Milken and the firm's chief executive officer, Frederick Joseph, had engineered a stunning revival at Drexel Burnham. The product of the 1971 merger of Burnham & Company and Drexel Firestone, two New York securities firms whose better days seemed to be behind them, Drexel had since become a powerhouse mainly because of the huge revenues that Milken brought to the firm. He had started as a lowly salesman of "junk" bonds, securities issued by corporations whose financial prospects were uncertain. These bonds paid high yields to investors because of the risk that their issuers might fail.

By 1986, the year that Michael Prozumenshikov joined Drexel, Milken was using his junk bonds to finance corporate takeovers. Raiders such as Carl Icahn and T. Boone Pickens were tendering staggering multibillion-dollar bids, backed by Milken's bonds, for some of America's best-known corporations. The takeover money itself came from big investors who eagerly gobbled up whatever bonds Milken issued. And as compensation for arranging the deals, Milken would collect massive fees for himself and Drexel.

The stardust spewed by Milken's money machine showered everyone at the firm, obscuring the traditional lines of rivalry and contempt among investment bankers, traders, and brokers. Whereas stockbrokers were considered plebeian at many establishment firms, at Drexel there was an excitement born of Milken's hot new money which suggested that these old rules need not apply. Stockbrokers were made to feel important, a vital part of the revolution their firm was staging on Wall Street.

Drexel was a newcomer to the national brokerage scene, but it was expanding rapidly. In the four years since 1982, the firm's retail network had ballooned from seven branch offices to forty, including the spanking new Minneapolis office. Throughout the Drexel system, Michael Milken's extraordinary success had instilled a ravenous appetite for profits. It wasn't the oldest or the largest, but in the retail stock brokerage arena, Drexel wanted to be the biggest badass on the Street. "We were very cocky," says an executive who helped to run the retail brokerage division. "I think we were the cockiest goddamn firm on Wall Street. Merrill Lynch? Who the hell's Merrill? Goldman Sachs? Forget it. We were *Drexel,* you know? I mean, if my kids acted like we did, I'd shoot them."

Brokers were encouraged to refer substantial clients who aspired to be corporate raiders to Milken's Beverly Hills office. Often, the biggest-producing stockbrokers were introduced to Milken personally. "It seemed like everybody over there had a pump line to Michael (Milken)," says Dean Hutton of Merrill Lynch. "A broker at Drexel could practically pick up the phone and call Milken, call his department, anyway, and talk to somebody about financing. A lot of brokers went to Drexel for that very reason. They found it exciting that they were on the cutting edge."

Drexel's openly aggressive corporate culture was the antithesis of the conservative image in which the brokerage industry had always cloaked itself. "If you worked at Drexel," says a former broker in the firm's Minneapolis branch, "you became aggressive just by the neighborhood you hung out in." One planned newspaper advertisement for Drexel's underwriting division pictured investment bankers as commandos, wearing helmets and fatigues and carrying automatic rifles. The ad never ran in any publication; Drexel executives decided it conveyed the wrong image, and killed it. Yet the coffee mugs that Drexel distributed to its brokers carried the motto "No Guts, No Glory."

Underlying these affectations was a disturbing trend of retail stock-brokerage in the 1980s—the emergence at many firms of a predatory attitude toward small investors. Hard sales to a rapidly shifting clientele were supplanting the stockbroker's traditional roles as financial adviser and retirement planner. Some brokers trolled for clients like dragnet fishermen, discarding the losers like so many drowned dolphins.

At Drexel, the retail division set the tone by lavishing perks upon its best brokers. Its incentive trips and conferences at resorts in Hawaii, California, and the Caribbean were becoming legendary in the industry, sought-after invitations to excess. Office expense accounts were bloated and widely abused. Some branch managers in the retail network pampered their best salesmen like gifted children.

Among his corps of brokers in Minneapolis, Bill Krebs presided over an atmosphere that was both collegial and overwhelmingly male, one that tolerated only those women who could—and cared to—hold their own in the macho camaraderie of the place. Krebs made liberal use of sports metaphors, calling an easy sale "a layup" and the enlisting of a deep-pocketed investor "a home run." Krebs also was fond of using what newspaper sportwriters call the "sports perfect" grammatical tense. For example, a dejected basketball player might describe a loss this way: "If I make that shot, we win the championship." In Krebs's parlance, the sports perfect was a motivational tool: "If you make one more call, we land that client."

Michael Prozumenshikov joined Drexel Burnham at the very pinnacle of its institutional arrogance, and the three years he spent there were to transform him by giving him his first taste of real luxury. In the minds of many of his Minneapolis colleagues, Prozumenshikov would come to personify the period's excesses. The people closest to Michael insist that he was misunderstood, that his chief failing was a naive optimism about his own abilities and the stock market. But others were amazed that the brokerage industry, reputedly one of the most regulated businesses in the world, would tolerate his hard-charging ways.

It was certainly true that Michael's final days at Merrill Lynch had left a bad taste in the mouths of his former bosses. Taking to heart Dean Hutton's warning about losing clients when he switched firms, Prozumenshikov had embarked on a vigorous and probably illegal program to avoid such a problem.

Michael had spent his last week at Merrill calling clients and urging them to move with him to Drexel. He joined Drexel on July 4, 1986, but his old boss, Dennis Kellner, was convinced that patriotism had little to do with his timing. Kellner had arranged a fly-fishing vacation in Canada that overlapped the holiday; it was Kellner's opinion that Michael had waited until his boss was gone so he could make the calls from the office without being caught. Michael correctly surmised that Merrill couldn't respond with its own efforts to keep his clients until Kellner, who knew his brokers' accounts better than anyone else, got back to Wayzata.

Sidestepping any talk of Kellner's attempts to discipline him, Prozumenshikov told clients the fiction that he was leaving because Merrill was pressuring him to sell lousy stocks underwritten by the firm's investment bankers. He warned his customers that Merrill brokers would call and try to woo them back, and he urged them not to listen. Making such preemptive phone appeals is common in the brokerage industry, but it didn't sit well with Dennis Kellner. "Me, personally," Kellner says, "I think it's wrong to be being paid by one firm and calling your clients and talking to them about going to another firm."

A more serious problem was the way Michael had handled the twenty or so of his clients who held stock mutual funds managed by Merrill Lynch. These funds couldn't be transferred to any other firm, so Michael decided to unload them before he left.

The federal securities law regulating mutual funds is very strict. Because many mutual funds levy "back-end" fees when they are sold, the law requires brokers to explain carefully such charges to clients before selling. These restrictions are in place because it normally doesn't serve an investor's best interest to swap one mutual fund for another. At Merrill Lynch, trading one fund for another was forbidden unless the customer wrote a letter expressly asking for the transaction.

Before leaving for vacation, Kellner had noticed Michael trading Merrill Lynch mutual funds for non-Merrill funds, and he wanted to know why. "My clients want them," Michael explained. "They understand the fees." In that case, Kellner said, get your clients to write letters confirming that they know they will be charged for the trades. If you don't, he said, Merrill will reverse the trades and charge you for any losses or fees.

In reality, some of Michael's clients had no idea they would be charged. "He did lie," says Michael Peltsman, one of two clients who later filed complaints against Prozumenshikov for his handling of the trades. "He said I wouldn't lose money. I thought it was unethical behavior." Meanwhile, as soon as Kellner was out of the way, Prozumenshikov resigned and left for Drexel. Kellner returned to find that Michael "had just literally gone through and sold out all his Merrill Lynch mutual funds that wouldn't transfer properly."

Prozumenshikov was deeply relieved to be free of Kellner and the Merrill Lynch culture he had found so stifling. Beneath the veneer of toughness he projected, he was actually very sensitive to criticism, and Kellner's constant hazing had hurt his feelings. Michael found Bill Krebs to be warm and supportive by comparison, and he was looking forward to working for someone who appreciated his talents. He truly wanted to please Krebs and find a niche at a brokerage house where his aggressive style was accepted.

At Drexel, all the early signs seemed promising. Krebs and his wife, Stacy, welcomed Michael by taking him and Ellen to dinner at L'Hotel Sofitel, a high-toned Minneapolis night spot. There, although Prozumenshikov had little reputation as a drinker, the Russian broker impressed Krebs with his fortitude. Michael ordered round after round of Absolut vodka and cheerfully drank his new boss under the table.

Krebs gave Michael the best office space in the branch, a corner unit so large it had previously accomodated four people. Through its floor-to-ceiling windows, Prozumenshikov enjoyed a vast view of Minneapolis and its sister city to the east, St. Paul. Far below, the Mississippi River meandered from north to south through the urban landscape, much like the broad expanse of the Neva River in Michael's native Leningrad. Nearby were the old Minneapolis grain exchange and the huge Gold Medal Flour milling plant, holdovers from a time when agriculture and grain processing had dominated Minnesota commerce.

Now, however, industrial, high-tech, and financial-service companies drove the diverse Minneapolis economy. They were pushing up skyscrapers as corporate headquarters, remaking downtown Minneapolis in a manner befitting their grandiose ambitions. Aging landmarks like the Foshay Tower mingled with such gleaming newcomers as the IDS Center, whose lofty corridors and vaulted ceilings looked like cathedrals dedicated to capitalism.

Mindful of Minnesota's fierce winters, architects had designed an elevated tunnel system to connect the skyscrapers. Called the Minneapolis Skyway, it hung over the streets like an elaborate spiderweb, linking the office buildings with department stores, restaurants, hotels, and bars. During his first winter at Drexel, Prozumenshikov would find that he could drive to work, spend the day at the office, step out later for dinner, and drive home—without once setting foot outside.

Drexel Burnham occupied the whole fortieth floor of a building called the Multifoods Tower. New York headquarters had dispatched an interior decorator to design the office, which featured a spacious reception area, warm blond woodwork, and corners that were rounded, rather than cut off at ninety-degree angles. The Drexel Burnham Lambert logo gleamed in brass above the entryway. The intent was to make Drexel's customers feel comfortable, and it worked.

Wasting no time, Michael went to work, cold calling even more furiously than he had at Merrill. From his office, Krebs saw that most of his brokers took a break each time they made a sale, sauntering down the hall to the order room with their tickets and stopping to talk with secretaries or other brokers along the way. Not Michael. He strode briskly up the corridor and back, his gaze rarely wandering to the side. Each month, a ranking of top-producing brokers in the Minneapolis branch made the rounds in the office; Michael told Krebs he was gunning for the top of the list. "The guy's working like a banshee," Krebs said. "I've never seen anybody work that hard in my life."

Prozumenshikov did take time out for a special errand—putting money down on a black 1986 Mercedes-Benz 560SEL sedan. It was, for him, a deeply meaningful acquisition, one that marked an important passage in his journey to personal success. "I sold a lot of cars in my life, but Michael was different than anyone else," says Stuart Kloner. "It was like he was buying this car to thank America for the opportunities it had given him."

But Michael didn't trust his Russian friends well enough to share the truth about his new Mercedes. He apparently decided that he needed to hide his escalating earnings from his less fortunate compatriots. To explain the Mercedes he now parked in Mark Goldburt's driveway, he concocted an elaborate lie: He claimed to have bought the car at a rockbottom price from a Chicago-based client who was divorcing his wife and didn't want her to have it. Goldburt, to his dismay, would learn the truth years later.

At Drexel, Prozumenshikov cast about for new ways to make money selling stocks, and he soon found one: a strange breed of investor whose huge stock trades generated commissions greater than he had ever earned. In the industry they were called hedge funds, or "flippers," a derisive reference to the way they traded stocks. By working for a hedge fund, a broker could reap a staggering commission of $50,000 or more on a single trade. Doing this kind of business could be dangerous, however, as Michael was about to learn.

Hedge funds were a controversial by-product of the bull market raging on Wall Street. As investors plowed money into the steadily rising stock market, corporations were capitalizing on the public's enthusiasm for stocks by releasing new issues of shares. The point of releasing a new issue was to raise money so the company could expand its business, whatever that might be. A chain of pizza joints might use the new capital to open more restaurants, while a medical-supply concern might spend it on research.

Securities firms such as Drexel Burnham earned fees by buying new stock issues from companies and reselling them to investors at a steep markup—a process known as underwriting. It was the underwriter's job to assess the growth potential of the company issuing the stock and set a per-share price for the issue that reflected the company's value. Most of the shares in the issue were sold privately to big investors such as pension funds and mutual funds. Then retail stockbrokers like Michael Prozumenshikov peddled whatever was left to their clients.

In 1986, the new-issue market was sizzling. The bull market helped ensure that the share prices of many issues surged as soon as the stock began trading publicly, reaping quick profits for investors. New issues were also attractive because the brokers' commissions for selling them were included in the per-share price and were, therefore, invisible to their clients. Brokers frequently claimed that new issues carried no commissions, although this wasn't strictly true.

The professional speculators who came to be known as hedge funds—often nothing more than stock traders working for obscure securities firms—dabbled exclusively in new issues. They traded stocks almost at random, buying up any issue they could get, whether the company made microchips, tennis shoes, or frozen yogurt. If the price of the stock rose after they bought it—even by a measly twenty-five or fifty cents a share—they would immediately resell it and take the profit. This tactic was called "flipping" a new issue. It wasn't rocket science, but it was extremely lucrative. (On Wall Street, the term "hedge fund" was also used to describe reputable money managers. But among retail stock-brokers such as Michael Prozumenshikov, the term was most often used to describe these new-issue speculators.)

"They were just looking for brokers who were unsophisticated or greedy," says one former Drexel broker. "They'd say, 'If you can get me the stock, I'm in for just about every deal.' They'd buy in five-thousand- and ten-thousand-share lots. Then they might flip the stock out in a couple of hours."

The main problem with flipping an issue was that it could wreak havoc in the fledgling market for the stock, plunging the share price into a tailspin. This infuriated the underwriters who had put the deal together. An underwriter was obliged to protect favored investors who bought the issue as a long-term investment; usually, when someone flipped a big chunk of the stock, the underwriter had no choice but to support the issue by buying back the shares at a substantial loss.

Michael Prozumenshikov knew nothing about such problems when one of his clients referred him to a stock trader named Louis Marin. Marin worked for a small Chicago firm called Brook Investments, but there was nothing small about Marin's trades. Marin told Michael he was looking to buy new issues underwritten by Drexel Burnham and other firms. If Prozumenshikov could deliver the stock, Marin would gladly buy ten thousand shares at a time.

Michael could hardly believe his good luck. He actually earned *more* in commissions handling new issues than he did selling ordinary stocks. And the volume of business Marin was talking about could double his commissions overnight. Michael enthusiastically phoned around to find out what new issues were available. Then he and Marin began to trade stocks.

At first, Bill Krebs knew nothing about Michael's deal with Marin. All he saw were the results: In Prozumenshikov's first full month on the job, the Russian broker grossed about $100,000 in commissions. This total was wildly high for any retail stockbroker, especially one who had just switched firms. Flabbergasted but delighted, Krebs crowed about Michael's production to Kurt Karmin, his boss in Drexel's Chicago-based Midwest regional headquarters. "We're happier than a son of a gun because Michael made all this money for the firm," Krebs says. "Makes me look good, makes Kurt look good, everybody's looking good, but we don't know what's really been going on here."

In fact, Krebs says, the stock was being flipped. If the share price rose, he says, Marin—or his clients—would immediately sell the stock for a profit. This, from the point of view of Drexel and its underwriters, was bad enough. Worse, though, was what was happening to the losing trades.

Capitalizing on a loophole in Drexel's accounting procedures, Marin was simply declining to accept trades that weren't profitable, Krebs says. If the stock's price had slumped after the issue was released, the bank that processed Marin's trades refused to acknowledge the trade. Through its computer system, the bank then sent the jilted stock order back to Drexel, which in turn automatically returned it to the bank. This process went on for days, with huge stock orders zinging back and forth in computer limbo, like bounced checks run amok.

The buck stopped at Drexel Burnham. Within a few weeks, it became clear that the trades had racked up losses of about $60,000. In Chicago, Kurt Karmin tried to get Brook Investments to own up to the debt; instead, Krebs says, Brook went out of business. Louis Marin left, apparently to go to some other firm. And in any case, it wasn't clear whether Marin bore legal responsibility for the losses, so Drexel was obliged to eat them itself.

For his part, Louis Marin admits that he did decline to accept some unprofitable new-issue trades, but says he did so only after Drexel Burnham tried to take away some of his winning trades. He denies he was acting as a hedge fund himself, but says he did handle stock orders on behalf of hedge funds.

Now Bill Krebs had a colossal mess on his hands, and Michael Prozumenshikov was in the middle of it. Enraged, Krebs stormed into Michael's office and demanded to know why he had processed Marin's trades. Michael pleaded ignorance, claiming that he thought the trades were legitimate. "Michael," Krebs shot back, "there's a $60,000 loss here. You're going to have to pay that." In the end, rather than forcing Michael to pay the losses out of his take-home pay, Krebs and Karmin decided to deduct it from his future gross production of commissions. Krebs also forbade Michael to trade with Marin again.

Even at freewheeling Drexel Burnham Lambert, the adventure raised eyebrows among the New York–based executives who ran the retail brokerage division. As one former Drexel executive put it, "With all due respect, to me Prozumenshikov was another young hotshot, and young hotshots made me nervous." The debacle also helped to sustain the nickname that Michael had learned to hate. At other Drexel offices, people who had never met Prozumenshikov were calling him the Mad Russian. Michael's success fueled his growing reputation as a wild man; if he hadn't made any money for the firm, no one would have cared.

But Bill Krebs found it hard to stay angry at someone who raked in such incredible commissions. While being forced to pay back the hedge-fund losses wounded Michael's pride, the damage to his personal finances wasn't devastating. In his second full month at Drexel, Prozumenshikov posted gross commissions of about $130,000—this time, with no hedge-fund orders to inflate the numbers. "Nothing stopped him," Krebs says. "If something happened, he just stepped over it and went right on."

To justify the unusually high trading volume in many of his accounts, Michael told his bosses Russian investors were uniquely adventurous—that they relished the big returns aggressive trading sometimes produced. It wasn't really true, of course—Prozumenshikov's lust for commissions had as much to do with his rapid-fire trading as any cultural predilection among his Russian clients—but Krebs didn't know that.

In Michael's accounts, meanwhile, problems were cropping up. A few Russian investors were breaking the code of silence, griping to Krebs that Prozumenshikov had executed trades without telling them and bought stock at prices higher than he promised. Three former Merrill Lynch clients had filed formal written complaints against him. And although Krebs was pleased with Michael's production, he worried that Michael might pose a liability to his Minneapolis operation. "I don't know if I trust this guy or not, because [clients] are telling me completely different things, almost in unison, than what he's telling me," Krebs said. "And he's saying they're lying."

To keep closer tabs on Michael, Krebs hatched a plan. He would plant an informant in Prozumenshikov's office—a sales assistant who would watch him and report to Krebs on the claims he made to his customers. Not just anyone would do, however. Michael's intense personality would overwhelm a timid soul.

It was Kurt Karmin's idea to place Mica Duncan in the job. Duncan, a nine-year veteran of the brokerage business, was assistant to the branch manager in Drexel's Kansas City office. Her husband, a broker for

another firm, was being transferred to Minneapolis, so she happened to
be looking for a job there. Duncan was smart, independent, tough, full of
energy and enthusiasm, and she knew securities law cold. She was a fit-
ness buff and a sports fan. Surrounded by aggressive male egos throughout her career, she had always held her own. Everyone at Drexel had
tremendous respect for her. And if anyone could handle Prozumenshikov, Bill Krebs decided after interviewing her, Mica Duncan could.

If Prozumenshikov knew that Duncan had been hired to ride shotgun
over him, he never said so. Instead of griping, he gratefully began heaping work on her. At first she sat at a desk outside his door, but he soon
asked her to move into the office itself.

The truth was that Mica had her own ideas about what the new job
would entail, and being a spy wasn't part of her plans. During her interview with Krebs she had tuned out his talk of informing on Michael. In
her mind, such a role wasn't appropriate, although she did intend to look
out for Drexel's interest in her own way. Duncan was confident that she
could rein in the Russian broker herself. And although Krebs and
Karmin had hired her to protect the firm, she would prove to be a god-
send for Prozumenshikov. For the next three years, she would work tirelessly for him, trying to keep him on the straight and narrow—and, when
that wasn't possible, taking calm, effective steps to protect him from
himself.

From the start, she didn't hesitate to tell her new boss what to do.
Mica took one look at the gaudy diamond ring and big Rolex wristwatch
he wore and strongly advised him to remove them while he was working. Less affluent clients who visited the office might find them offensive, she said. To Prozumenshikov, it came as a revelation that anyone
could be put off by the accoutrements of wealth, but he saw her point.
From that day, his first act upon arriving at work was to slip off the jewelry and stow it in a desk drawer.

Mica listened carefully to Michael's phone conversations, even those
he conducted in Russian, a language she didn't understand. "After a
while I knew what he was saying just by the inflection," she says. "I
could always tell if the conversation was going well, because of the tone
of his voice." In a number of ways, Duncan noticed, Michael tried to
convey the notion that he was omniscient about the market. He implied
that he had access to inside information that would move stock prices,
and he often made promises he couldn't keep. "So many times," Mica

says, "he would say, 'That's no problem; we can take care of that.' He would get off the phone and I'd say, 'Michael, you know we can't do that.'"

Other troubling points were the rapid pace of trading in Michael's accounts and the number of his clients using margin accounts to trade. Somewhere along the line, he had gotten into the habit of aggressively turning over stocks in many of his clients' portfolios. And while more conservative brokers thought it imprudent to recommend margin accounts to investors with limited means, Michael apparently didn't.

It wasn't Duncan's job to advise Prozumenshikov's clients to invest more conservatively, but she did know a way to help keep Michael out of trouble. "If I thought an account was too active," she says, "I would go and tell the manager: 'You need to send an activity letter on this account.'" In an activity letter, a branch manager thanks a broker's client personally for doing business with the firm and asks the client to phone if there are any problems. Failure to respond to such a letter substantially weakens a client's case if he later files a complaint or a claim for restitution.

To Mica's great relief, Michael didn't send out much correspondence of his own. "You love for brokers not to write letters," she says, "because then there's nothing in writing that can be held against you."

With two such strong personalities working in close quarters, sparks sometimes flew. Michael continued to be susceptible to hedge-fund traders and other smooth operators who offered to boost his commissions. It irritated him when Duncan told him someone was trying to take advantage of him, yet he seldom lost his temper with her. "I think he was a little afraid of her," says Dan Marcus, Kurt Karmin's right-hand man at Drexel's Midwest headquarters. "The only reason that Michael lasted as long as he did is because she worked goddamned hard to try to keep him out of trouble."

Despite Duncan's moderating influence, Michael remained indiscriminate about whom he would take as a client. At one point, he enlisted a client who was doing time in a California prison. The man ordered stock trades from prison by calling Drexel's toll-free phone line, and Drexel mailed his account statements to a Minnapolis post-office box. Mica didn't see any reason to object, but she often kidded Michael about it: "There's a call from Sing-Sing on line two," she would say.

A month after Mica arrived in Minneapolis, Michael got a rude shock. An ominous letter from the New York Stock Exchange arrived at Drexel, notifying Prozumenshikov that the exchange had launched an investigation into his business practices. Investigators, the letter said, were looking into the three complaints filed by Michael Peltsman, John Beskar, and a client named Jon Dahl. They were seeking evidence that Michael had misrepresented sales costs, executed unauthorized mutual-fund trades, and churned Beskar's account.

This first run-in with regulators rattled Michael. Just as his career was beginning to flourish—as he was finally reaping some rewards for his years of hard labor—he now had to worry about being thrown out of the brokerage business. At Krebs's request, Prozumenshikov wrote responses to the three clients' allegations. Drexel's legal department then reviewed Michael's statements and forwarded them to the New York exchange. Meanwhile, the Exchange mailed a letter to Beskar asking him to turn over his trading records and testify against Prozumenshikov. "They kept pestering me to cooperate," Beskar says. "They were hot to put him away."

For a while, Michael's fear of losing his newfound affluence forced him to be more circumspect in his sales approach. He now redoubled his efforts to develop such legitimate skills as researching stocks. Paging through news reports and financial documents, he scrutinized Minnesota companies for signs of unappreciated value. "He'd be looking for situations where he really thought something was going to happen, where there was going to be movement in the industry or movement in the company," says a former Drexel broker. "There was a company here in town that offered AIDS-awareness training. It was a series of training programs about AIDS that somebody had developed, and he thought it was going to be a hot stock because of the AIDS scare."

Prozumenshikov was also becoming quite good at spotting bargains among the blue-chip stocks of national companies. Unlike other brokers, he seldom overpaid for the stock of a nationally known company, and—with a couple of notable exceptions—he was rarely suckered in by a bad recommendation from Drexel's research department.

Inevitably, however, every broker made mistakes. And even at his best, Prozumenshikov was hampered by a reluctance to own up to them. For example, one Drexel broker who became friends with him says Michael was overly enthusiastic about preferred stock in the Western

Union telegram and money-wiring company. The stock was trading for about $57 a share, and Michael swore it was going to rise to $100.

On Prozumenshikov's strong recommendation, the broker bought two hundred shares for his own account, and immediately its price began to plummet. "I got busy and I didn't see him for a week," the broker says. "The stock continued to go down. So I stopped by and said, 'Michael, what do you think? It's sinking like a rock. What should we do? Should we buy more or should we sell it?' And then he was busy on the phone, because his recommendation hadn't worked out. His personality was such that he couldn't acknowledge that he was wrong. I finally sold it at a big loss."

Mica, meanwhile, was doing a number of things to help boost Michael's sales. In their daily relationship, roles were solidifying—they were becoming a team. Michael did the selling, and he was the one who called clients when there was good news to report about trading profits. If the news was bad, Mica was usually the one who called. She also walked his stock orders down the hall and fielded incoming phone calls, enabling him to cold call new prospects with fewer distractions. The two of them even devised a set of hand signals to communicate while Michael was on the phone.

As indefatigable as ever, Prozumenshikov was now able to stay on the line practically every minute of the day. And even when the story he was telling about a stock was far-fetched, his enthusiasm and conviction often made the sale. Each February, for instance, he would tell cold-call prospects that they should position themselves in Reebok stock. It would soon be spring, he explained, and people would start running and walking again, boosting athletic-shoe sales and Reebok's stock price. Prozumenshikov told the tale as if he were delivering the Gospel, but the stock-price run-up rarely panned out. "It was," Mica says, "just something for him to say."

Duncan's help enabled Michael to bring in commissions that exceeded even Bill Krebs's expectations. In just the second half of 1986, he generated about $500,000 in gross commissions—more than most brokers made for the whole year. This placed Prozumenshikov among Drexel's top two hundred brokers nationally and in the lower level of Drexel's perquisite incentive system, the President's Club. Members of the group took expense-paid trips to opulent resorts. At the beginning, these junkets served as Michael's vacations, for he refused to take any other time off. "I had to beg him to go on vacation for a week," Ellen Prozumenshikov says. "I said, 'Michael, you have to take care of yourself.'"

Despite his big earnings, Prozumenshikov rarely had any cash in his wallet, and Mica usually ended up paying for lunch. Sometimes, as the two of them ate sandwiches at their desks, she tried asking him about Russia, but he wasn't much interested in talking about it. What she knew about his previous life she learned mainly from hearing him describe it to his clients.

One day Michael brought a photograph of his wedding in Leningrad to the office. It portrayed his wife, his relatives, his in-laws, and a younger, thinner version of himself, all posing somewhat stiffly for the camera. Mica was surprised to note that the expressions on the faces were bland—even, in some cases, slightly grim. She studied it for a moment and then looked up at Michael. "Nobody's smiling," she said. A quizzical expression passed over Michael's face, changing quickly to a scowl—not at Mica, but at some long-buried remembrance of his native country. "Why should they?" he said. "They lived in Russia."

Despite Duncan's tendency to admonish Michael, they were discovering that they liked each other. Michael's charisma was at its peak while he was working the phones, and his dry jokes about his clients kept Mica in stitches. Sometimes, when the phone rang, they would both be laughing so hard that neither of them could answer it. Even their quarrels seemed to draw them closer.

Almost in spite of herself, Mica was developing respect for Prozumenshikov—an appreciation of the hardship he had endured and admiration for his resilience. She thought she understood how deprivation had spawned his strong desire for material things. It was clear that he expected no favors from anyone, and this trait she found refreshing. "I had never met anyone with a work ethic like that," she says. He was obviously the purest sort of bootstrap capitalist, determined to elevate himself and his family as far as he could in one lifetime.

Michael's rugged individualism was not without its unfortunate side effects, however. One of them was his nihilistic personal code, which rejected higher authority and was especially skeptical of restrictions and rules. Prozumenshikov didn't like it, for instance, when his born-again colleague, John Noonan, tried to talk to him about Christianity. Prozumenshikov respected Noonan, a driven salesman who was Michael's only real equal among the retail brokers in the branch. But he resented Noonan's proselytizing. "Michael was an adamant atheist, and he was pretty proud of it," Noonan says. "He didn't believe in a God. He was the God—you know, you make or break whatever you got. I bought him a Russian bible once and tried to share the Gospel with him, and he was pretty hostile toward that."

Professionally, Michael and John shared a healthy competition that they both enjoyed. One day, however, Noonan decided that Prozumenshikov had taken the rivalry a step too far.

A stockbroker in the office had decided to call it quits and go into another line of work, and Drexel's policy called for Krebs to parcel out the names of the broker's clients among other salesmen, giving the biggest accounts to brokers who had the best chance of persuading the investors to stay with Drexel. Krebs gave several names to John Noonan, including one of the plums—a wealthy Drexel client known to be very active in the stock market.

"But unbeknownst to me," Krebs says, "[the broker] has given all the accounts to Michael. I'm passing the accounts out to everybody in the office, and two days later we find out that these accounts have been prowled, that Michael is doing business with them."

It was John Noonan who made the discovery. When he called the first name on the list, the man said he had already signed up with someone named Michael Prozumenshikov, a Russian fellow. Noonan was surprised, but it didn't seem like a big deal. Some kind of mix-up, maybe. But when Noonan called the second client on the list, the story was the same. Michael had been there first.

Suddenly livid, Noonan bounced from his chair and strode briskly down the long hallway toward Prozumenshikov's office. Bill Krebs, whose own suite lay between Noonan's and Prozumenshikov's corner units, saw John hustle past and wondered where he was off to in such a hurry. People standing in the corridor scurried out of Noonan's way.

Directly across the hall from Michael's office, stockbrokers were gathering for the regular Monday afternoon sales meeting. Through the plate-glass wall of the conference room, they could see Prozumenshikov leap up as Noonan wheeled into his office. Conversations trailed off in mid-sentence as the brokers stared at the scene playing itself out across the hall.

Noonan was clearly furious about something. A former nightclub bouncer, he was built like an oak tree. Thick cords of muscles bulged beneath his shirt and tie. In a booming voice that carried all the way down the hall, he accused Prozumenshikov of stealing clients before anyone else could phone them. Prozumenshikov was underhanded and unprincipled, Noonan shouted.

Prozumenshikov, a big man in his own right, stood right in Noonan's face, not giving up an inch. At first he merely defended his honor, arguing that he was doing what the clients wanted. But as Noonan continued to level charges, Michael lost his temper. "You're a liar," he finally retorted. And at this Noonan clenched his fists, apparently ready to fight.

Across the hall, two dozen brokers watched in amazement. A few of the younger salesmen, eager for the main event to start, began hollering encouragement.

But by now Bill Krebs had emerged from his office, and he came sprinting down the hallway. He arrived as the screaming reached a fever pitch, and he stepped between the two men and pushed them apart. His voice was louder than either of the enraged stockbrokers, and his message was clear: If you don't stop this right now, Krebs thundered, you're both out of the business. "They were going to get to blows," he says. "I know they were going to get to blows."

Prozumenshikov suddenly seemed to become aware of his surroundings. Glancing across the hall, he could see that the entire brokerage staff had witnessed the confrontation. He was glad that Mica, who had left for the day, hadn't seen it. As Krebs led Noonan down the hall, the big Russian returned to his desk and slumped into his chair. Soon Krebs was back with a grimace on his face. He marched into the office and slammed the door shut so no one could hear him chew Michael out.

To Michael's surprise, Krebs didn't take sides in the dispute over clients. Instead, he chided Prozumenshikov for acting childish in front of so many people, and he ordered Michael to stay away from Noonan. "You don't want to mess around with him," Krebs said. "He'll hurt you."

"He's your favorite," Michael returned in a wounded tone. "You always side with him. You never side with me. Anyway, I'm not afraid of him. I have no reason to be afraid of John Noonan or anyone else. In Russia we used to settle our arguments with knives." And to emphasize the point, Michael unbuttoned his shirt sleeve and rolled it up to show Krebs an ugly scar.

Afterward, there was a great deal of speculation in the office about whether Michael had, in fact, stolen Noonan's accounts. Neither man wanted to talk about it, and Noonan played it down, insisting that the confrontation hadn't come as close as people thought to a fistfight. Many brokers took Noonan's side, convinced that Michael wasn't to be trusted. Others were disgusted by the whole episode. "Most of the older guys, they just thought it was outrageous that that kind of thing could go on in a brokerage firm," one broker says.

The competition between Prozumenshikov and Noonan redoubled, but without its previously amiable tone. "We were each very aware of what the other was doing on a gross production basis—almost on a daily basis, a minute-by-minute basis," Noonan says. "I never had any animosity after that, but I was never close with him. I knew he didn't like to be beat. So when I beat him, I let him know it, and vice versa." The rivalry was to continue for years, even after both men had gone on to different firms.

To some extent, Michael was now on Bill Krebs's shit list. Krebs lived with a nagging fear that the Russian broker was up to no good, yet he felt powerless to change Prozumenshikov's ways. Michael's huge production of commissions gave him clout at Drexel—a special status that Krebs felt he had to respect. "I'm in a bad situation," Krebs said. "I can't fire the guy, but I've got to report him if he's doing something." The Drexel manager's frustration frequently boiled over, and he and Michael now had loud quarrels of their own.

"I'll never forget one argument," Krebs says. "I don't even know what it was about. He was doing something I told him he couldn't do. We got into a real heated discussion about this. And right in the middle of the discussion, when I'm really pissed off, he started laughing at me. It got my goat. I wanted to go right down and pull his guts out with my hands." Yet despite the anger of the moment, Krebs didn't seem to take any of the clashes personally. For him, they were simply part of managing a difficult employee. In his heart, Krebs says, he had a genuine affection for Michael.

Years later, Krebs sat in the living room of his suburban home and ruminated on his stormy relationship with the Russian stockbroker. "Actually," Bill Krebs said quietly, "that's intimacy. If you can fight with somebody like that, that's intimacy. I guess that's one of the reasons why I feel like I feel about what happened to Michael. I feel real bad that it happened."

CHAPTER 7

Short, slight and soft-spoken, Dennis Carlson didn't look at first glance like a self-made multimillionaire. His face was too boyish, his hair too tousled and casually clipped. He shunned suits and ties for open-collared sports shirts and blue jeans. Yet Carlson, a high-school dropout, had earned a fortune before he was forty and now ranked among Minnesota's business elite.

The clues to Carlson's success could be seen in his manner. He was capable of clever, witty banter, but he became bored easily. In restaurants, he scowled and grumbled if asked to wait for a table. He gave orders reflexively and seemed accustomed to being obeyed.

People who had more than a cursory acquaintance with Carlson understood that his personality was rooted in contrast. Despite his studied dishabille, for instance, he opted for cosmetic surgery when his face began to sag. He favored such high-risk hobbies as motorcycling and amateur aviation, yet was concerned enough about his personal safety to install rocket-propelled parachutes in his three small airplanes. If one of the aircrafts became disabled, the rocket would activate the giant chute, and the entire plane would float to the ground intact.

In business Carlson projected a relaxed, big-picture style, but in fact he was good at identifying problematic details in any deal, and he was a formidable negotiator in the clutch. He took pride in pointing out that he had never taken a dollar from the government—in student loans, unemployment benefits, small-business assistance, or any other form. "I'm one of these people who want the government to protect our shores and deliver the mail and stay the fuck out of my personal life," he said.

Carlson could have owned the biggest mansion on Lake Minnetonka, but he chose instead to live in a relatively modest four thousand-square-foot house on Minnetonka's southern shore. He used the lake as a runway for his airplanes, outfitting them with pontoons for water landings and switching to skis in winter, when the lake froze. On sunny days, he sometimes flew north to lunch at lakeshore restaurants in Wayzata. There, crowds of gawkers gathered as his small, parachute-equipped plane circled for a landing. After gliding to a stop along the shore, Dennis Carlson would emerge from the cockpit, beaming like Charles Lindbergh after his historic flight across the Atlantic.

Carlson had made his money in factory close-outs. He bought surplus goods from manufacturers and resold them to the public at a markup. In 1974, he had founded a company he called C.O.M.B.—an acronym for Close Out Merchandise Buyers—and soon began advertising its wares in national newspapers. Within ten years, Carlson had built C.O.M.B. into a mail-order and retail network with forty stores and $60 million in annual sales. C.O.M.B. issued stock and went public in 1984. By 1986, Carlson had left the company and sold his stake in it for about $18 million.

These achievements only whetted Carlson's appetite. Compared with the feats of men like Irwin Jacobs and Carl Pohlad—the Minnesota financiers who had bought much of his C.O.M.B. stake and who ranked, according to *Forbes* magazine, among the four hundred wealthiest Americans—Carlson's successes remained modest. Suddenly free of the business he had built, he now was dabbling—talking with would-be entrepreneurs about raising money for their ventures and involving himself in whatever growing company he thought held promise.

Carlson was in hot pursuit of stock in one such emerging corporation, Home Shopping Network, Inc., when he first crossed paths with Michael Prozumenshikov. At the time, Prozumenshikov was working at Merrill Lynch.

Home Shopping Network had pioneered a new approach to mass marketing—news-style television broadcasts anchored by glib, attractive men and women who sold consumer products such as jewelry and electronics. The concept was enormously successful. As the company's sales boomed, Merrill Lynch was planning to take Home Shopping Network public by underwriting a new issue of its stock. Merrill's underwriters had priced the soon-to-be-released issue at $18 a share.

Carlson, an old hand at mass marketing, smelled a bargain. He was sure the stock price would shoot skyward as soon as the issue was released, and he was looking to buy as much Home Shopping Network stock as he could find. So far, however, he had been unable to land so much as a single share. At $18, everybody wanted it. Favored Merrill Lynch clients seemed to be the only people who could get any of the stock, and Carlson didn't have an account there. Then he remembered meeting a friendly Russian stockbroker while visiting the Merrill Lynch branch in Wayzata. It couldn't hurt, he decided, to give the man a call.

Unlike most brokers Carlson knew, Michael Prozumenshikov was charming on the telephone. He knew a great deal about C.O.M.B., and he seemed genuinely pleased that Dennis had called. And even though Carlson wasn't one of his clients, Michael said he could easily put his hands on some Home Shopping Network stock. Carlson enjoyed the conversation, but was skeptical that Prozumenshikov would be able to deliver.

The next day, however, Prozumenshikov called Carlson with the good news. He had managed to get ten thousand shares.

Michael was only too happy to explain how he did it. He had combed computerized financial news services for reports about Home Shopping Network and found one that said regulators in South Dakota refused to approve the stock for trading in their state. Then he phoned Merrill's South Dakota branch—which, as it turned out, had been allocated ten thousand shares of Home Shopping Network stock but wasn't allowed to sell it. "He went directly to that office and just said he had a client who would take it all, and he wanted it right now," Carlson says. "It was legal, and it was clever."

When the Home Shopping Network issue was released for public trading, its price soared to $42 a share—more than twice what Carlson had paid for it. The price continued to rise, and within a few weeks the stock split three-for-one. Carlson had turned a quick profit of about $80,000.

After this coup, Carlson often called Michael to chat. Carlson liked to say that he "collected" interesting people, meaning that he looked for unique sparks in his friends. And the traits he liked in Prozumenshikov, besides the Russian broker's exotic background, were the confidence and optimism that allowed Michael to ignore the conventional wisdom and transform complicated problems into simple tasks—such as getting his hands on sought-after stock when everyone else said it couldn't be done.

Strangely, Prozumenshikov didn't hound him about opening a substantial account at his firm, as brokers usually did. Instead, Michael seemed content to share vicariously in Carlson's pleasure about the profitable trade. While Michael might mention offhand some stock he was recommending to his clients, he didn't pressure Dennis to buy it. The anonymous prospects whom Prozumenshikov hammered in his cold calls would have been stunned to hear Carlson describe the Russian broker's sales approach. "He was mild-mannered, pleasant, low-key," Carlson says. "Oftentimes he called just to say 'Hi' and made you feel warm and fuzzy. He was not high-pressure at all. Whatever he did, he did it right."

Prozumenshikov had good reasons for taking it easy on Carlson. In the first place, the hard sell probably wouldn't work with such a canny businessman. And it wasn't as though Michael, as he did in his cold calls, had to push to get a foot in the door; the Home Shopping Network deal had swung Carlson's door wide open. It was, Michael hoped, only a matter of time before Dennis decided to reward him for his resourcefulness.

Besides, he absolutely revered Dennis Carlson. Carlson was the personification of Michael's own goals—living proof that the capitalist system placed no limits on personal achievement. Prozumenshikov was grateful simply to be associated with the quiet millionaire.

One afternoon, Dennis phoned Michael and asked him to stop by his house after work. When Michael showed up at the prescribed hour, Carlson presented him with a gleaming Concorde watch made of fourteen-carat gold. It was, Dennis said, a token of his appreciation for Michael's help in the Home Shopping Network transaction. For Carlson, Prozumenshikov's reaction to the gift was gratifying. "He became almost childlike," Carlson says. "He looked as though he was going to get a tear in his eye, as though no one had ever given him anything before, especially something as valuable as a gold watch."

When Michael left Merrill Lynch for Drexel Burnham Lambert, his contact with Carlson increased. Like many other investors at the time, Carlson was attracted by the aura of success that Michael Milken's operation brought to Drexel. And Carlson wanted to know whether Drexel, with its underwriting clout, could help raise money for companies in which he took an interest. For example, he was high on a small Minnesota company called Ballistic Recovery Systems, Inc., that made the rocket-propelled parachutes he installed in his planes. He was also interested in Seahawk Deep Ocean Technology, Inc., a firm that developed equipment to look for sunken treasure.

Bill Krebs, Michael's boss, knew that the firms Carlson was touting were too tiny to pay Drexel's underwriting fees. But Krebs was interested in getting Carlson to open an account at Drexel.

Despite his affinity for Prozumenshikov, Carlson never seriously contemplated turning his money over to Michael—until, that is, he had a falling out with his broker at the New York–based Goldman Sachs securities firm. Dennis was angry about transactions the Goldman broker executed while Carlson was in Brazil, which he believed lost about $1 million of the $17 million in his account. He filed a claim for restitution, and he began looking for someplace else to put his money.

The Carlson account was large enough that Drexel executives decided to put on a full-court press. Prozumenshikov spent hours at Carlson's house, describing the strategies he would employ if Dennis chose Drexel. Kurt Karmin, chief of Drexel's Midwest headquarters, flew up from Chicago to talk with Carlson about the advantages the firm could offer to a substantial investor. Drexel even arranged to fly Carlson and Prozumenshikov to New York, where Dennis was introduced to the executives in the firm's retail brokerage division. The coup de grâce was a meeting with Frederick Joseph, Drexel's famous chief executive.

In *The Predators' Ball*, reporter Connie Bruck describes Fred Joseph as Michael Milken's "face to the world . . . so politic, so polished, so affable, so disarming, this silver-haired, soft-spoken Bostonian, that he would lend his mantle of legitimacy to the Milken operation." Only the biggest of Drexel's retail brokerage clients ever met him. And Dennis Carlson, although he realized Drexel's dog-and-pony show had but one purpose, couldn't help but be flattered by Joseph's attention.

It happened that Carlson's meeting with Joseph took place soon after the well-known arbitrageur Ivan Boesky pleaded guilty to securities fraud and agreed to cooperate with the Securities and Exchange Commission's investigation of insider trading on Wall Street. It was to be a fateful period for Drexel Burnham Lambert. Boesky's testimony would precipitate the biggest insider-trading scandal in history. Eventually, it would end Michael Milken's reign as junk-bond king and bring mighty Drexel to its knees.

There had been suggestions in the *Wall Street Journal* that Drexel figured prominently in the SEC's investigation, but no one yet had any idea how hard the scandal would hit the firm. Among other things, the *Journal* had reported that Boesky received inside information on pending takeover bids from a Drexel investment banker named Dennis Levine. The newspaper even suggested that Boesky had stiffed Levine for $2.4 million—the Drexel man's share of Boesky's ill-gotten gains. Dennis Carlson, an avid reader of the *Journal*, had perused these accounts, but they hadn't soured him on Drexel.

When Carlson and Prozumenshikov were ushered into Fred Joseph's pine-paneled office in Manhattan, they found the chief executive in repose, the knot in his tie loosened and his feet propped up on his desk. "He looked so damned comfortable that I said, 'Don't get up; stay there,'" Carlson said. "I took the chair opposite his desk and put my feet on his desk. And we both sat with our feet on the desk." Prozumenshikov knew better than to join them. After introducing himself to Joseph, he eased into a chair and tried to remain as inconspicuous as possible.

Joseph had no way of knowing whether the bad publicity about the Boesky affair had given Carlson reservations about moving his money to Drexel. But after some small talk, Joseph forced the issue. What did Carlson think of all that, he asked, of Ivan Boesky and the insider-trading scandal?

"The son of a bitch deserved to go to jail," Carlson declared without hesitation. Pleased at seeing surprise register on Joseph's face, Carlson barreled ahead with his analysis. "Not because he allegedly traded on inside information," he went on. "He was paying a young man for the information—I think the guy's name was Dennis Levine—and Ivan Boesky stiffed his informant. Anyone who does that is a fink and ought to go to jail. Here you got a guy giving you information worth hundreds of millions of dollars and all he asks for is a couple of (million) bucks in a brown paper bag. And the dirty son of a bitch stiffs him. I mean, that's a louse." Here Carlson wound down his diatribe, and, after a moment of stunned silence, everyone in the room had a good laugh.

In the end, Drexel got Carlson's money—not all of it, but a $7 million chunk. It was enough to satisfy Michael Prozumenshikov. Landing Carlson as a client substantially boosted the assets the broker controlled at Drexel.

Most of the money Michael managed for Dennis was put into conservative vehicles, including blue-chip municipal, state, and federal bonds. Prozumenshikov urged Carlson to open a big margin account for stock trading, but Carlson declined. However, to Michael's delight, he did set aside more than $1 million of his own money for aggressive speculation in takeover stocks. "It was the eighties," Carlson says. "We didn't buy equities with an eye for growth and for long-term appreciation. We were trading, and we were trading on deal stocks. Michael liked deals, and by the way, I did too. Most of the ideas were mine. Whenever he mentioned a stock to me, I had already known about it. It was in play, or an offer had already been made. He didn't have to hype it to me."

Although Carlson and Prozumenshikov didn't limit their trading to companies based in Minnesota and the Midwest, there were plenty of exciting regional corporations to choose from. These companies manufactured all kinds of goods: Food products, high-tech equipment, and medical supplies were a few of the regional specialties. Local business benefited from the presence of sophisticated regional securities firms such as Piper Jaffray and Dain Bosworth, which underwrote stock issues and then supported the companies by making markets in their stocks.

For Prozumenshikov, the vibrant Minnesota business environment was a playground of investing possibilities. And he wasn't alone in his enthusiasm for his area's stocks. As a rule, stockbrokers in the Twin Cities of Minneapolis and St. Paul pay closer attention to local companies than do brokers in other cities. It was easier to get good information about firms that were close to home, and brokerage offices became clearinghouses for rumors about them. "Minneapolis is a very clannish town as far as investments are concerned," said John Petcoff, Prozumenshikov's client in nearby Milwaukee. "Everybody knows every goddamn thing."

Carlson knew a thing or two as well. Michael was thrilled by Carlson's extensive knowledge of business in Minnesota—and elsewhere. By his reckoning, Dennis was well-nigh omniscient. To be sure, Carlson had assembled an impressive list of business contacts during his years at C.O.M.B. And Dennis was always networking, meeting more people through business deals and parties. Michael pumped his new client for details about virtually everything—the people Dennis knew, the companies he was interested in, the companies they both knew were the targets of takeover plays. Because of his total confidence in Carlson, Prozumenshikov was to follow his new idol into at least one stock that would cost Michael's other clients dearly, that of Zondervan Corporation, a bible publisher based in Grand Rapids, Michigan.

For months now, Carlson had been accumulating a large position in Zondervan, which like so many companies recently had become the target of corporate raiders. Through its national network of bookstores, Zondervan was the nation's fourth largest book retailer. In addition to its evangelical line, the company had published the autobiographies of such noted Christians as drug-trafficking automobile mogul John DeLorean and former Nixon aide Charles Colson. The music-video network MTV had recently rejected a Christian rock video called "Six, Six, Six," distributed by a Zondervan subsidiary, which contained a frightening scene of the Antichrist perishing in flames.

Out of Great Britain had swooped a raider named Christopher J. Moran, who accumulated 8.5 percent of Zondervan's stock and then offered to buy the rest of its outstanding shares in a friendly transaction. Moran asserted that the company's assets were undervalued. Zondervan, he said, was neglecting the opportunity to profit from the popularity of born-again Christianity in the United States. "It's a company, not a church," he told the *Chicago Tribune*.

Even as the Zondervan board of directors rejected Moran's offer, more sharks began to circle the company. Investors in New York and California announced they had also acquired stakes in Zondervan and were willing to participate in a takeover. Emboldened, Moran continued buying Zondervan shares and said he was considering a hostile bid for the company.

Dennis Carlson got to know Christopher Moran through Jeffrey Wendel, a Minneapolis stockbroker, and flew to New York to meet Moran and discuss joining his Zondervan investor group. In person, Moran cut an impressive figure. His speech spilled out in a melodic brogue. He wore the finest Saville Row tailored suits, and he possessed a sly, old-world charm that bewitched many Americans.

Moran also had a keen appreciation for the bottom line. Zondervan's assets—its sixty-one stores and its publishing facilities—were worth vastly more than the combined value of the company's 4.1 million outstanding shares of stock, Moran told Carlson. The only way to maximize the hidden value of the company, he said, was to change the way it did business, either by acquiring it or forcing it to sell itself to someone else.

Carlson began buying Zondervan shares as part of a group that included Jeffrey Wendel, but Carlson didn't use Michael Prozumenshikov as his broker in the transactions. He bought the stock for more than $20 a share—a price already inflated by Moran's takeover talk, far higher than Zondervan's usual $10 to $15 trading range.

Like scores of embattled companies in the roaring eighties, Zondervan was now "in play." At corporate headquarters in Michigan, Zondervan employees gathered in an emergency prayer rally, imploring God for protection from the British raider and his allies. Finally, in October 1986, the company relented to the pressure and announced it had hired an investment banking firm to explore selling itself.

Soon Moran passed along to Dennis Carlson a juicy tidbit about Zondervan. The British raider, Carlson says, told him that Zondervan was about to be bought by the giant New York–based MacMillan Publishing Company. "Moran was saying MacMillan was going to take it over," Carlson says. "There were conference calls between myself, Wendel, and Moran where Moran would make the statements. He said he had had meetings with them and reported back to us that a sale was imminent, in the forty-dollar-a-share region." If true, the rumor seemed certain to push Zondervan's stock price sharply higher and enrich Moran, Carlson, and their fellow investors.

It is clear that Michael Prozumenshikov knew about the MacMillan rumor—even though it hadn't surfaced in news reports—because he used it to sell Zondervan stock to his clients. It isn't clear where Michael heard the takeover rumor.

In May 1987, Christopher Moran shocked his allies by liquidating more than half of his 560,000-share stake in the company. Later, the Securities and Exchange Commission would sue Moran for insider trading, alleging that he sold the shares after being told Zondervan was making no progress in finding a buyer. In any case, his dumping of the stock prompted a number of other big investors to bail out as well. Zondervan's stock price went south; by mid-May it had plunged to about $15 a share.

Prozumenshikov still thought MacMillan was about to buy the Michigan bible company. It was at this point that Michael began hawking Zondervan stock to a few of his fellow Russians and his wealthiest American clients. "Michael didn't sell it to everyone," Duncan says. "He was kind of careful sometimes, when he really had insider information."

What Michael was doing was illegal, whether his customers made money on the trades or not. And for all he knew, the New York Stock Exchange's investigators were still hot on his trail. And during business hours, at least, he was coy about passing along the MacMillan tip. "I've heard there are some people looking at taking it over," he would say. "We won't hold it for a long time. If the story proves wrong, we'll get out of it."

Outside the office, however, Prozumenshikov couldn't help boasting about what he knew. One of those he approached was Valery Gilevich, the surgeon's assistant he had met in the hospital eight years earlier, and whom he had later enlisted as a client. One Friday afternoon, Michael phoned Val and, speaking in Russian, urged him to invest in Zondervan stock. Prozumenshikov said he was sure the stock price would rise substantially, and quite soon.

Gilevich was skeptical. Why, he asked, should I invest good money in a religious publishing company? Even speaking in Russian, Prozumenshikov was uncomfortable holding forth on the telephone. Instead, he asked Val to stop by his house that weekend. "I'll explain when I see you in person," he said.

On a warm Sunday afternoon, Gilevich drove to Michael's suburban home, where Michael greeted him with a smile and led him into the family room. There Prozumenshikov eagerly told Gilevich about MacMillan's supposedly pending bid for Zondervan. "He was convincing me that he knows everything about the company, that they are lined up to be taken over by MacMillan," Gilevich says. The next day, through Prozumenshikov, Val bought about $15,000 worth of Zondervan stock for about $15 a share.

Within two weeks, although MacMillan hadn't made an offer for the bible company, Zondervan's price surged to more than $18 a share. Gilevich, who stood to earn a $3,000 profit if he liquidated his stake, urged Prozumenshikov to sell. But Michael balked. He was convinced that a takeover might occur at any moment, and the resulting profit would make $3,000 look like a pittance. In his own way, he was trying to look out for what he thought was Val's best interest. "He refused to sell it," Gilevich says. "He said it's going to be higher. I said, 'Are you sure?' He almost was like swearing on a mother's grave, you know, he was so convincing."

Michael also used the MacMillan rumor to sell Zondervan stock to Zachary Persitz, whose wife, Julia, had been so helpful during Ellen Prozumenshikov's pregnancy. At the time, Michael was managing most of Zack's savings—a total of about $100,000—and, so far, the returns had been spectacular. In just six months, the stocks Prozumenshikov chose for Persitz had reaped a profit of more than $35,000, minus commissions, for a robust gain of more than 5 percent a month. When Prozumenshikov strongly recommended the Zondervan stock, Persitz didn't hesitate. In three transactions over the next few weeks, Zack invested a total of about $24,000 in the bible company.

The MacMillan rumor didn't pan out. Weeks turned into months, and still Zondervan's board received no offers. Once again, the stock price began to slump. Christopher Moran faded from view, apparently no longer interested in acquiring Zondervan. MacMillan, it turned out, had considered bidding for the company but had balked when Zondervan declined to provide information on its financial operations.

Now other big investors, worried by news reports suggesting that Zondervan might never find a buyer, rushed to sell their stakes. Among them was Dennis Carlson, who sold his position for a huge loss. He, Wendel, and other members of their Minnesota group sued Moran, alleging that the raider had reneged on a commitment to indemnify them from losses on the stock. Eventually, they won a judgment for $2.2 million—which they couldn't collect because courts in Scotland, where Moran lived, wouldn't honor the ruling.

Both Val Gilevich and Zack Persitz held onto their Zondervan stock for months in the vain hope of a takeover. And both suffered what were, for them, major losses. Gilevich lost about $10,000 of the money he had salted away from his modest hospital salary. What irked Val most was that, in his view, the investment needn't have been a loser. Testily, he reminded Prozumenshikov that he had asked the broker to sell when the stock price was high. What happened, he demanded, to Michael's sure-thing MacMillan tip? "It's not *my* fault," Prozumenshikov shot back. "It's not my fault that MacMillan didn't buy it."

But Val's annoyance was nothing to the fury of Zachary Persitz. As a rule, Zack monitored activity in his Drexel account zealously. Despite the big profits Prozumenshikov was earning for him, he became irrationally angry if even one of the stocks Michael chose lost money. Persitz had never lost as much in the market as he did on Zondervan—a total of about $12,800. As the bible publisher's stock price limped lower, Zack complained bitterly to Michael and Mica Duncan.

Persitz chose to leave the remainder of his savings in Prozumenshikov's hands, but seemed unable to let go of his resentment about Zondervan. Even months later, it flared up unpredictably during conversations about unrelated transactions. This struck Michael as both unfair and ironic, because in the past Zack had always made a show of how little he and Julia Persitz cared about material things. It was hard for Michael to shrug off Zack's fits of temper, however; their wives were friends, as were their young sons, who shared the same name.

Dennis Carlson, who had more money to lose, didn't take his Zondervan losses as hard as Persitz did. Dennis simply turned the matter over to his lawyers and moved on. In 1987, there was no shortage of new deals to occupy his attention.

That summer, Carlson was approached by three mid-level United Airlines executives who wanted to take over a publicly traded airline called Air Wisconsin. It was the largest regional airline in the country, and the executives wanted to run it. They came to Carlson because they knew nothing about the mechanics of takeovers and had little money of their own to use as equity in such a deal. They had decided they needed a deep-pocketed partner to help with the details and the financing.

In typically informal style, Carlson hosted the first meeting about Air Wisconsin at his house, on a sunsplashed mid-July afternoon. There, the United men lounged around Carlson's private pool, sipping cool drinks, and mulling Air Wisconsin's assets. They all agreed that the airline's lucrative business shuttling passengers from the upper Midwest to Chicago's O'Hare International Airport made it a worthy target. Air Wisconsin owned about thirty airplanes, ten of them jets. It also owned valuable arrival and departure gates in United Airlines's new terminal at O'Hare. Judging by its stock price of $10 a share, the commuter airline was grossly undervalued. "Their gates and slots at O'Hare were worth as much as the stock itself," Carlson says.

For the time being, the men agreed to keep their discussions secret. Neither United, which was affiliated with Air Wisconsin, nor executives at the Wisconsin airline itself were likely to welcome their advances. More to the point, Carlson and his partners needed to keep any potential takeover bid out of the newspapers. Reports that Air Wisconsin was in play would inflate the stock price and make a takeover less attractive, just as Christopher Moran's media hype had done to Zondervan.

Carlson was intrigued. Here he saw an opportunity to step into the ranks of big-league corporate raiders who sought to acquire companies, sell off some of their assets, and control the rest of the company more or less for free. Carlson estimated he would need to raise about $100 million to acquire the airline. For financing, if he decided to go ahead with the deal, he might need to look no further than Drexel Burnham Lambert.

Michael Prozumenshikov had often bragged that the link to Michael Milken's all-powerful junk-bond department was encouraged throughout his firm. If a Drexel stockbroker had a big client who wanted to get into the takeover game, Prozumenshikov said breezily, Milken's people would be happy to look him over. Carlson now told the Russian broker that he was exploring a bid for Air Wisconsin, and asked whether Michael could set up a meeting with someone in Drexel's high-yield bond department. Prozumenshikov fairly bubbled with enthusiasm for the project. He assured Dennis it would be no trouble to tap into Milken's outfit, which, as they both knew, was the sun in Drexel's universe.

Soon Carlson received a phone call from someone named Dennis McCarthy in the Beverly Hills office. McCarthy's tone was enthusiastic and upbeat, as if there weren't a doubt in his mind that a takeover could be accomplished. He asked a few questions about Air Wisconsin's assets and stock price, then scheduled a meeting with Carlson in California. Between now and then, McCarthy said, he would do some research on the company and put together estimates of what it would take to tender a bid.

Carlson packed everything—the three-hour flight to Los Angeles, an afternoon meeting at Drexel headquarters, and a late dinner with McCarthy—into a single day. He had heard that Milken's people were workaholics, and McCarthy certainly seemed to fit the mold. McCarthy had looked into Air Wisconsin, he said, and he shared Carlson's conviction that the company was undervalued. "He said, 'You want to make a tender offer? Go ahead. We'll finance you with junk bonds,'" Carlson says. "If the tender offer was to be one hundred million dollars, and if I had twenty million dollars of my own money in it, they'd provide bonding for the remaining eighty percent, just like that. It came so quick, so simple, I couldn't believe my ears." Drexel's main requirements were that Carlson sink a substantial share of his personal worth into the deal and, of course, that he pay enormous underwriting fees.

The ball was left in Carlson's court. He was to return to Minneapolis and begin buying Air Wisconsin stock. He wouldn't, at first, accumulate as much as 5 percent of the company's shares, because at that level he would have to disclose his holdings publicly. Carlson, his partners from United, and McCarthy would settle on an appropriate date. Then Carlson would quickly acquire an additional 10 to 15 percent of the stock and announce his junk-backed bid for the company.

Michael Prozumenshikov, again flouting securities laws, meanwhile had taken it upon himself to peddle Air Wisconsin stock to other clients, without telling Carlson about it. Despite his best intentions, his Zondervan tip hadn't worked out for small investors like Gilevich and Persitz. This time, Prozumenshikov decided to reveal his inside knowledge only to his most aggressive, well-to-do clients. One of them was Milwaukee native John Petcoff.

Prozumenshikov told Petcoff that Carlson was looking at taking over Air Wisconsin, and had just returned from a meeting with Milken's people in Beverly Hills. "Michael said he was involved in intimate things, and he's privy to this information," Petcoff says. "He said Carlson was taking a large position in the stock." On Michael's recommendation, Petcoff bought two thousand shares of Air Wisconsin for about $10 a share.

Prozumenshikov also advised broker friends at Drexel to recommend Air Wisconsin to their clients. He even mentioned the stock to Alex Bernstein, the other Soviet-born broker in town. When fellow brokers asked why they should put their customers into such a nondescript Wisconsin company, Michael smiled mysteriously. "Because it's going to go up" was all he would say. Other brokers concluded that Prozumenshikov spread the rumor simply to stoke his own ego.

Dennis Carlson bought about $400,000 worth of Air Wisconsin stock and continued to explore the details of acquiring the company. His research, however, suggested that the deal was not as straightforward as McCarthy had made it out to be. There was, for one thing, considerable risk involved in sinking most of his personal fortune into any single venture. Moreover, Carlson was having trouble verifying what landing slots at O'Hare were actually worth. And Air Wisconsin's board of directors was bound to resist the takeover as vigorously as it could. It was all becoming too complicated for Carlson's taste.

As summer turned to fall, the Wisconsin legislature delivered what Dennis decided was the killing stroke to his fledgling deal. An Australian raider named Alan Bond had tendered a $1 billion hostile takeover bid for Wisconsin's Heileman Brewing Company, brewer of

Old Style beer and other beverages. Called into special session by the governor, the state legislature quickly enacted one of the most vigorous antitakeover laws yet seen in the United States. Among other things, it gave the board of any Wisconsin company the right to veto unwanted takeovers, regardless of whether the bid benefited shareholders.

Three months after they began, Carlson's takeover talks were finished. "I decided that I wouldn't take on the whole Wisconsin legislature," he says. "Hell, I couldn't even manage my girlfriend." Carlson later noted with disgust that the Heileman deal went forward despite the antitakeover law, after the company's directors voted to accept a sweetened offer of $1.2 billion.

Prozumenshikov tried unsuccessfully to talk Carlson into going ahead with the bid. "To him, to take over Air Wisconsin was real simple," Carlson says. "Just get the money and go do it and you can run that airline. To him, nothing was complicated. And as much as one would like to believe the world is built that way, the world is not built that way."

Yet Michael's regrets were tempered by the fact that his clients who bought Air Wisconsin stock did well in the end. In November, Carlson's erstwhile partners in the deal resigned from United Airlines and made an $85 million, $11.50-a-share takeover bid for Air Wisconsin, with financial backing from Citicorp. Although Air Wisconsin directors rejected the offer, the publicity attracted other investor groups, who weighed in with sweetened offers of $14 and then $16 a share.

These offers drove up Air Wisconsin's stock price, and Prozumenshikov's clients were able to sell their shares for a profit. Michael was immensely proud of having been ahead of the curve on the takeover plays, and heedless of the laws he had violated in the process. "He didn't care what rules there were," John Petcoff says. "There were no rules as far as Michael was concerned."

It was Prozumenshikov's strong conviction that the biggest players on Wall Street shared his contempt for the law. The widening insider-trading investigation on the Street merely reinforced his unorthodox view. Clearly, he decided while reading the *Wall Street Journal*'s coverage of the scandal, just about everyone with access to confidential information was using it to trade stocks. His own dabbling with insider trading, he suspected, paled beside the schemes of big players like Michael Milken.

Disappointed that Dennis Carlson hadn't met Milken during his trip to Beverly Hills, Prozumenshikov soon had the consolation of meeting the great man himself. That year, Milken was the featured speaker at a three-day retreat for top-producing Drexel stockbrokers at the Greenbrier Hotel, a colonnaded structure nestled within 6,500 acres of lush gardens in the mountains of West Virginia. Prozumenshikov was among the two hundred brokers who gathered to hear Milken talk about the world economy. After the speech, Milken descended from his podium and pressed the flesh with the brokers for more than an hour. There, surrounded by opulence Prozumenshikov had never known as a child, he met the man who embodied everything he wanted to be. He introduced himself, shook Milken's hand, even exchanged views on a couple of stocks—and later gushed about the encounter during a long-distance conversation with Mica Duncan.

Ever after, Milken was Michael Prozumenshikov's personal hero. Even later, when Milken was indicted and anointed by the financial press as the standard-bearer for greed in the 1980s, Michael continued to worship him. The federal investigation, Prozumenshikov told one colleague, was a witch-hunt, and Milken was no more guilty of impropriety than anyone else in the securities industry.

Just as fears were mounting in Drexel's corporate hierarchy about the fallout of the SEC investigation, however, executives in Drexel's retail division were becoming concerned about goings-on in the Minneapolis branch. The prevailing perception at Midwest headquarters was that the atmosphere of the branch was too permissive, even for profit-hungry Drexel Burnham. Compliance problems such as Prozumenshikov's run-in with the New York Stock Exchange were seen as warning signals. Compliance officers and others who tried to get records from the office found Minneapolis staffers defensive or openly hostile. Some brokers were complaining about Bill Krebs's management style and about inefficiency in processing their stock orders. Morale was said to be low.

Also worrisome to some executives was a power struggle between Krebs and his assistant manager, which Krebs resolved by demoting the deputy. Midwest chief Kurt Karmin had visited Minneapolis and came away with the impression that the political strife in the branch might be a tip-off to deeper problems.

Matters came to a head when Karmin, seeking an unbiased opinion, dispatched two assistants to Minneapolis. One was Dan Marcus, Karmin's top deputy in Chicago. The other was Janice Brennan, an administrator who knew more about critical "back-office" brokerage operations—i.e., the transmission of stock orders to New York and the processing of payments, among other things—than anyone else at Midwest headquarters.

Marcus and Brennan spent two days in Minneapolis interviewing brokers and support staff and reviewing records. They learned that Minneapolis employees had divided themselves into pro- and anti-Krebs camps. A few said Krebs was a good administrator who wisely avoided heaping restrictions on his brokers; others complained that he played favorites. Krebs's critics tended to be more vocal than his supporters, who seemed to think that loyalty meant keeping their mouths shut. Krebs, for his part, defended himself vigorously, describing instances in which he had cracked down on brokers and pointing to the dynamic growth in commission revenue under his leadership.

The last straw for Brennan and Marcus was a confidential conversation with Mica Duncan.

While Prozumenshikov did his best to hide his most flagrant abuses from Duncan, she nevertheless had a good idea what he was up to. She didn't blame him for breaking rules so much as she blamed Krebs for failing to stop him. Her loyalty to Michael hadn't wavered, but Mica felt strongly that she needed to alert someone to the problems she saw in the office.

Duncan met Marcus and Brennan after work at a restaurant in the downtown Minneapolis Marriott Hotel. She asked for, and received, assurances that what she was about to say was strictly off the record; it wouldn't find its way into company files or be used, on its face, to discipline anyone. Then, over dinner and a few glasses of wine, Duncan delivered a distressing report on the state of the Minneapolis branch.

If Marcus and Brennan suspected that discipline was lax in Minneapolis, she said, they were right. From her point of view, coming to work in the branch had been like taking a job at some other, more profligate firm. Brokers there, Duncan said, were allowed to ignore margin calls and violate trading rules.

The problems were hurting Drexel's image, she said. People in the local business community were talking about Drexel, and what they were saying wasn't good. The newspaper reports about the scandal brewing in New York were bad enough. Locally, Duncan said, the scuttlebutt was that Drexel didn't adequately supervise its stockbrokers and that clients suffered as a result.

Now that she had started, her words tumbled out in a torrent. She was worried about Prozumenshikov, she said, for his own sake and Drexel's. He wasn't getting the direction he needed. She had little doubt, she said, that problems such as Michael's hedge-fund debacle could have been avoided if the broker's bosses kept closer tabs on what he was doing.

On the flight back to Chicago, Brennan and Marcus discussed what they would tell Kurt Karmin. Marcus had known Duncan for years, and he trusted her opinion. The urgency of her appeal worried him, drawing the problems he had observed himself into sharper perspective. At a minimum, there was rampant disloyalty in the office to Bill Krebs. Moreover, Brennan believed, the branch's back office was a mess.

By the time the plane touched down at O'Hare, the two of them had decided their report to Karmin would be grim indeed. "You couldn't fail to notice there was a problem," Brennan says. "I don't care how blind you are, you couldn't fail to see that."

CHAPTER 8

Before he moved his savings to Drexel Burnham Lambert, Zachary Persitz had never cared much about money. A hydroelectrical engineer for the state of Minnesota, he knew a few things about mortgages, IRAs, stocks, and bonds. But it was clear that his priorities lay elsewhere.

A self-styled intellectual, sometime poet and sculptor, Persitz was dedicated to improving his mind. He immersed himself in books, often huddling beneath a reading lamp until late at night. He loved art and music, tastes he shared with his wife, Julia, a violinist in a local chamber orchestra. Frequently, at the dinner table, he surprised her by trotting out well-informed opinions on Christian televangelism, computer science, cardiology, and other obscure topics.

Persitz was an organizer, a list maker, meticulous about researching even the most routine matters. When he decided to buy a dog for his young son, Daniel, he spent weeks studying breeds from A to Z before settling on a rare long-haired species renowned for its obedience and lack of shedding. When he scheduled family vacations, he mapped out each day's activities in advance. He strove for precision in all facets of his life, and he hated nothing so much as wasting time. The dry cleaner was near the grocery store and the drugstore, and the gas station was on the way, so of course all these errands must be saved for the same trip—even if it meant doing without something in the meantime.

Zachary found it necessary to give unsolicited advice to his two younger brothers, who had immigrated to the United States after he did. The next youngest, Leonard, had been diagnosed as a manic depressive and needed, in Zack's view, considerable shepherding. Alex, the youngest, was stable, married, and gainfully employed, but this didn't dissuade Zachary from besieging him with unsolicited advice. Zack, irrationally worried that his brother might somehow contract AIDS, once spent the better part of an hour trying to talk Alex out of traveling to California without his wife.

Other worries plagued Zachary. For example, he mistrusted doctors and other professionals who made judgments he didn't understand. When a friend was stricken with cancer, Zack phoned Valery Gilevich at the Metropolitan Medical Center—dozens of times—to probe for flaws in the diagnosis of his friend's physician. Persitz endlessly interrogated Gilevich about all the technical details: morphology, chemotherapy, the implications of his friend's urine output and heart rate, the credentials of the surgeon who was to operate. "Maybe it was a little excessive," Gilevich says.

Persitz stood more than six feet tall, but his frame was lean, giving the impression of a shorter man. His face was prototypically Russian, with a soft, downturned mouth, a strong chin, high cheekbones, and dark, sad eyes that were accentuated by thick eyebrows. His wavy spray of hair was black.

Zack, or Zorik, as he was called by others in the Russian community, was known to be aloof in social situations. At parties, he could often be found at the center of a group of youngsters, leading games or engaging them in earnest conversation, endlessly patient with their prattling and short attention spans. "He loves kids," Julia Persitz often said, "and kids love him."

No one, his wife thought, was a more devoted father than Zachary. Before Daniel reached school age, Persitz had spent hours with the boy in the evenings, teaching him to speak and write both Russian and English. Convinced that hearing spoken words would enhance his son's writing ability, he read aloud to Danny each night from Dr. Seuss and other children's books. Zack adhered to this routine even when he and his wife had guests, vanishing upstairs for a half-hour at Danny's bedtime. And he gave his son elaborate birthday parties; for one of them, he wrote a poem and hand-painted a T-shirt for each child.

While Julia appreciated her husband's dedication, the couple didn't always agree on the proper approach with Danny. It was very important to Zack, for example, that the boy excel at sports. Julia was inclined to let Danny decide what he wanted to do, to let things take their natural course. But Zack, who wanted his son to be strong and masculine, insisted that Danny learn to play soccer and baseball.

Zachary's strong opinions about parenting seemed to result from his own unhappy childhood in Russia. His parents had divorced when he was six. After the split, which was acrimonious, Zachary seldom saw his father, Boris Persitz, and his mother soon remarried. Zack became increasingly moody and yearned for privacy. But in crowded Leningrad, he was obliged to share one of the two cramped bedrooms in his family's flat with his brother, Leonard Persitz, and, before long, his half brother, Alex Shifrin.

Young Zachary seemed to his family to be attuned to a muse that no one else heard, one that filled his head with the poetry and resolutions for self-improvement that he scribbled constantly in his notebooks. Of the three boys, Zack was the best student. He enjoyed studying and excelled at all subjects, from physics to literature and foreign languages. He had hung a curtain to cordon off a corner of his crowded bedroom, and he often sequestered himself there at a small desk, reading or writing for hours. He liked to keep the area tidy, his books in alphabetical order, his possessions arranged neatly on a shelf.

Leonard and Alex liked nothing better than to try to invade Zachary's curtained sanctuary. Some nights, after bedtime, the two boys would steal up quietly to rifle through the private things Zack kept hidden in a box under his desk—sea shells, colored pictures, coins, and his precious notebooks.

When he awoke and caught them, as he inevitably did, Zack attacked Leonard, the ringleader, with appalling ferocity. Zack would hold the younger boy down and pound him with his fists until Leonard's shrieks woke their mother. As these nighttime invasions continued, Zack took to keeping a pair of pliers near his bed. When he caught his brothers trespassing, he exacted a terrible punishment.

Zachary seemed to record incidents like these on some scorecard in his psyche, silently tallying grievances against each of the members of his family. For instance, he resented Alex, the only child of his mother's second marriage, because he felt that his half brother received more than his fair share of attention.

Lowest, in Zachary's estimation, was his stepfather, David Shifrin, whom he simply ignored. When they passed in the hall or sat at the dinner table, Zack pointedly avoided the man's gaze. And while some children might give their parents the silent treatment for a few hours or even a full day, Zack had refused to utter a single word to his stepfather for a period of seven years. At first this was embarrassing, an awkward gap that was difficult to explain to relatives and friends. With the passing years, however, it became a matter of family routine.

Zack's reticence derived from a single incident. One evening, his mother and stepfather had gone out for dinner, leaving ten-year-old Zack to watch over Leonard and Alex, who was only two. When the couple returned, they found baby Alex bleeding from a gash on his head. Zack said Alex had fallen out of his crib. Horrified, Shifrin had reddened and screamed at Zachary. When the boy yelled back, Shifrin, who didn't believe in spanking children, gave Zachary a shove. This single gesture had terminated their relationship.

Still bitter about his parents' divorce, Zack also refused to acknowledge his natural father's surname of Persitz. When Zack entered high school, he called himself by a fictional name, Zachary Severov. He chose Severov, a variation of the Russian word for north, because it was consistent with his most romantic notion of his own identity. Leningrad, situated in far northern Russia, was almost a country unto itself, the cultural and intellectual capital of the vast Soviet Union. Young Zachary wanted to be as strong and independent himself. When he was old enough, he changed his name legally to Severov.

At seventeen, Zack was admitted to a prestigious Leningrad engineering school. And soon afterward, his family received permission from state housing authorities to move into a bigger flat. After years of contending with Zack's reclusiveness, his parents had wearied of his bizarre behavior. Shifrin, in particular, was adamant that Zack either change his ways or remain in the old flat when the family left it.

On the appointed day of the move, matters came to a head. Zack, who planned to accompany his family to the new apartment, had packed his belongings. His mother and brothers tried to talk him into speaking to his stepfather, but Zack still refused. He sat in his room amid a heap of boxes, a forlorn expression on his face.

In one last attempt to make peace with the wayward teenager, Shifrin strode into the room and tried to engage Zachary in conversation. As Zack's mother, Maria, stood in the doorway, her husband asked whether Zack planned to be sociable if he came along to the new apartment—whether he was willing to forgive and forget.

Zachary stared off into space, declining even to acknowledge his stepfather's presence. Disgusted, Shifrin turned to his wife. "If he doesn't want to talk to me, I see no reason why he should come with us,"

he said. "I've spent years with him, not talking to him, and I don't want
to put up with it anymore."

Young Zachary Severov said nothing. But for the first time in seven
years, he fixed his stepfather with his dark eyes. His gaze had malice in it.

Years had passed since then, years full of turbulence, growth, and
change. Zack had matured, settled into a career, and his relations with
his family had slowly improved. His wife, Julia, did what she could to
salve the old wounds. After she and Zack immigrated to the United
States, before the birth of their first child, she insisted that they both
change their surnames back to Zack's original name of Persitz. She
maintained cordial relations with Zack's mother and stepfather, helping
to persuade them to leave Russia and settle in Minnesota.

Julia also urged her husband to reestablish ties with his natural
father. And although Boris Persitz refused to leave Russia permanently,
Julia prevailed upon him to fly across the Atlantic and visit his son in
Minneapolis. To Julia's relief, the visit was pleasant for everyone. On the
day Boris Persitz was to return to Russia, she was pleased to see her persistent campaign for reconciliation rewarded. Pushing aside his long-
nurtured resentment, Zachary had hugged his father and, in a gentle tone
of voice, called him "Dad."

Yet not everyone was as tolerant of Zachary's idiosyncrasies as his
wife. Michael Prozumenshikov, for instance, had always found Zachary
peculiar. The Persitz and Prozumenshikov families carried on a relationship that revolved mainly around their sons, who were inseparable. The
families gave their children nicknames: Daniel Persitz, who was tall for
his age, was "Danny Big," and Daniel Prozumenshikov, thinner and
shorter, was "Danny Little." Their mothers, Ellen and Julia, constantly
ferried the boys back and forth for visits, sleepovers, and parties.

Michael and Zachary, although they indulged their wives' and sons'
friendships, didn't especially care for one another. But that hadn't prevented Michael from pursuing the Persitzes as clients. Julia and
Zachary maintained IRAs with a broker at another firm, Prudential-
Bache Securities, and in the past Michael had encouraged them to transfer their money to Merrill Lynch. "He would say that he could make
lots of money for us," Julia says, "and he did have lots of Russian
clients at that time." At first, however, the Persitzes had resisted
Michael's solicitations. "I had this idea that friendship and business do

not go together," Julia says. Her good friend, Ellen Prozumenshikov, felt the same way.

Then, in 1986, Julia received $67,000 from the settlement of a personal-injury lawsuit, which she filed after her car was rear-ended on an expressway. Her lawyer in the case was the same attorney Prozumenshikov had used after his own traffic accident, years earlier. The award meant they could build a bigger house. It also eased one of Zachary's most pressing concerns. Together, he and his wife earned only $65,000 a year. He wanted his children to attend high-quality private schools and colleges, but until now he had fretted about where he and Julia would find the money for tuition.

When Prozumenshikov heard how much Julia had won, he redoubled his efforts to enlist the Persitzes as clients. Now working at Drexel Burnham Lambert, Michael phoned Zachary constantly, extolling the stock market's strength and his own stock-picking acumen. Zachary's money wasn't working for him in a lowly bank account, he said. His best clients, he boasted, were earning 20 percent a year on their savings.

Zachary discussed Michael's pitch with Julia, and the two of them agreed to give the broker a try. "We had decided maybe we should give Michael ten thousand dollars and see what he can do with it," Persitz said later. Over dinner one evening at Michael's house, Zachary proposed investing the $10,000 with Michael.

That sum, Michael said quickly, wasn't enough to generate the best returns. He knew that Persitz had more than $100,000 in the bank, including the accident settlement and about $33,000 of his mother's money. They should invest it all at Drexel Burnham, he said. The sale closer, one Michael had used before, was this: "Are you going to make the big decision for your children?"

Zachary asked Michael a number of questions about the safety of investing at Drexel Burnham. "My main concern was how secure the investment would be," he says. "I wanted it very secure, because part of that money was my parents' money and Michael knew it." In addition, he said, he wanted access to his money, to build a new house, give his parents money to take vacations, and pay for any other expenses that came up.

Michael's eyes lit up as he anticipated where this line of conversation was headed. He could guarantee the couple an annual return of 18 percent, he said, far more than Zack could earn investing the money at a bank, and he could do it by investing conservatively.* After a moment's hesitation, Persitz pulled out his checkbook and wrote Michael a check for $100,000.

During the next couple of weeks, as Prozumenshikov processed the papers for the Persitz account, Zachary pressed Michael to formalize their agreement. "I told Michael that I would like to have an agreement that would specify our discussion and his promises . . . signed by both of us, maybe notarized," Persitz says. "He told me that since we were friends that wouldn't be necessary. His position was that this would be just a meaningless piece of paper, and so I didn't press him for an agreement. I believed him."

For the first few months of his business relationship with the Persitzes, Prozumenshikov delivered even more than he had promised. With remarkably consistent success, he invested their money in stocks whose prices he expected to rise rapidly, a mix of local shares such as C.O.M.B., General Mills, and Tonka and national companies like the Coca-Cola and Disney corporations. He often waived commissions for the Persitzes. And when Zachary inundated Michael with long lists of stocks he wanted researched, the broker did the work for free.

Yet despite the tremendous gains in his account, Zachary didn't appear to be satisfied. Not trusting the accuracy of Drexel's computer-generated account statements, he micromanaged the account himself, keeping detailed notes on each transaction. He phoned Mica Duncan constantly to be sure Prozumenshikov hadn't paid more for any stock than the agreed-upon price. And he continued to suggest stocks himself, most of which Michael dismissed as "dogs" and refused to buy for the account. Zack followed these stocks especially closely, phoning to berate Michael if even one of them did well later.

In the past, it turned out, Zachary had been easygoing about money mainly because he had none. Now, though, he was proving to be as obsessive about money as he was about everything else. He read personal-finance magazines and the business page of his newspaper with intense interest. And he seemed determined to put Michael through the

*Mica Duncan disputes that Prozumenshikov promised Persitz a guaranteed 18-percent return, while Julia Persitz says Michael did make such a guarantee. Ellen Prozumenshikov wasn't asked about the matter when she later testified in court. The guarantee, if it occurred, violated both Drexel's rules and the Minnesota fraud statute.

same inquisition he inflicted on doctors, dentists, and other professionals who performed services for him and his family. Zack's first losses trading with Michael—about $1,500 on Edgcomb Metals Company, a processor of steel and aluminum, and $4,000 on a company that conducted AIDS-awareness training—sent him into a rage.

Zack's behavior was a matter of great consternation to both Prozumenshikov and his assistant, Mica Duncan. For a man making as much in the market as Persitz was, his constant bickering seemed ridiculous. Particularly outrageous was his habit of phoning Mica and demanding that she calculate the balance of his account to the penny. Although she was busy, Mica dutifully hauled out her calculator and did the math, then phoned Zack to inform him of the total. "Pretty close," he would say. "You're only off by three bucks."

These encounters annoyed Mica. Naturally cheery on the telephone, she tried her best to be cordial to Zachary, but his tone often pulled her up short. On his best days he was reserved; at other times, his accent-tinged voice carried an intense and intimidating edge. The undercurrent of hostility was the only clue to Zack's hair-trigger temper, for he never shouted or cursed when he was angry. "There was something creepy about him," Mica says. "I don't know if he was testing me, or what."

Prozumenshikov, meanwhile, didn't hesitate to ridicule Zack's obsessive behavior. Once, after the Persitzes and Prozumenshikovs returned from a week's vacation together at a villa in the Cayman Islands, Michael vowed to Mica that he would never again share the same quarters with Zack. "Zachary researched the entire trip," he moaned. "He planned what we were going to do at every moment." Zack's rigid recreation schedule, Michael said, had made the trip seem more like work than a holiday.

Another night, as the Prozumenshikovs and Persitzes relaxed together after dinner at the Prozumenshikov home, Zachary mentioned that he had enrolled his son in Little League baseball. Zack readily admitted that he didn't know much about America's national pastime, but he had heard, he said, that it was a sophisticated and compelling game. Zack said he planned to go to the library, check out books on baseball, and research the game's nuances so he could teach them to Danny.

Michael threw back his head and laughed. In his opinion, baseball was a stupid sport. He had been to a Minnesota Twins game, he said, and it moved at a snail's pace, with little athleticism or drama to recommend it. And in any case, he added, it was silly to try to bone up on sports at the library. "You don't learn about baseball by reading books," he told Zack scornfully. "Go to a baseball game." Zachary's only response was to glare at Michael, and Julia quickly changed the subject.

One reason for Zack's edginess about his Drexel account was the scuttlebutt he was hearing about his broker's business practices. Prozumenshikov's aggressive pursuit of clients had made him famous among his fellow immigrants. Their society was close-knit, and their culture was bound up with discretion. And now, in the widely dispersed Russian and Ukrainian community, Michael's reputation was taking a beating.

There was talk that Prozumenshikov promised returns he couldn't deliver. His machinations, it was said, had cost certain elderly people substantial portions of their retirement savings. Rafail Shirl, a Ukrainian immigrant, prepared tax returns for people who were also Michael's clients. More than a few of them told Shirl that Michael had promised tax-free income on investments they later learned were taxable. When Shirl phoned to ask him about it, Prozumenshikov was defensive. "You don't understand what you're doing," the stockbroker snapped. Still, Shirl persisted in calling Prozumenshikov whenever a problem cropped up on an income-tax form. After a while, Michael stopped returning the calls.

From time to time, Zack Persitz asked Michael about the rumors he was hearing from other immigrants. Michael dismissed the talk as nonsense. "Don't worry," he would say. "These people don't understand the market." Rather than easing Zachary's anxiety, Prozumenshikov's airy disclaimers heightened it. Perhaps, Zack worried, Michael was secretly as indifferent to the profitability of the Persitz account as he seemed to be about the earnings of his other clients.

Prozumenshikov, for his part, was convinced that Zachary's histrionics were merely an extreme example of a trait common among his Soviet clients. Many of them, he concluded, naively believed that the stock market was a one-way elevator to riches. They wanted only gains, he groused to other stockbrokers, and they were too bitter about the losses. Never mind that Prozumenshikov's bad habit of guaranteeing stock market returns had helped to create the attitude he deplored. He was a professional now, he said, and he wanted to deal with clients whose attitudes toward the stock market were also professional.

In Michael's mind, too, there was more than one kind of Soviet immigrant. In conversations with Mica Duncan, he described the over-simplified class distinction he saw: There were, he said, "blue-collar Russians" and "white-collar Russians." The former were laborers and merchants, many of them from Ukraine and other southern provinces of the Soviet Union. The latter were professionals, most of them engineers, doctors, or psychologists who hailed from Russia's urban north. And Michael clearly identified himself with the professional class, even though he had failed to win accreditation in his chosen field of dentistry.

The Prozumenshikovs' closest friends in the immigrant community were mainly of the latter type. Michael and Ellen were part of a regular social circle that included five or six couples. These people got together on weekend nights to have dinner or go out to movies, plays, or the symphony. Almost everyone in the circle was from Leningrad, and most of them were also Michael's clients. Prozumenshikov's old friend, Mark Goldburt, was a fixture in the group. So was Valery Gilevich, who still worked at the Metropolitan Medical Center.

The long-standing friendship between Goldburt and Prozumenshikov had managed to survive an early test, one that arose from Michael's investing advice. On Prozumenshikov's recommendation, Goldburt had bought stock in two companies, both of which promptly tanked. After selling out for a loss, Goldburt sat down for a heart-to-heart chat with Michael. "We are friends," Mark said. "Do me a favor. If you want to continue to be friends, let's forget about business. I don't feel that your advice is very good." This was a bitter pill for Michael to swallow, but it worked. By avoiding trading stocks in Goldburt's brokerage account, the two men had managed to remain close.

For other members of the circle, however, doing business with Michael was a source of continuing friction. Prozumenshikov and Valery Gilevich, for instance, traded stocks even as they socialized together. When Gilevich was on call at the hospital, Michael constantly phoned Val on his hospital beeper, hounding him with stock ideas. "The situation," Gilevich says, "was like this: Somebody comes to your house uninvited, and you shut the door in front of this person. But he is so persistent in attempts to get inside, he tries to get through the window. So you shut the window. So he tries to get inside the house through the chimney. He will not take no for an answer." Later, the Zondervan stock

debacle, which cost Gilevich thousands of dollars, further strained relations between the two men.

Business dealings were also disrupting Michael's friendship with
Mark Tsypin, a telecommunications specialist at the US West phone
company. Tsypin's English was a little rough, but his consistently excellent work and his calm, self-assured manner had inspired his supervisors
to put him in charge of an entire department at US West. Tsypin, a
Leningrad native, was warm and witty, well-liked by his friends and
peers. He was a well-groomed man who wore wire-rimmed glasses, his
salt-and-pepper hair combed neatly into place.

Tsypin had been Michael's client since 1985, when Prozumenshikov was at Merrill Lynch. From the start, the stocks Michael chose
for him had been a mixed bag. Some were profitable, but big losses on
others erased most of the gains. Despite the mediocre performance of
the account, Tsypin noted with some bemusement that Michael himself
was prospering: The Mercedes, the huge corner office at Drexel Burnham, and the split-level suburban home all testified to this fact. "I was
surprised how he was able to do so well," Tsypin says. "If he did so
well for himself, why did almost all my stocks turn bad?" The worst
was yet to come, however. Michael persuaded Tsypin to open a margin
account, promising that the expanded buying power of borrowing
money from Drexel would enable him to earn better profits. Ultimately,
the stocks that Tsypin traded on margin were the ones that would hurt
him most.

Chilliest to Prozumenshikov, at least lately, was Michael Brezman,
another member of the group of Leningrad expatriates. As Prozumenshikov's client, Brezman had lost more than $1,000 investing in a Hous-
ton-based, oil-exploration company called Apache Corporation. It irritated him that Prozumenshikov never apologized for the loss, or even
acknowledged it.

And it hadn't taken long for Brezman to tire of Prozumenshikov's
status-seeking. The flashy watch and jewelry Michael wore were "too
much," Brezman says. Brezman also noted with distaste that when
friends bought Prozumenshikov an expensive Montblanc fountain pen for
his birthday, the broker chortled with delight and repeatedly called it "the
Rolls Royce of pens." On another occasion, Prozumenshikov had taken
Brezman on a tour of the mansions along the shore of Lake Minnetonka.

As the two men rode in Prozumenshikov's Mercedes, Michael pointed to each rambling house and told Brezman the name of the rich man who lived in it. Brezman couldn't have cared less who lived in the houses. And for him, a pen was a writing instrument, not a status symbol.

Perhaps sensing that Brezman disapproved of him, Prozumenshikov began to reciprocate in subtle ways. After dinners at individual homes, husbands and wives separated in the old-world way: The women congregated in the kitchen, preparing coffee and dessert, while the men retired to the living room to smoke and talk among themselves. When Brezman spoke in this setting, Prozumenshikov would often roll his eyes and smirk—"a mysterious smile," Brezman says—as though he thought Brezman's opinions were hopelessly backward.

People in the group were also uncomfortable with another of Michael's new habits: his lying. He bragged, for instance, that the super-rich financier Irwin Jacobs was one of his clients. He even showed Mark Goldburt and others a gold watch, claiming that Jacobs had given it to him. "He was very proud of that," Goldburt says. "He said: 'See what kind of clients I have?'" The story didn't seem to add up, however. "We didn't believe it," Mark Tsypin says. "Why would Irwin Jacobs go to some unknown guy when he has the best resources and accountants available?"

The fact was that the closest Michael had come to meeting Irwin Jacobs was seeing the financier have gas pumped into his Rolls Royce once at a service station.

One Saturday evening, the Goldburts and the Prozumenshikovs went out with a third couple, Alec and Bella Buzhaker. Alec, another client of Michael's, was quarreling with him about a stock that Michael had recommended for his account. The previous day, Buzhaker said, this stock's price had closed at $10 a share. Prozumenshikov, eager to put the best face on things, insisted it had closed at $12 a share. To settle the matter, Alec produced a copy of the *Minneapolis Star Tribune*, opened the business section, and pointed to a stock listing. There, in black and white, was the price: $10 a share.

Prozumenshikov, flustered, retorted that the newspaper must have gotten it wrong. "This is a mistake," he said. "It's a misprint." Mark Goldburt tried to intercede. "A newspaper can make a mistake, Michael," Goldburt said, "but I don't believe it's the case here." Michael reddened and began talking fast. He knew it was a mistake, he said, because he had checked the price before he left the office the previous day. What's more, he said, he was shocked that his friends didn't believe him.

Later, at home, Mark Goldburt and his wife discussed Michael's wild-eyed claims. "How can he say this?" he asked her, agonizing over his friend's dishonesty. Goldburt had always been Michael's staunchest supporter, quick to rise to his defense if someone else criticized him. But even Mark, who was very fond of Michael, could see the changes that his friend's new values were wreaking.

Michael Brezman complained that Prozumenshikov was "closed"— that he shared little of himself in social situations. And Goldburt, although he wasn't ready to give up on his friendship with Prozumen- shikov, could no longer deny that Brezman was right. "When you have a simple life," Goldburt said later, "you don't have anything to hide. But when you become a big cheese, talking about millions and all these famous names, you become much more difficult to penetrate. When Michael was just a simple guy who tried to pass his dental exam, he was very nice—very *open*. But when he became a big person, big investor, he changed."

One by one, the members of Michael's circle of friends scaled back their accounts at Drexel Burnham. All of them had lost some money early on; the losses, coupled with Michael's unwillingness to admit his mistakes, brought home the notion that business and friendship didn't mix. Now, within the group, only Mark Tsypin was still acting on Michael's stock recommendations with any regularity.

But Zachary Persitz—who wasn't part of Mark Goldburt's social cir- cle—was more invested in Prozumenshikov than ever. At his broker's behest, Zack had recently transferred his and Julia's remaining assets—a total of about $50,000, in their joint account at Prudential-Bache, their custodial account for their son, Daniel, and their own retirement accounts—to Drexel. This placed the Persitz family's finances almost entirely in Michael's hands.

Up to this point, lucky timing had allowed Persitz to do much better in the market than Michael's original Merrill Lynch clients. Zack had begun buying stocks in November 1986, as the great bull market of the 1980s entered the final frenetic year of its race to the heavens. Since 1984, the value of the thirty stocks in the Dow Jones Industrial Average had doubled, and the market was continuing to surge at a blistering pace. In November 1986, an investor could have earned money in the market by throwing darts at a stock table and buying whatever companies they hit.

In any case, Prozumenshikov was better now at picking stocks. In the past he had been too quick to believe whatever optimistic fluff a company's investment bankers and public relations staff served up. Lately, his research skills had improved, and he had begun to eye companies more skeptically. For the most part, he had learned to steer clear of the dogs.

Michael wasn't infallible, however; greed often skewed his judgment. And in February 1987 came the biggest mistake of Prozumenshikov's career.

Underwriters at Drexel Burnham Lambert and other Wall Street firms were releasing a huge new issue of shares in Texas Air Corporation, the holding company run by airline executive Frank Lorenzo. In the brave new world of deregulated air travel, Lorenzo hoped to create a massive airline conglomerate composed of regional carriers that had once been independent. Texas Air was on the prowl, having gobbled up Continental Airlines, People Express, parts of Frontier Airlines, and, most recently, Eastern Airlines.

Airline employees despised Frank Lorenzo as a union buster. In 1983 he had taken Continental into bankruptcy proceedings, canceled its union contracts, and cut salaries in half. Now, many people expected him to do the same with Eastern, which was struggling under the weight of heavy debt, high operating costs, and stiff competition from other carriers.

But as much as the unions hated Lorenzo, Wall Street loved him. As a rule, the market responded to executives who were capable of winning givebacks from historically strong unions by bidding up the stock prices of their companies. And now Wall Street firms such as Prozumenshikov's Drexel Burnham Lambert were rewarding Lorenzo with a $48-a-share new issue of Texas Air stock, which was intended to raise money so the company could restructure its business. "Everybody on the Street got some" of the Texas Air issue, Mica Duncan says. "I mean everybody. And everybody was pushing it."

Drexel Burnham was no exception. Drexel's research department was telling stockbrokers that Lorenzo was going to grind Eastern Airlines's rebellious unions into submission. Lorenzo was tough enough, the analysts said, to make Texas Air a dominant player in the deregulated airline industry. And the $48-a-share new issue—from which, incidentally, Drexel's underwriters were collecting fat fees—was going to be the greatest thing since the Home Shopping Network.

Michael Prozumenshikov's own opinion about the prospects of Texas Air Corporation was somewhat less sunny. Lorenzo had strung together a couple of quarters of decent profits, but Prozumenshikov could see that Texas Air had problems. There was, for one thing, its huge debt. In an interview with *Forbes* magazine a few months earlier, Lorenzo himself had acknowledged the debt that aggressive acquisition of airlines had heaped on his company: "At Texas Air," Lorenzo said, "we have a substantial debt-to-equity ratio. But leverage is okay as long as you maintain significant liquidity and profitability." Since then, Lorenzo had added Eastern Airlines to Texas Air's holdings, and Prozumenshikov noted that Eastern had more than three times as much debt as it had assets.

It was also apparent to Prozumenshikov—and to any other stockbroker who read the newspapers—that Lorenzo would face tougher resistance from the unions at Eastern than he had encountered at Continental. After Lorenzo's successful union-busting in 1983, Congress had enacted a law that required executives to negotiate with unions before abrogating their contracts. Lorenzo would also have to prove conclusively that such a step was financially necessary. Moreover, the Airline Pilots Association had apparently learned from the Continental episode. After years of refusing to honor other unions' strikes, the pilots' union was now espousing the rhetoric of solidarity. That February, the *Wall Street Journal* warned that despite recent profits at the company, Texas Air's consolidation of airlines was "anything but problem-free."

But Michael's reservations about Texas Air didn't stop him from grabbing a big chunk of the new issue when it came out. "I don't think Michael was that big a fan of Texas Air," says one former broker in Drexel's Minneapolis branch. "But he went along and did his share. Michael would always take a big piece of these issues. He might have had half the whole branch's allocation."

His misgivings about the company notwithstanding, Prozumenshikov had a powerful incentive to sell the Texas Air stock to his customers. A broker earned higher commissions on new issues, particularly those underwritten by his own firm, than on ordinary shares. And as usual, the commissions weren't tacked onto the $48-a-share price. So to an unsophisticated investor it looked like the shares carried no commission at all, which made them easier to sell. And from Michael's point of view, easy money was always too good to pass up.

So, straight-faced and enthusiastic, he sold the issue to his clients. With Dennis Carlson, Prozumenshikov stuck to the script written by Drexel's research department: Lorenzo was the man who could impress pampered airline unions with the hard realities of doing business in the 1980s. "He was just touting the stock," Carlson says, "because Lorenzo was consolidating airlines." Carlson bought $250,000 worth of the Texas Air issue.

For Mark Tsypin's benefit, Michael concocted a completely different story. At a party, Prozumenshikov told Tsypin he had heard from a reliable source that Texas Air was going to be taken over. The tender offer, he said, would be announced within a couple of weeks. "He called it 'a sure deal,'" Tsypin recalls. "I'm not sure that he used the word 'guaranteed' but he was very damn sure that it would happen." Tsypin bought about $10,000 worth of the issue.

Michael also sold the stock to Zachary Persitz, despite Zack's reservations about it. "I knew from the newspapers that Texas Air was experiencing problems between the owner, Frank Lorenzo, and the unions," Persitz says. "I told Michael I don't particularly like this kind of investment because I don't think it's conservative. He told me that it is conservative and that he has some kind of inside information that this stock would do real well soon." So Michael sank nearly half of the Persitzes' worldly assets into Texas Air—about $48,000 for one thousand shares of the stock.

Almost immediately, Texas Air's stock price sank, as many big investors "flipped" the issue. Unperturbed, Michael soon bought more Texas Air for Zachary's account—five hundred shares at $42 a share on March 19, and two hundred shares at $35 on May 8.

When Zachary received his monthly statement in June, he was baffled. Not only had he not authorized the trades, Persitz knew that all the money in the account was tied up in other stocks, and he had no idea how Michael had paid for the seven hundred new shares. "He told me that he opened a margin account for us for about a hundred thousand dollars," Zack says. "I was very uneasy. I didn't like it. I didn't ask him to open the margin account." Michael pacified Zack by praising Texas Air and telling him the company would do well. The decline in the stock price, he said, was only temporary. If Texas Air had been a good buy at $48, it was a better buy at $35.

The market seemed to bear out Prozumenshikov's analysis. Within a week, the stock price fought its way back to $40 a share, and Michael sold the two hundred shares he had bought at $35 for an $800 profit—minus his own $155 commission. Personally, Prozumenshikov was relieved by the resurgence of the stock price. Dozens of his clients owned Texas Air, and a rout could hurt them very badly.

Together, Michael and Zachary decided that the Persitzes should hold onto their remaining fifteen hundred shares of Texas Air. After all, Dennis Carlson and many other savvy investors had decided to hold their shares. Selling them now for a substantial loss didn't seem to make a lot of sense, especially with Drexel's research department still high on Texas Air's prospects. Besides, Prozumenshikov knew that taking a big loss on the investment would drive Persitz into one of his fits. Michael didn't relish sitting across the dinner table from Zachary and enduring his stony glare.

Unfortunately, Texas Air's nosedive had only just begun. And with it would go Zachary Persitz's dream of sending his children to private school.

CHAPTER 9

The first warning came on October 14, 1987, although neither Michael Prozumenshikov nor anyone else recognized it for what it was. That day, a Wednesday, the Dow Jones Industrial Average tumbled ninety-five points in rampant selling of stocks on Wall Street. It was the biggest single-day drop in the Dow's ninety-one-year history, greater even than on Black Tuesday, the stock market crash of October 29, 1929.

No one panicked. A ninety-five-point drop, while unsettling, was less than 4 percent of the value of the stocks in the Dow Jones average at the time. By contrast, the Dow's thirty-point decline on Black Tuesday represented a far greater swoon for its era, about 12 percent of the market's total value.

The next day, Thursday, Michael watched the market fall out of bed again. After a day dominated by selling, it closed fifty-seven points lower. Seeing his clients lose money was no fun, but neither, Michael decided, was the two-day drop anything to get worked up about. He regarded it as an opportunity, a chance for his customers to buy the stocks he liked at discounted prices.

On Friday, however, the market's funk deepened. By lunchtime, the Dow was down 130 points, spoiling Michael's normally relaxed Friday afternoon routine. The time slot reserved for catching up on research and planning for the following week now found him riveted to his computer screen, contemplating damage control.

Bewildered, Prozumenshikov tracked the plunging prices of the stocks he had spread around among his clients. He waded through a series of news stories about who was selling on Wall Street, and why. He did his best to find strong industry sectors—utilities, airlines, banks, chemical companies, and so on—but none presented itself. The stock traders were hammering them all.

Michael drew a couple of conclusions. First, much of the decline was the result of program trading, the computer-driven transactions of sophisticated institutional investors. These big players brought their stock transactions to market tens of thousands of shares at a time, triggering selling and buying programs whenever the Dow broke through significant price levels. Like most retail stockbrokers, Michael didn't view the market in this way. He judged companies' prospects individually, balancing the strength of profits, the savvy of managers, and the demand for products. As breathtaking as the three-day rout was, he couldn't see where it changed these so-called fundamental factors.

Besides, the market's decline was too broad-based to flee. Other than bailing out of stocks altogether and moving money into bonds or CD accounts, there was no safe haven from the storm. Thus, he decided, there was little he could do for his clients other than phoning some of them and asking whether they wanted to get out of a particular stock. In most cases, Michael didn't favor this recourse. Selling now, he told his customers, amounted to locking in losses.

As trading on the New York Stock Exchange drew to a close that Friday afternoon, its last flurry of activity seemed to bear out Prozumenshikov's analysis. A rush of buying in the final ten minutes helped the Dow regain some ground; it rallied about 22 points to finish the day 108 points lower. Jostling with a couple of younger brokers on the elevator down to the parking garage, Michael was all smiles and bravado. By Monday, he assured them, the bull market would reassert itself.

Over the weekend, the *Wall Street Journal* prepared an elaborate package of articles on the previous week's drawdown. The lead story was a meticulously balanced "think piece"—newspaper parlance for an article more like an essay than a news story—heavy on interpretation and historical comparisons. While amply quoting gloomy market strategists, the article pointed out that a similar downward spike in 1984 had been nothing more than a brief break in the bull market.

On Monday, when Prozumenshikov strode into his office at 6:30 A.M. as usual, the *Journal* was waiting for him. He quickly devoured the front page, then turned to the inside of the paper. There he found a couple of charts, one of which leaped out at him. It showed two lines, one above the other, each ascending from the bottom left quadrant toward the top right. One line tracked the Dow Jones average during the eight years of unprecedented prosperity that preceded Black Tuesday in 1929.

The other depicted the Dow's surge during the 1980s, the past seven years of Michael's life.

But for the ominous plunging slash that represented Black Tuesday, they were identical.

When Mica Duncan arrived at work that morning, Michael's eyes were wide and his jaw hung slack, his round face bathed in the green glow of his Quotron screen. The numbers and symbols there gave grim testimony to the lives being wrecked on the floor of a stock exchange more than a thousand miles distant. The Dow Jones average had begun plunging from the moment the exchange opened at 9:30 A.M. eastern time—8:30 A.M. Minneapolis time. Dozens of stocks weren't yet trading because massive orders to sell shares had befuddled the stock specialists who made markets on the floor of the New York Stock Exchange. Specialists are normally the reason an investor can sell shares when no one else wants to buy, but now some of them were stalling to assess the damage in other stocks. Their hesitation was fueling the general panic.

The Dow was dropping in increments of ten points or more every ten minutes, each point representing about a billion dollars in investors' losses. By 9:15 A.M. central time, the industrial average was down ninety-five points and reeling toward another record single-day drop.

Prozumenshikov told Duncan he had tried to sell, to get his clients out of some of their biggest positions. But everyone, in every brokerage office across the country, was trying to do the same thing. Traders on the floor of an exchange in Chicago were using financial instruments based on an index of five hundred leading stocks to bet that stock prices would continue to plummet. Big program traders were unleashing waves of computer-assisted sell orders. The cataclysm took on a momentum of its own. Prozumenshikov had never seen anything like it.

Drexel's trading desk in New York wasn't taking phone calls. A little later, a peremptory voice on the Drexel "squawk box" informed stockbrokers that no orders were going to be accepted by telephone today. No orders, the voice repeated. None. Throughout the day, the periodic comments emanating from the speaker on Michael's desk offered little comfort. "We don't know what's going on," the voice said. "Please don't call us."

Prozumenshikov spent much of the morning staring into his screen with the kind of horrified fascination usually reserved for bad automobile accidents. He also phoned some of his clients. Michael forced himself to speak slowly into the receiver, betraying little of his anxiety to his customers.

The big speculative stock holdings of substantial clients like Dennis Carlson and John Petcoff left their accounts utterly vulnerable to the carnage. Michael couldn't reach Carlson, who was out of his office at a business meeting. So he called Carlson's home and talked to Debbie Smith, Carlson's girlfriend. A few of Carlson's positions, he told her, were protected by offsetting options trades: as the stocks' prices dropped, the values of the options rose. But most of the stocks, Michael said, weren't hedged in this manner. "Nobody knows what to do," he admitted.

The catastrophe on Wall Street led the noon television newscasts, and soon all the phone lines in Michael's office were ringing at once. For an hour or more, Prozumenshikov fielded calls from one panicked client after another, calmly predicting that the downturn was temporary. "It's a one-day thing," he said, again and again. "We'll get some of it back tomorrow." As Prozumenshikov delivered his canned oratory, he noticed that the Dow was down more than 250 points.

After a while, the incoming phone calls tapered off. By now Michael had ceased to marvel at the calamity, having exhausted the superlatives in his English vocabulary. Now he sat slumped in his chair, trying to block out the mental arithmetic that whispered his clients' mounting losses into his ear—and trying not to think about all the promises he had made.

Elsewhere in the Drexel Burnham branch, brokers drifted in and out of one another's offices, shaking their heads. Younger men, just getting started in the business, clustered around more senior colleagues. Even the minicrash after the assassination of John F. Kennedy, the worst one-day downdraft in recent history, was nothing like this, the veterans agreed. Dull resignation was written on every face in the branch, from the biggest broker to the lowliest secretary. "We all just sort of sat there and watched it tumble," Mica Duncan says. "There was nothing you could do."

Michael talked with Debbie Smith several more times that afternoon. They discussed which stocks might bounce back quickest after the market finally found its bottom. Buying more of those shares might help to reduce the damage, Michael said. With Prozumenshikov's help, Smith put together a list of suggestions to present to Carlson.

Unbeknownst to Debbie and Michael, however, Carlson had pro-
ceeded from his business meeting to a bar. During the meeting at Kraus-
Anderson, Inc., a big Minneapolis construction company, a secretary had
kept coming in to update Carlson and the others on the market's collapse. Carlson didn't know exactly how much he was losing, but he
knew it was in the millions. He also knew that today, at least, there was
nothing he could do about it. So he headed out to a favorite watering
hole with a group of employees and fellow businessmen. It would be
quite late when Carlson's friends finally dropped him off at home. "I
was drunk," Carlson says. "Plenty."

By 3 P.M., when the market closed, Prozumenshikov and Duncan
were exhausted. The Dow had settled about five hundred points lower,
although the besieged stock specialists in New York had yet to declare a
precise tally. What was clear was that $500 billion invested in the stock
market—millions of which belonged to Michael's three hundred clients—
had simply vanished.

Black Monday. The stock market crash of 1987. The worst day in
Wall Street's history.

Michael, as usual, was trying to look at the bright side. "It's going to
be fine," he told Duncan. "It's going to come back. Not to worry, not to
worry." For once, Prozumenshikov's cheeriness rang hollow in Mica's
ears. "He always tried to look at things like, it's going to be okay," Duncan says. "Sometimes that was a fault of his. It wasn't going to be okay,
but he wouldn't address it and take care of it. That's just the way he
was."

For both of them, the next two days went by in a blur. The over-the-
counter market in smaller stocks, which had resisted the momentum of
the crash on Monday, made up for it with a wild rout on Tuesday.
Michael spent his time trying to explain to clients how things could have
gone so wrong. He tried to be reasonable, to express hope that, with
patience and judicious investing, they might recoup their losses. Most of
his clients were in shock, scarcely comprehending what had happened.

Then, on the third day after the crash, came a black rain of margin
calls that left no room for doubt.

Most of Michael Prozumenshikov's clients had bought stocks with
borrowed money. And in all too many cases, Michael had persuaded his
clients not only to open margin accounts, but to plow as much money as
they could borrow into the stock market. Everyone who traded on mar-

gin had signed a consent form that alluded to the risks involved. But most people didn't know how truly grave these risks could be.

What Michael's clients were receiving now were demands from Drexel Burnham for immediate payments, lest the now-devalued assets in their portfolios—the collateral for their loans—be forcibly sold at catastrophic losses. "Due to market fluctuation," a telegram might read, "you owe Drexel Burnham Lambert $15,000. You have five days to deliver this sum to the firm or the securities in your account will be subject to liquidation." Michael's clients received more margin calls than those of any other broker in the Minneapolis branch. "Almost every client that Michael had was hit," Mica Duncan says. "That was hard for everyone."

Even for the Mad Russian himself. For all his recklessness with other people's money, Michael had never intended to hurt anyone. The margin calls anguished him so much that in most cases he couldn't bring himself to deliver the bad news personally. Each day after the crash, Drexel's New York operations department faxed Prozumenshikov a list of margin calls that were being sent to his clients; it was Michael's job to phone people before the telegrams arrived and "hold their hands," Duncan says, coaxing them through the difficult period. But Michael couldn't bear it. "I'll tell them later, I'll tell them later," he told Mica.

In this grim business, however, Mica Duncan wouldn't tolerate delays. Rather than letting Michael's clients receive unannounced demands for money, she made the calls herself. And she prevailed upon Prozumenshikov to phone Russian clients who didn't speak English.

Still, the margin calls took some people by surprise. For John Petcoff, Michael's big client in Milwaukee, tallying the $600,000 paper loss the crash inflicted on his $1-million Drexel portfolio was painful enough. The telegram he received demanding $150,000 to cover margin losses was an extra slap. Annoyed that Prozumenshikov had said nothing before it arrived, Petcoff phoned his broker in Minneapolis. "Michael," he said, "what are you *doing* to me?" Prozumenshikov's reply was a scarcely audible mumble. "Don't worry about it," he said. "We'll work it out, we'll work it out."

But John Petcoff was a rich man, capable of paying margin calls and withstanding his heavy losses. Others weren't as lucky. Among the less affluent, Michael's client list had become a litany of personal tragedies, recounted prosaically by columns of numbers.

Perhaps worst was the case of Clement Seifert, the retired carpenter and navy veteran who had turned over his retirement savings to Michael. Seifert and his wife had recently withdrawn thousands of dollars to buy land and build a vacation home in northern Minnesota. Removing the equity had left the account precariously leveraged, which hadn't seemed like a problem at the time.

In a stroke, the crash relegated Clem Seifert to poverty for the rest of his life. Having sunk his money into the vacation home, there was nothing left—no ready cash at all—to pay Drexel's margin calls. In a few days, Drexel began selling out the stock in Seifert's account. When Mica spoke to Clem on the telephone, she could tell that he didn't yet understand what was happening. He was, she noted sadly, still clinging to his dream of a retirement spent drifting between his two homes, fishing in the rural north and returning to relax among family and friends in the Minneapolis suburbs.

Soon the liquidation was complete. All that was left of Seifert's $70,000 nest egg were two hundred shares of stock worth about $16,000. "He never should have been put on margin," Duncan says. "He was an older man, you know, limited income. Those types of people don't belong on margin. And when Michael saw that he was taking out all this money (for the vacation home), he should've said, 'Hey, let's back up here.'"

A few days later, Seifert came in to survey the damage. He sat in a chair in front of Michael's desk, his eyes red-rimmed, his hands shaking. He realized now, he said, that his social security checks and small pension wouldn't be enough to pay the mortgage on his vacation home. Now that his savings were gone, he would have to sell it. Worse, Seifert said, there wouldn't be enough money for him and his wife, Kathryn, to travel, or even to have dinner at their favorite restaurants. "You've ruined my whole life," he told Michael.

Prozumenshikov was genuinely sorry about Seifert's situation, but he didn't blame himself. Was it his fault the market had crashed? Michael's tendency in confrontations was to diffuse them by changing the subject—or, when he didn't want anything more from his adversary, to lash back angrily. Neither response seemed appropriate here. Michael didn't know what to say, so he said nothing.

Unfortunately, as Seifert continued to rail at him, a slight smirk stole onto Prozumenshikov's face. Seifert couldn't tell whether it was an expression of nervousness, defiance, or something else. Whatever it was, it outraged him. "He was coming back with that smile on his face," Seifert says, "like nothing can touch him . . . like it wasn't his fault."

Now Seifert paused, staring coldly at his stockbroker, dragging on one of his True menthol cigarettes. Then he spoke again. "Michael," he said slowly, "you are going to do this to people, ruin their lives. I'm not going to do anything against you. But one day, when you're doing this to other people, you are going to run into the wrong person."

For two weeks after the crash, a parade of the downtrodden trooped through Michael's office, many bearing checks to pay their margin calls. These were the lucky ones. Those who, like Seifert, couldn't afford to pay had their portfolios stripped of the most valuable stocks. "A lot of them couldn't come up with it," Duncan says. "So we had to liquidate their positions. And when you sell out to meet a margin call you really take a bath."

Hardest for Prozumenshikov was dealing with his fellow Russians. His tool in selling stocks to these people had been trust, the solidarity implied by their common situation in the new world. And from the point of view of his clients, Michael had breached the trust. While many of Prozumenshikov's American clients absolved him from moral responsibility for the crash, the immigrants tended to blame him personally. They had awoken one morning to find their American dreams shattered; Michael Prozumenshikov, they were sure, was the agent of their destruction.

Some people phoned Prozumenshikov to scream at him, while others sobbed or wailed into the receiver, as if there were something he could do—and ought to do, as a fellow Russian—to repair the damage. For the first time, Michael began to dread coming to work in the morning. Each day posed some new crisis, some fresh assault of anger and recrimination.

One of Michael's biggest problems was the ruination of Texas Air Corporation. The crash had pounded investors in Frank Lorenzo's airline conglomerate, erasing 30 percent of the stock's value in a single day. Yet for the many of Prozumenshikov's clients who had bought Texas Air, the crash was simply a final, humbling stroke.

The stock, Wall Street's darling just eight months earlier, had proved to be one of the Street's most spectacular blunders. Since the day the underwriters had released their $48-a-share Texas Air issue, virtually every red flag that market analysts use to downgrade a stock had been unfurled at Texas Air.

Management at Texas Air's subsidiary airlines had been a revolving door. Lorenzo either fired popular executives, such as Continental Airlines president Thomas Plaskett, or watched them resign, such as People Express chairman Donald Burr. Little sours Wall Street on a stock faster than instability at the top of the corporate hierarchy. It betrays a lack of confidence in the direction of a company's most basic business strategies.

As for the notion that Lorenzo was destined to dominate the airline unions, the opposite seemed to be true. The unruly unions at Texas Air's new Eastern Airlines unit had vexed Lorenzo from the start. Eastern's pilots were campaigning to reverse the labor concessions Lorenzo had won at Continental in 1983 by unionizing Continental's four thousand pilots. And machinists at Eastern had dealt Lorenzo another blow by reelecting Charles Bryan, the firebrand who headed their union, by an overwhelming 88 percent majority.

Texas Air's acquisition of airlines had been overly aggressive, it turned out, and merging them had proved harder than Lorenzo anticipated. Using proceeds from the $48-a-share stock issue in February 1987, Lorenzo had lumped the operations of People Express, Frontier Airlines, and New York Air into Continental. The results had been unhappy employees and notoriously bad service, with Continental consistently ranked near the bottom in passenger satisfaction surveys.

But what rattled investors most were Texas Air's losses. Every publicly held corporation in the United States must report its earnings or losses four times a year. On Wall Street, these earnings statements are regarded as report cards on the performance of a company's executives. After the two profitable quarters in 1986 that got Wall Street's underwriters so excited about Texas Air, the company had posted three consecutive quarterly losses. Its newly consolidated Continental subsidiary was losing millions a month.

Even before Black Monday, these problems had reflected themselves in Texas Air's stock price. It had slipped below $40 a share the previous summer, hovering for months in the mid-thirties. In September, a month before the crash, the price had fallen below $30.

Many of the big investors who jumped onto Frank Lorenzo's bandwagon in early 1987, such as prominent New York investor George Soros and the money-managing pension funds for government and corporate employees, had long since bailed out. These investors' huge sales of Texas Air stock drove the price lower still. In late summer, a skeptical *Wall Street Journal* article had proffered various detailed explanations for the appalling performance of Frank Lorenzo's stock. Dennis Carlson, who lost $150,000 on his own Texas Air stake, had a simpler theory. Lorenzo "turned out to be a jerk," Carlson said.

Now, after the crash, Texas Air was trading for a $15 a share. Michael Prozumenshikov didn't need to be a genius to grasp what this frightful figure meant to his clients. Investors who had trusted his enthusiastic solicitations to buy the Texas Air issue for $48 a share had watched two-thirds of their money vanish like rain on parched earth.

During the traumatic weeks that followed Black Monday, other brokers in the Minneapolis branch noticed a change in Michael Prozumenshikov. For a while, the Mad Russian became uncharacteristically contrite. In the past he had tended to think of his clients in numeric terms: how much their individual accounts added to his growing pool of assets, how much of their money was available to spend, and generate commissions, on any given day. Now Michael was forced to confront the reality that the numbers represented people's lives, their dreams of owning homes and sending children to college.

Prozumenshikov had told Clement Seifert and others that he could get them out of the market "in seconds" in the event of a major market downturn. When it came down to it, he had been powerless to do anything of the kind. "I think it really scared him," says one former Drexel broker. "He'd just shake his head and say: 'This is a terrible thing.'"

Michael knew he had a tendency to underestimate risk, to be a little too upbeat about the stocks he sold. But that was the business, he had rationalized to colleagues, the way the game was played. In truth, Prozumenshikov had found the brokerage business ridiculously easy to navigate. Before Black Monday, it had all been so much fun, an unexpectedly quick route to the personal wealth he sought. "He had probably got to a point where he felt that he was omnipotent," says Dan Marcus, then second in command at Drexel's Midwest regional office. "A lot of these guys get this feeling in a rising market: They think it's easy."

Now, finally, Prozumenshikov understood why his bosses at Merrill Lynch had counseled against putting small investors into margin accounts. "He learned the market can go down," one broker says. "He'd never known that before."

But Michael Prozumenshikov hadn't come this far—halfway around the planet, to a strange and wonderful new culture—to watch his career founder in self-pity. It didn't take long for his vast reserve of optimism and ambition to reassert itself.

The road back, oddly, began with the steely resolve of Dennis Carlson. Carlson had lost $3.5 million in the crash, but he wasn't whining about it. In fact, Carlson had enthusiastically returned to the market after Black Monday, convinced that this was a great time to pick up stocks at bargain prices. Carlson, Michael noted, was strong and independent, a real rugged individualist. This was the kind of man that Michael himself wanted to be.

Faced with mass defections and crippling losses among his current clients, Michael went back to the basics: research, referrals, cold calling. It was harder now, to be sure, with most of the investing public still reeling from the crash. Ever the canny salesman, Prozumenshikov changed his pitch to confront this problem head-on. The crash, he argued forcefully to strangers on the phone, had created a rare opportunity. Those who failed to invest now, he said, would regret it later. "If you're not ready now," he would say, "do you know somebody else who might be?"

Prozumenshikov worked feverishly to identify high-quality stocks whose values the crash had discounted. For John Petcoff, who remained Michael's client, the Russian broker crafted a portfolio of pure blue chip, which was aimed at recouping Petcoff's massive market losses. "I'll make it up to you," Prozumenshikov told Petcoff. "We'll make it all back."

Despite the crash, Prozumenshikov would finish 1987 number one among retail salesmen in Drexel Burnham's Minneapolis branch. For the year, he grossed $663,000, nearly as much as brokers in the branch who peddled to institutions rather than to individuals. Michael still had his job, his house, his Mercedes. Why despair? Other brokers admired the strength of Michael's will. "The world was falling apart," one of them recalls. "And Michael said, 'Hey, this is opportunity.'"

A regrettable corollary of Prozumenshikov's retooled optimism was his belief that the market's losers—primarily, in his mind, the timid and backward Russians—somehow deserved what they got. The Russian investors who berated him and abandoned the market after losing much of their money in the crash, he said, were "stupid." Smart capitalists such as Dennis Carlson—and, by implication, Michael himself—would never wind up in poverty after a lifetime of labor. As for the queasy tweaks of conscience he had felt on Black Monday and the dark October days that followed it, Prozumenshikov exiled them to the mental compartment where he stowed all his counterproductive emotions.

"It's funny how quickly that whole thing went away," Mica Duncan says. "By the end of November, he was back. It was: 'Back to square one, and let's go from here.'"

PART 2
RECKONING

CHAPTER 10

Small investors like Clement Seifert weren't Black Monday's only victims. Like an earthquake along a fault line, the crash touched off a series of aftershocks, rattling and reshaping the financial landscape in every direction.

At Drexel Burnham Lambert's Minneapolis branch, the first casualty was the boss, Bill Krebs. Krebs's hot-blooded management style had been perfect for staking Drexel's territory in Minneapolis, for raiding other firms to build a strong sales team in a new market. But now his superiors felt it was time for a change. Even before the crash, many on Wall Street sensed fatigue among small investors, a growing weariness of the hard-selling ways of the 1980s. More suddenly than anyone expected, Black Monday had brought the changes to a climax. No one knew what the new world would look like, but securities-industry executives could be sure it would abide less barefaced aggression than in the recent past.

A few weeks after the crash, Bill Krebs's superiors found the excuse they needed to oust him. Three stockbrokers in the branch had been managing a "discretionary" account—an account whose owner consented to let the brokers trade stocks without telling him first. But trading in the account had been inordinately active, and now the investor was griping about losses. Worse, the documents supposedly granting discretionary authority had disappeared. Krebs alerted New York to the problem and called for an internal audit to try to find the missing papers.

When the two auditors arrived in Minneapolis, they seemed to have their own agenda. They spent a morning interviewing the three stockbrokers, briefly reviewed some records, then marched into Krebs's office. "You're in serious trouble," one of them said. For days, no one would tell Krebs exactly what he was accused of doing. "To make a long story short," he says, "they called me to New York at the end of November and they fired me."

Krebs was sure he was being made a scapegoat for a problem he himself had uncovered, and he resented it. He had put a great deal of hard work dousing fires after the crash. He pointed out that the Minneapolis branch had lost only about $30,000 of Drexel's money on Black Monday, versus hundreds of thousands or millions in losses at other branches. But nobody was listening. Krebs refused an offer to stay on at Drexel as a broker. And in a statement to the National Association of Securities Dealers, which keeps a disciplinary file on every stockbroker in the country, he protested his firing vehemently. A Drexel executive later said he believed the discretionary account incident was simply "the excuse that [Drexel] used to say, well, it's time to get rid of Bill Krebs."

The Drexel manager's firing was front-page news in Minneapolis. Eager for a local angle on the crash, the *Minneapolis Star Tribune* reported that Black Monday had unearthed questionable trading practices at Drexel's local branch that prompted the firm to relieve Krebs of his management duties. Around town, managers of competing firms crowed about the plight of the man whose hiring practices had so vexed them. Krebs would land on his feet, joining Drexel rival Shearson Lehman Hutton, the securities operation of the mammoth American Express Company, as a broker. Yet when Krebs left on December 31, 1987, many Drexel brokers felt they were witnessing, for good or ill, the passing of an era.

They weren't far wrong. The Dow Jones Industrial Average rallied back within a couple of months after Black Monday, but small investors didn't come with it. Many of them—the true neophytes, whose money hadn't rested comfortably in stocks to begin with—would never return to the market. And among those who did, caution supplanted greed.

Many brokers, trying to respond to the shifting tide, were now peddling certificates of deposit, or CDs, and blue-chip stocks and bonds. These were vehicles that produced reliable, if unspectacular, returns. "The crash changed the way people looked at the business," says a former Drexel broker. "There wasn't an emphasis on trading. Clients were more conservative."

Inevitably, fewer clients and more sedate investing strategies meant diminished earnings for stockbrokers. Weak salesmen were being forced out of the business, and even strong salesmen had to work harder for the new accounts they opened. Competition for scarce deep-pocketed investors had never been this fierce—or this ugly. Some brokers told investors about other brokers' disciplinary problems, hoping to grab the clients for themselves. A survey by the Securities Industry Association found that stockbrokers' income slumped 30 percent during the six months after the crash.

The ruin and alienation of the small investors who drove the mid-1980s market translated to sharp declines in the assets managed by Wall Street firms. As assets dried up, profits plunged as well. Trading volume was down on all the big stock exchanges. Mutual-fund sales and underwritings of new stock issues were also down sharply. Of Wall Street's previously powerful profit centers, only mergers and acquisitions remained hot. Small investors were the ones who paid the biggest per-share commissions—often more than ten cents a share for stocks—and their absence exacted a heavy toll on the Street.

The bull market, it turned out, had papered over years of self-indulgence and bloated payrolls. And now firms were forced to begin looking for ways to trim their huge operating costs.

Few stockbrokers were actually laid off. Brokers, as a rule, earned commissions rather than salaries; if they didn't sell, they didn't earn. Therefore, the expenses they created for their firms were minimal—the phone calls they made, the space they sat in, and the support staff to process their trades. Yet many brokers did leave the business, usually because their managers hounded them so relentlessly to produce that many became too miserable to go on, and quit.

Support staff was a different matter. These salaried employees—administrators, secretaries, clerks, computer operators—were being dismissed in record numbers. Many national firms were cutting costs by closing entire branch offices; Shearson, for instance, closed about 90 of its 590 branches. The period that followed the crash became known in some circles as "the year of the knife," during which more than 15,000 securities-industry employees lost their jobs in one way or another.

Firms that couldn't make ends meet were being consumed by stronger companies. By August 1988, more than a dozen major mergers or acquisitions would transform and consolidate the brokerage industry. And when one brokerage firm bought another, it generally wanted only the salesmen, their clients, and perhaps the top traders and investment bankers; most everyone else at the target firm was let go. In a blockbuster deal just after the crash, Shearson paid $964 million to gobble up the previously influential E. F. Hutton brokerage firm. Hutton had endured an especially severe drubbing in the crash and now, contrary to a well-known advertising slogan of the time, was neither talking nor being listened to.

In their advertising and public relations, in fact, the dominant firms of Wall Street were now paying lip service to investors' new conservatism. They were heralding a return to the roots of their business—retirement planning and sound financial advice. Slogans like "No Guts, No Glory" would give way to such soothing jingles as "One Investor at a Time" and "Rock Solid, Market Wise."

Yet beneath the surface, the industry was hungrier than ever. Many brokerage firms, in fact, had become addicted to the big revenues of the pre-crash era, and a sudden slump in brokerage revenues was unacceptable. New York executives pressured their branch managers to maintain production despite the mass exodus of small investors. And although all signs now pointed to an inexorable decline in commissions, sales managers did everything they could to work against it.

Mainly this meant stealing away big producers from other firms. Few branch managers were willing now to commit themselves to the expense of training entry-level stockbrokers. They wanted proven salesmen who could walk into an office and generate big numbers from day one. Consequently, securities firms were throwing around ever more fantastic sums to woo such brokers. They were devising clever incentive-laden bonus packages—"golden handcuffs," as they were called, which used the promise of future earnings to lure an established broker and chain him to a firm for years.

And so it was that during the seeming austerity of the post-crash period, the culture of stockbrokers as hired guns flourished as never before. The securities industry had long since dispensed with the niceties other industries imposed on career moves—protocol stipulating weeks or months of notice before a job change. When stockbrokers resigned, they quit and left on the same day and took most of their clients with them.

Within the widely dispersed brokerage community of Minneapolis and its wealthy suburbs, people were moving so fast that some in the industry had trouble keeping track of their former colleagues. It wasn't unusual to come to work on a Monday morning and, without warning, find a friend's office dark and empty. In one particularly gossip-worthy defection, the entire six-man contingent of Smith Barney, Harris Upham's elite Wayzata branch left for PaineWebber just eight days before Smith Barney was to open swank new headquarters for the brokers.

Yet the scramble for good salesmen couldn't forestall macroeconomics. The securities business was entering a sustained and stultifying recession—the worst days it had seen since the stock market funk of the Jimmy Carter era—and there was nothing anyone could do to stop it.

Drexel Burnham Lambert was as vulnerable as any firm to the lean times that followed the crash, but it also had some unique problems of its own. Using Ivan Boesky as a witness, the Securities and Exchange Commission and the New York U.S. Attorney's office were preparing civil and criminal cases that centered ever more narrowly on Drexel. Newspaper articles about the scandal rained down daily. "We were getting a lot of press," says a former Drexel broker, "and it wasn't good press. People were less trusting of Drexel. It was getting tougher and tougher" to land new clients.

There were those in Drexel's retail brokerage division who sought to shed the firm's cowboy image, as executives at other firms were striving to do. Yet even as investigators laid siege in New York and Drexel executives devised public relations countermeasures, the old ways died hard in outposts such as Minneapolis.

One infamous instance had an executive from Drexel's Beverly Hills office creating an uproar at a get-acquainted session with Minneapolis stockbrokers by suggesting that they sell their clients stock in the Minnesota-based Pillsbury Company. Pillsbury, the Minneapolis brokers knew all too well, was a notorious dog. Its ineffectual marketing of America's favorite food products was matched only by absurd management turmoil of its single biggest business, the Burger King hamburger chain.

Months earlier, a rumor that Pillsbury might be the target of a hostile takeover had made the rounds on Wall Street, but this talk had come to nothing. In fact, the best takeover defense specialists in the business— those at Drexel Burnham Lambert itself—had helped Pillsbury executives put together an arsenal of antitakeover measures. Why, the brokers wanted know, should they recommend such a go-nowhere, do-nothing stock to their clients? The visiting executive refused to explain. "Just buy the stock," he said.

Two weeks later, Grand Metropolitan PLC, a British food and liquor company, announced a $5.23 billion, $60-a-share tender offer for Pillsbury. Instantly, the stock price shot from $39 to $57 a share, for a stunning one-day gain of nearly 50 percent. Any Drexel broker who had acted on the tip looked like a genius to his clients. And when Grand Met overcame Pillsbury's defenses and completed the takeover for a sweetened $5.75 billion, or $66 a share, the clients of some brokers in the Minneapolis branch made small fortunes. The brokers themselves were forced to conclude that a few Drexel executives, even as the firm accepted millions of dollars in fees to protect Pillsbury from predators, were passing along inside information about its impending demise.

In the aftermath of Black Monday, incidents like this bred a kind of institutional schizophrenia in Drexel's retail brokerage division, with one personality shaped by the fear of retribution for past sins and another steeped in the usual Drexel arrogance.

It was in this climate that Michael Prozumenshikov displayed the full measure of his resourcefulness and his formidable will. Many brokers, having weathered hundreds of rejections, simply gave up on cold calling. But when someone slammed down the phone on Prozumenshikov, the broker broke into a self-confident chuckle that suggested he actually got a kick out of other people's rudeness. It was this striking ability to lay aside his basic human frailty that set Michael apart from the pack. The fact that some of his former clients thought him an evil man bothered him little—at least not until later, when the death threats started.

But Michael couldn't help but be worried by the carnage in the lives of brokers around him. He watched weaker producers lose their jobs. There was disturbing talk on the Street of trimming the 40 percent share of gross commissions that brokers were allowed to keep. Michael saw his most gifted colleagues scaling back their plans to buy big-ticket luxury goods. Many were having trouble sustaining the conspicuous consumption to which they had become accustomed—some were losing their homes, their cars, their wives.

Prozumenshikov was, by now, ruminating about the dream house he one day would build in a far-west suburb of Minneapolis. Already, he carried enormous debt and paid awesome bills to support his lifestyle. He knew he couldn't afford to let his earnings sag.

Michael set about maximizing his income in any way he could. He scoured the hinterlands of Minnesota for emerging companies to recommend to his clients. He mined his best sources for any hint of inside information. He pondered ways to act on his long-standing dream of starting a company that would buy and resell goods from the Soviet Union. He began pitching this import-export idea to potential partners such as John Petcoff, to whom he shipped bottles of Soviet champagne and other cheap Russian goods.

Meanwhile, some of Prozumenshikov's bad habits got worse. Most of his current clients—those who had survived the crash—were tired of rapid trading and high-risk penny stocks. But Michael continued to encourage the new clients he enlisted to trade aggressively. He chased after other brokers' clients, including, in some cases, the customers of brokers in his own Drexel branch. He made a deal to share commissions with a young broker who referred a big client to him, then reneged on it.

And, sometimes brutally, Michael cut off emotional connections to clients whose lives the crash had wrecked. One such instance was his apparent indifference to Clement Seifert, whose lifetime of hammering two-by-fours and installing drywall had built the nest egg he lost on Black Monday. That blistering hot summer of 1988, a drought year in the Midwest, Seifert was found wringing his hands and mumbling to himself in his soon-to-be-sold vacation home, agonizing over his ruined retirement. It was ninety degrees in the house, and the elderly carpenter hadn't eaten in days. His wife had him committed to the psychiatric ward of a local Veterans Administration hospital. When an employee of Merrill Lynch called to ask Michael about the Seifert family's allegations of churning and unauthorized trading in the past, Prozumenshikov dismissed them as misguided ravings.

Michael's lack of contrition for his clients' losses was also evident in the advice he gave younger brokers. It was, actually, genuine compassion that motivated Michael to take a couple of less experienced salesmen under his wing. He was good at communicating his ideas, so good that Mica Duncan told him that he should have been a teacher. "He loved to hear himself talk," she says, "and he loved to explain stuff to people." But Michael's help, one young broker says, amounted to a primer on hard-selling methods from a vanishing buccaneer era.

Not long after the crash, Prozumenshikov befriended a salesman named William Humphries. Humphries was a former football star for the University of Minnesota, a hulking man, tall and powerfully built. Once a highly regarded prospect for pro football, Humphries had suffered a serious shoulder injury that prevented him from passing the Dallas Cowboys's physical examination.

Now a rookie stockbroker at a time when the industry tolerated few novices, Humphries was floundering. He approached Michael one afternoon, hoping to pick up a few pointers from the number-one salesman in the Minneapolis branch. "I asked him how he did his business," Humphries says, "and why was he so successful."

In the weeks that followed, Prozumenshikov became a mentor to William Humphries. They talked every morning at 6:30 A.M. On Friday afternoons, William planted himself in a chair in Michael's office, and the Russian broker reached into a desk drawer for the bottle of cognac he kept there. Over a drink, the two brokers talked stocks and sports. Humphries even began to pick up some Russian. Among the many things the two men had in common were that both had been athletes and both had grown up poor.

Michael told William about the simplicity of his own cold-calling technique. He advised Humphries to abandon the elaborate sales scripts Drexel handed out, to shorten his pitch, and get right to the point. "He broke it down into real simple terms," Humphries says. "The bottom line is to make people money." Prozumenshikov advised Humphries to cold call doggedly, regardless of how many clients he currently had. "Michael would still cold call even though he was doing eight hundred thousand to one million dollars (a year) in business," Humphries says. "I said, 'Damn, you don't have to cold call.' But he was always trying to add more clients, because you never know when one's going leave you."

Many clients were eager to invest in CDs. They were safe and, at the time, they were paying healthy interest rates. Yet selling CDs generated next to nothing for a broker, so Michael urged William to resist them. He also told the young broker not to sell mutual funds. "Stay away from mutual funds, because they are illiquid," Prozumenshikov would say. "You make money buying and selling. You cannot buy and sell mutual funds."

Michael also advised an aggressive trading style. "He traded equities (stocks) like commodities," Humphries says. Prozumenshikov exhorted his young charge to alter the stories he told clients about stocks in order to keep buying and selling and generating commissions. "Tell them the story changed," Prozumenshikov said. "Sell it. Buy something else. We make money, right? You make more than the bank, right? Okay, then, we sell. We buy something else. We make more money." The advice, Humphries says, paid off. "All of a sudden, my business just started booming."

Yet as the weeks passed, Prozumenshikov's apparent lack of conventional morality became a point of friction. Among the stocks Michael recommended as fodder for Humphries's clients was Lonrho P.L.C., a diamond-mining company. The stock did well for investors, and William earned plenty of commissions handling their trades. Soon, however, he learned that Lonrho was based in South Africa. One reason for the company's big profits, he found out, was that Lonrho paid black South Africans little for their dangerous toil in its mines.

Humphries, who was black, immediately stopped selling the stock. And he told Michael he ought to stop selling it too, because in Humphries's view such trading supported the racist policies of apartheid. Michael scoffed. Politics didn't matter, he declared, "as long as you make money."

Humphries found this deeply offensive—and surprising for a member of an ethnic group which, in Russia, had been an oppressed minority. At the time, however, he kept his feelings to himself. Later, a grave expression fixed itself on William Humphries's face as he recounted the episode and others in his complicated relationship with Michael. "That's the attitude," he said, a little mournfully. "That's what he exposed me to."

As manager of the Minneapolis branch, Bill Krebs had been replaced by two veteran Drexel brokers who ran the office together. One of them, Mort Greenberg, made a special effort to be nicer to Prozumenshikov than Krebs had been. Michael was the biggest producer in the branch, and, consequently, Greenberg decided to treat him with respect. Not long after Greenberg was promoted, he rewarded Michael for posting a strong monthly commission tally by buying the broker a set of Waterford crystal.

Prozumenshikov, in return, wasted no time taking advantage of Bill Krebs's departure. His passion to rebuild his depleted client base drove him back into the arms of a former client, new-issue trader Louis Marin. Prozumenshikov hadn't spoken to Marin since the trader left Brook Investments in Chicago, where Marin's big stock transactions had cost Michael thousands of dollars.

Marin was now working at a Denver-based concern called VIP Financial Co., which was run by a soft-spoken Coloradan named Timothy Vasko. VIP was a tiny firm, but Vasko aspired to expand it by bringing in a high-powered broker to sell securities to financial institutions. Louis Marin was to be his institutional broker.

Prozumenshikov had never found it in himself to get really angry at Marin, even during the nasty business involving Brook Investments. Perhaps this was because of the many traits he and Marin shared. Marin, a Latino, had anglicized his first name from Luis to Louis, just as Prozumenshikov had transmuted his name from Mikhail to Michael. Like Prozumenshikov, Marin spoke with an accent. But he was nevertheless a smooth talker and a natty dresser. Said Timothy Vasko, Marin's boss at VIP Financial, "You'd have to meet Louis to understand. He's a salesman." In Marin, it turned out, Michael Prozumenshikov had met his match. The best salesman at Drexel Burnham Lambert's Minneapolis branch was about to be sold by a better one.

One summer day in 1988, Marin phoned Prozumenshikov and announced he was working for VIP. He was sorry, he said, about the losses Michael had suffered during their previous encounter. Now Marin wanted to bury the hatchet. He had money to invest in new issues of stock, and he wanted to do the trading through Drexel so Michael could earn commissions.

Bill Krebs had forbidden Prozumenshikov to trade with Marin, but that, by Michael's way of thinking, was immaterial now. Michael's new bosses knew nothing about the prohibition, so he was free to do business with Louis if he wanted to. Mica Duncan was against it, of course. But with Marin dangling huge trades that could pay commissions of $50,000 or more a month, Michael was inclined to give him the benefit of the doubt. Mica, though wary, finally relented. "We just have to be very, very careful," she said.

Louis Marin opened several new Drexel accounts which, Duncan says, "were structured a little strange from the beginning." For one thing, the new accounts were in other people's names. These, Marin explained, were clients of VIP Financial, for whom he would be buying and selling stocks. Yet rather than providing addresses or phone numbers for most of the clients, Marin asked Prozumenshikov to mail their account statements to VIP's Denver address, Duncan says.

Another potential problem: The new accounts were set up to buy stocks using the "delivery versus payment" method of trading. Delivery versus payment was the brokerage industry's version of the old saw, "The check is in the mail." It was a kind of gentleman's agreement that allowed stocks to be delivered to an investor's bank, rather than directly to the investor himself. The understanding was that the investor would authorize his bank to pay for the shares within five business days.

Traditionally, delivery versus payment had been the loophole hedge funds used to reject unprofitable stock trades while immediately reselling, or "flipping," winners. By 1988, some brokerage firms had wised up to the tactic and instituted rules to prevent it. Merrill Lynch, for one, refused to pay a stockbroker a commission for any new-issue trade that was flipped for a quick profit. This took away the broker's incentive to sell stock issues to unscrupulous hedge funds.

Marin's intentions in using the names of VIP's clients aren't clear. What is certain is that securities regulators would later discipline Marin for the practice, charging him with executing trades in VIP client accounts without the investors' authorization. These clients, the National Association of Securities Dealers would allege, knew nothing about the big trades Louis Marin and Michael Prozumenshikov were about to execute. Marin himself disputed this, saying his clients were aware of the trades.

Trade the two salesmen did, in huge volume, often ten thousand shares at a time. Marin spread the shares around among the Drexel accounts. When Prozumenshikov presented Marin with some hot new stock issue, Marin might order five thousand shares for one account and five hundred shares for another. Some stockbrokers had a hard time convincing underwriters to turn over thousands of shares of coveted new issues, but not Prozumenshikov. "Michael was really able to get a lot of syndicate items, a lot of new issues, because he moved a lot of stocks," Mica Duncan says.

In his lust for easy commissions, Michael got a little sloppy. Within the retail division, Drexel's New York–based underwriters circulated copies of something called a syndicate calendar. This calendar, which alerted brokers to promising new stock issues, bore the bold label: "For Internal Use Only." Yet as soon as he got his hands on it, Prozumenshikov faxed the calendar to Marin. Then Marin "would just go down the calendar and say, 'I'll take this, this, this, and this,' " Mica Duncan says.

Both Drexel's and the securities industry's rules required Marin to submit forms, signed by VIP's clients, granting permission for him to execute trades in the accounts he opened for them at Drexel. Whenever Louis phoned Michael to discuss a trade, Duncan jumped onto the line and demanded that Marin turn over the forms. Uneasy about sending account statements to Marin rather than to the investors themselves, Duncan hectored Louis for their actual addresses. "I would say, 'Okay Louis, I have to send duplicate confirmations to the clients. What's their address?' He'd say, 'I'll send it to you later,' " Duncan says.

Prozumenshikov was too busy trading to worry about such details, but the trades—their sheer size and volume—unnerved Mica. She was afraid they would plague Michael later, as Marin's trades at Brook Investments had done. To her credit, Duncan never stopped hounding Marin for the required documentation. "Louis kept saying, 'I'll give you that information; I'll get you their addresses,' " Mica says. "In some of the accounts he did; the majority he didn't." Mica warned Michael that she would take up the matter with Drexel's legal people if Marin didn't comply. "No, don't tell, don't tell," Prozumenshikov pleaded, though he knew she had only his welfare in mind.

In the legal department of Drexel Burnham Lambert's New York headquarters, Nolan Sheehan's phone rang mainly when people had problems. Sheehan wasn't an attorney, but he was a seasoned administrator. Among other things, it was Sheehan's job to help clean up stockbrokers' messes. He kept meticulous files on the 1,500 brokers in the retail division, and he usually knew what to do when one of them was bending the rules. Today, when he picked up the telephone receiver, Mica Duncan was on the line from Minneapolis. And she had a problem.

Duncan, phoning from an empty office down the hall so Michael wouldn't overhear, briefed Sheehan on the trading her boss had been doing with Marin. "Since I've got your attention," she said, "let's look at some things." Working on a common computer system, Duncan and Sheehan simultaneously punched up files on the accounts Marin had opened. There was silence on the line as Sheehan pondered the huge dollar value of the transactions—then, as his eyes wandered to the addresses registered for the accounts, a sharp intake of breath.

"My God," Sheehan said. "None of them have any addresses. They're all going to VIP."

A blinding glimpse of the obvious, to be sure, but Duncan held her tongue.

"I know that," she said.

"Do you have trading authorizations?" Sheehan wanted to know.

"No," Mica said.

"Well," Sheehan sputtered, "we've got to stop trading in these accounts. We just can't do it. Tell Michael not to do any more trades until you've got the proper paperwork in."

"Hey," Duncan retorted, "it's going take a bigger person than you and me to make him stop. You've got to go to a source higher than me to say that to."

Which is exactly what Sheehan did.

But it was too late. As Duncan says, "Things were really starting to go to hell in the accounts." The stocks Marin ordered had been delivered as scheduled, she says, but by settlement day no payment had arrived. Mort Greenberg, Michael's boss, tried calling Marin's boss, Timothy Vasko, in Denver, but couldn't get him on the phone. The National Association of Securities Dealers would later conclude that Marin was intercepting phone calls that could have alerted Vasko to the problem, an allegation Marin denies. Finally, Greenberg sent Vasko a telegram asking him to call regarding urgent business.

Soon Vasko phoned Greenberg and listened as the Drexel manager described the problem. "I'm sure Louis is handling it," Vasko said at first. But by the end of the conversation, Vasko says, he realized what was going on: "Louis had been trading through Michael and not paying for the trades." This, too, Marin denies.

It was Greenberg's view that VIP should pay for the trades now, but Vasko refused. "You don't have any trading authorizations on file to take these orders," Vasko told Greenberg. He was right. And no arbitration panel in the land was likely to make VIP pay for trades its clients had never authorized.

Now, Duncan says, Drexel Burnham was sitting on a loss of $140,000—a sum big enough to draw unwanted attention from the firm's top brass. Allan Sher, the all-powerful executive vice president, and Herb Dunn, chief of Drexel's newly reorganized western region, soon were phoning Mort Greenberg and demanding to know what was going on.

Prozumenshikov "panicked," Duncan says. He was afraid someone would dredge up the old records and realize this wasn't his first encounter with Louis Marin. Prozumenshikov phoned Marin and screamed at him, demanding that Louis pay for the trades. Marin, Duncan says, said he didn't have the money. Prozumenshikov slammed down the phone in disgust. "I'll never talk to him again," he said.

Meanwhile, Timothy Vasko says, he discovered that Marin's unauthorized trades weren't the only problem. A bill arrived from American Express demanding $6,000 for goods charged on a corporate credit card Vasko says he didn't know Marin had. A call to American Express, Vasko says, solved the mystery. Months earlier, Vasko had loaned Marin a card to fly to San Francisco on company business. After returning the card, Vasko says, Marin phoned American Express and reported it missing. The company then mailed him a new one, which Marin since had used liberally, Vasko says.

Marin disputes this account. He says Vasko gave him a permanent American Express card as part of Marin's hiring at VIP. "I was traveling back and forth to Chicago with the card," Marin says. "He wanted to make me comfortable."

Furious, Vasko confronted Marin about the card and the stock trades at Drexel Burnham. "He tried to explain it away," Vasko says. "I was so angry, I didn't really listen to him. I just went back to my office and shut the door."

Marin left VIP for good. But he refused, at first, to return a company-owned Saab turbo sports car that Vasko had loaned him. Marin kept the car, he says, because he believed Vasko owed him money for the Drexel stock trades. Vasko had to take Marin to court to get the car back. By then, Marin had applied for Chapter 13 personal-bankruptcy protection, citing debts that included $160,000 in back taxes and $3,500 in delinquent student loans. Despite the bankruptcy proceedings, a Denver judge ordered Marin to return the car to VIP, which he did.

Vasko reported the episode to the National Association of Securities Dealers, which began investigating. To Vasko's dismay, the NASD soon filed complaints against both Marin and Vasko himself. Marin, the agency noted, had worked for eleven firms in the previous five years. This transience should have deterred Vasko from hiring him, the NASD asserted. Vasko protested that he had phoned Marin's three previous employers, that none of them had anything bad to say about the trader. The NASD nevertheless slapped Vasko with a ten-day suspension from his job and a $10,000 fine for failing to adequately supervise Marin.

As for Marin, although he managed to land jobs at two more firms

I ЛЕНИНГРАДСКИЙ МЕДИЦИНСКИЙ ИНСТИТУТ имени академика И. П. ПАВЛОВА

Факультет *Лечебный* группа № *35*

ЭКЗАМЕНАЦИОННЫЙ ЛИСТ № *891*

Фамилия *Прозуменщиков*

Имя *Михаил* Отчество *Иосифович*

Протокол о допуске к вступительным экзаменам № *12* от *20 июля* 19*70* г.

Дата выдачи *20 июля* 19*70* г.

Ответственный секретарь
приемной комиссии _____ (подпись)

_____
(подпись поступающего)

I. Оценки, полученные на вступительных экзаменах

№ п/п	Наименование предмета	Дата	Оценка	Фамилия, И. О. экзаменаторов	Подписи экзаменаторов
	I — По профилирующим дисциплинам				
1	Физика (устно)	0.5.VII.70	(пра)	Смирнов Л.В. Руанова Н.В.	
2	Химия (устно)	5/VII-70	3 (три)	Шмелёв Л.Н. Марке В.Н.	
3	Биология (устно)	14 авгуса На	4 (четыре)	Семенова 4.4.2. Тюрина Л.Я.	
		ИТОГО			
	II — По непрофилирующим дисциплинам				
1	Русский яз. и литература (письменно)	1/VII-70	3 (три)	Дмитриева К.А. Кадычева К.В.	

Ответственный секретарь приемной комиссии

ПРИМЕЧАНИЕ: 1. Экзаменационный лист служит пропуском на экзамен.

2. По окончании приема экзаменов экзаменационный лист должен быть возвращен в приемную комиссию.

3. Не зачисленный в учебное заведение получает обратно свои документы после сдачи экзаменационного листа.

4. Опоздавшие и не явившиеся в срок допускаются к экзамену лишь с разрешения ответственного секретаря приемной комиссии.

Р-нт I ЛМИ, з.48, т.5000.3/3-70г.

As an aspiring dental student, seventeen-year-old Michael Prozumenshikov profited from his prowess at the hammer throw, an athletic event popular in Russia. His performance on his dental school entrance exams, to which he carried this identification card, was less impressive. Michael was nevertheless admitted to the First Leningrad Medical Institute, the city's best.

Transplanted to the United States, Prozumenshikov abandoned his dental career for the booming stock-brokerage business. Michael, ensconced in the Minneapolis branch of Drexel Burnham Lambert, made millions for the junk-bond firm. From his fortieth-floor window, he could see downtown Minneapolis and the Mississippi River, rolling through the urban landscape like the Neva in his native Leningrad.

At a costume party, Michael donned prison stripes to pose as the jailed
Wall Street arbitrageur Ivan Boesky, who received insider tips from an
investment banker at Drexel, Prozumenshikov's own firm. Ellen
Prozumenshikov, Michael's wife, sits beside him.

Michael, by now employed at Prudential-Bache Securities, let his hair down
at a toga party thrown by a fellow Russian expatriate. He wasn't always so
relaxed. His profane outburst at another party marked an ugly rupture from
his circle of Leningrad friends. Valery Gilevich, Michael's longtime friend
and fellow stockbroker, is at far right.

Zachary Persitz, self-styled intellectual, sometime poet and sculptor, turned over his family's savings to Michael Prozumenshikov. A doting father, Persitz taught his elder son, Daniel, to speak and write both Russian and English before the boy was six. For his younger son, Jonathan, Zachary wrote and illustrated a book about the importance of reading.

Michael, Zachary, and
their families vaca-
tioned together in the
Cayman Islands. Here,
while basking with
Zachary in the generous
Caribbean sun, it was
impossible for Michael
to foresee the coming
explosion.

Foraging crows led a maintenance man to a gruesome discovery at this site, a
Christmas tree dump in the Minnesota countryside.

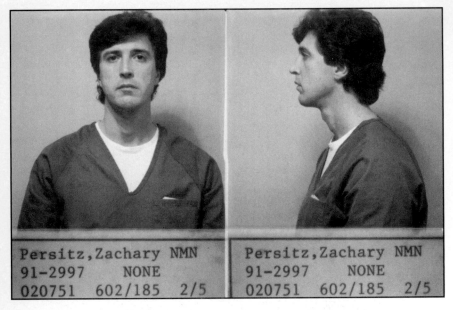

Persitz,Zachary NMN
91-2997   NONE
020751 602/185   2/5

Persitz,Zachary NMN
91-2997   NONE
020751 602/185   2/5

Jail was a dehumanizing experience for Persitz. Shortly after these photos were snapped, an officer took samples of his blood, saliva, and hair, including pubic hair. Later came suicide attempts and electroshock therapy.

after he left VIP, his career as a stock trader would soon be finished. In 1990, the NASD would censure him for the stock trades at Drexel, fine him $25,000, and throw him out of the business.

Prozumenshikov got little out of his second encounter with Louis Marin except liability for the $140,000 loss. Drexel soon replaced Mort Greenberg with a new manager from outside the firm named Jerry Shaughnessy. Shaughnessy's mandate was to come down hard on any broker who operated outside the rules. And, although it enraged Michael, Shaughnessy insisted that the loss come out of Michael's gross commissions.

The final indignity for Prozumenshikov was a close encounter—his second—with industry regulators. When Vasko reported the matter to the NASD, he took pains to detail Prozumenshikov's role in it. In one conversation with an NASD lawyer, Vasko went so far as to suggest that the NASD "chase down" the Russian broker, who had clearly broken industry rules by accepting Marin's trades without client authorization forms. Soon Vasko got an angry call from Prozumenshikov. "Why did you drag my name into it?" Michael wanted to know. Vasko, in no mood to talk to the man he held partially responsible for his own misfortune, told him to call VIP's lawyer and hung up. In the end, however, Michael would slip through the regulators' fingers, just as he had after churning mutual funds at Merrill Lynch.

The messy business did start Prozumenshikov's relationship with Jerry Shaughnessy, his new boss, on a sour note. And in the depressed post-crash securities industry, all Michael needed was a boss who watched his every move and jumped all over him when he made a mistake.

Prozumenshikov spoke to Louis Marin only once more. The trader phoned one fine autumn morning while Michael was still in the process of paying off the $140,000. Marin said he needed money to fly from Denver to Chicago. He wondered whether Michael could loan him $500.

Gently, Prozumenshikov returned the receiver to its cradle. He looked at Mica Duncan, his round face as blank as a refrigerator door. "Louis wants to borrow money," Michael said gravely. "Do you think I should loan it to him?"

A full minute passed before either of them could stop laughing.

CHAPTER 11

On the wall of Michael Prozumenshikov's office hung a map of cold-war Leningrad. The work of Central Intelligence Agency cartographers, it rendered the city's labyrinthine streets, canals, and alleyways in painstaking detail. It was, Prozumenshikov told visitors proudly, more accurate than any map available in Leningrad itself. Beside the map dangled an even rarer memento of pre-Soviet Russia: paper money bearing the visage of Nicholas II, the last czar, who was executed after the revolution.

These were gifts from Valery Gilevich, whose friendship with Prozumenshikov had flourished since Gilevich abandoned his medical career and became, like Michael, a stockbroker.

The year was 1988, and in March Gilevich had joined a small Minneapolis brokerage firm. A new job was what he needed, for he had tired of his late hours and low station at the Metropolitan Medical Center. The securities business seemed an appropriate second career, given Val's long-standing fascination with free markets. As a teenager in Leningrad, his ceaseless talk of the United States and its capitalist system had won him the nickname "American Boy."

Gilevich, of course, had heard all the stories about Prozumenshikov's supposed crookedness. Who hadn't? By now Russians and Ukrainians were disparaging Michael everywhere Val went. An indelible memory for Gilevich was the occasion on which he told a fellow Russian about his new job as a stockbroker. "Oh?" the man responded amiably. "To be a thief like Michael?"

Yet Val's loyalties remained with his friend. Michael and Ellen were gracious hosts, preparing elaborate dinners and offering fine wine and liqueurs to their guests. Not long ago, Val and his wife had vacationed with the Prozumenshikovs at Lake Tahoe. "We had a ball," Gilevich says. The rub in Val's friendship with Michael had been their squabbling about bounced checks and trading losses while Michael was managing Val's savings. And this Gilevich resolved by moving his money from Drexel Burnham to his own brokerage firm.

Lately, Michael had been a big help in lining up job interviews and giving Val tips on how to sell himself. When Gilevich went to work as a broker, the single piece of advice Prozumenshikov gave him about the brokerage business seemed self-evident. "Persistence," Prozumenshikov had said. "Call and call and call and call."

But acting on the suggestion wasn't as straightforward as it sounded. Cold calling, Gilevich found, was tedious work, a process of speaking to strangers and their suspicious secretaries all day long. Gilevich had an agile mind and a good sense of humor, but isolating himself from the punishment of the phone calls wasn't as easy for him as it was for Michael. There was another difference as well. Mindful of Michael's many feuds with former clients, Gilevich resolved that his own approach to the business would be conservative, his investing strategies attuned to his customers' true financial goals.

It was in appreciation of Michael's help in introducing Val to potential employers that, over dinner, Gilevich ceremoniously presented his friend with the framed antique paper money. Neither man mentioned it, but both understood the symbolism of the gift. The czarist currency and the CIA's Leningrad map, an earlier present from Gilevich, were nothing less than acknowledgments of the central conflict of their mutual ancestry—their love for Russia, its culture and its history, and their contempt for the thugs and imbeciles who ran it.

Now, for Michael Prozumenshikov, these souvenirs of his native country served as troubling reminders of his villification in the U.S. immigrant community. Whatever the merits of the rumors circulating about him—and many of them were exaggerations or outright lies—he was becoming a pariah among his own people, notorious not only in Minneapolis but in places from Brooklyn to San Francisco. And Michael's hot temper was only making matters worse.

A few months after the stock market crash, Prozumenshikov phoned police in St. Louis Park, the suburb where his parents lived. He complained that two former clients, a couple named Yefim and Nina Sheynin, had been making threatening phone calls to his parents' home.

The two of them had lost $200 at Drexel Burnham, Michael told the police, a paltry sum that nevertheless prompted them, he said, to vow to "destroy him." Yefim Sheynin, Prozumenshikov said, had used an old Russian death threat: "They will find you in a coffin with white shoes on." The Sheynins, Michael claimed, had also threatened his six-year-old son, Daniel.

An officer who visited the Sheynin home found that the elderly couple spoke little English. In halting speech, the Sheynins offered to phone a friend—Zina Shirl, the beautician who had been an early U.S. contact both for them and for Prozumenshikov. This woman, who had also lost money trading with Michael, would be happy to translate, they said.

Through Shirl, the Sheynins rebutted Prozumenshikov's complaint against them point by point. They said they had lost thousands, not hundreds, of dollars, and the losses had occurred in a supposedly stable retirement account. They fervently denied threatening Michael's son or parents. Yefim Sheynin admitted using the "white shoes" phrase, but said he did so only after Prozumenshikov debased his wife. According to Sheynin, Prozumenshikov had said, "Tell your old whore to shut her mouth, or I will cut her tongue out." Moreover, the couple insisted, Nina Sheynin had been in the hospital on the day Michael claimed she called to threaten him.

The St. Louis Park police officer apparently believed at least some of what the Sheynins had to say. A few days later, he visited Michael at his office in downtown Minneapolis and pointed out discrepancies between the stories. When he told Prozumenshikov he was closing the case, Michael flew into a rage. Calmly, the officer told the angry Russian he should contact police in his own suburb of Plymouth if he wanted to continue to press charges.

Michael's conclusion was that the law couldn't, or wouldn't, protect him and his family from angry former clients. Not long after the Sheynin incident, he bought a handgun and learned how to use it. Michael kept the pistol in his bedroom.

Such confrontations were becoming all too common for Michael. Another occurred when Merrill Lynch tried to extract money it had mistakenly turned over to one of his estranged clients.

Boris Panich, an immigrant living in San Francisco, had opened an account with Michael after friends in Minneapolis gave the broker his name. One month in 1986, Panich had noticed that the account balance was about $16,000 too high. "I called Michael right away," Panich says. "I said, 'Why this jump for one month?' He said, 'I forgot to tell you. I made this money for your daughter.' I said: 'I think this is a mistake.'"

Yet when the next monthly statement arrived, the total was the same. And so it remained the next month, and the next. Thrilled, Panich had referred his friends to Prozumenshikov, telling them Michael understood the American stock market and could make their money grow. When Michael left Merrill for Drexel Burnham, Panich's account went with him.

After the stock market crash, Panich received a telegram from Drexel demanding $4,500 to protect the devalued stocks in his portfolio. And soon Merrill Lynch was badgering him for $16,000 more, saying it had erroneously credited his account with that sum in 1986. Dennis Kellner, Michael's old boss at Merrill Lynch, later theorized that Prozumenshikov knew all along that the $16,000 didn't belong to Panich. "There's no question in my mind that Michael knew what was going on," Kellner says. "You would have to be totally ignorant not to have known that the guy didn't deserve the money. Any broker who was trying to do the right thing would've gotten it back immediately."

Unfortunately, most of the money Merrill sought had since been lost investing in Texas Air stock. Panich, who earned a small salary as a shuttlebus driver at an automobile dealership, owned only one major asset—his home—and he was terrified of losing it.

Thus Panich's good humor was in short supply when he arrived in Minneapolis with his attorney for an arbitration hearing in the Merrill Lynch case. The hearing played itself out in a drab hotel conference room, before a panel of three professional arbitrators. Panich sat quietly until he heard Prozumenshikov deny that he had ever said the $16,000 was a trading profit. At this Panich exploded, screaming at the stockbroker in Russian as the arbitrators watched silently and Panich's lawyer winced. Prozumenshikov said nothing. When the outburst ceased, Michael calmly resumed his testimony. In the end, Merrill would win its case and, because Panich couldn't afford to pay, place a lien on his house in California.

During a break in the proceedings, Panich and Prozumenshikov ran into one another in a hotel bathroom. Panich's lawyer had warned him not to speak to Michael, but he was too furious to comply.

"Michael," he said, "why are you doing this? Why are you lying?"

Prozumenshikov, who was rinsing his hands, refused to look at his former client. "I don't want to talk to you," he said, staring into a mirror.

Panich opened his mouth to say something, then thought better of it. "I got so mad I felt like hitting him," he says. Silence hung in the white-tiled room as Michael finished at the sink and dried his hands with a paper towel. Finally, Panich spoke. "God will punish you," he said, spinning on his heel and stalking out of the bathroom.

While Panich was in Minneapolis, he heard plenty from friends and relatives about Prozumenshikov—all of it bad. They said Michael was "a fancy guy" who drove a Mercedes, ate at the most expensive restaurants, and lived in a big house. The prevailing view among these immigrants was that Michael paid for his perks with money he stole from clients. Zina Shirl, also a friend of Panich's, was talking about suing Prozumenshikov. Shirl had lost $20,000 trading stock and stock options with him. Despondent about the losses, she had decided to channel her distress through the courts.

It wasn't hard to find a lawyer who would take the case. In September, the SEC concluded its long-standing investigation of insider trading at Drexel Burnham by filing civil charges alleging securities-law violations by Michael Milken and others. Criminal charges were expected soon. It would take time to try the government's charges, and there was no guarantee the authorities would win. But Drexel's reputation was in the toilet. Across the country, enterprising securities lawyers were filing lawsuits and arbitration claims against Drexel brokers, betting that the besieged firm would rather settle for big money than fight.

Shirl, Panich, and two other immigrants pooled their trading records and helped a Minneapolis lawyer put together a lawsuit against Michael and his firm. It accused the broker of fraud, churning, unauthorized trades, and, in a unique twist, civil violations of a federal law governing Mafia activity, called the Racketeer Influenced and Corrupt Organizations, or RICO, statute. Among other things, the lawsuit claimed that Prozumenshikov had forged Boris Panich's signature on a consent form to trade stocks with borrowed money.

But when the lawsuit arrived at Drexel, neither Michael nor the firm's lawyers were impressed. "We laughed," Mica Duncan says. "I mean, there wasn't one thing in there that I couldn't refute." Drexel's lawyers would soon file a document rebutting virtually every allegation in the suit and denying that Michael had forged Panich's signature.

Lawyers at the firm also argued that the case had been inappropriately filed in U.S. District Court. Securities firms limit their legal exposure by requiring investors to agree in advance that any disputes will be moderated by industry arbitrators. Under industry rules, the case belonged in arbitration, not in federal court. Drexel's lawyers were confident the judge would throw it out.

So, for Michael, the real problem wasn't the lawsuit. It was the publicity that accompanied it.

One afternoon, a reporter from a weekly newspaper called *CityBusiness* phoned Prozumenshikov and told him she was doing a story on the court case. She interviewed him briefly, then hung up. The conversation worried Michael. The reporter, he told Mica, seemed to think he was guilty.

On the day the article appeared, Michael heard about it from a client. Nervously, he asked Mica to run down and buy a copy of *CityBusiness*. At the time, Prozumenshikov and Duncan were sharing their office with a young broker named Mark Stein, whom the previous branch manager, Mort Greenberg, had asked Michael to tutor. When Duncan returned, she made two photocopies of the article, one for herself and one for Stein.

The reporter had balanced the piece by quoting Michael liberally, but its tone was nonetheless harsh. Jeffrey Robbins, attorney for the four immigrants, implied in it that Prozumenshikov had used his Russian clients' naivete to cheat them out of their life savings. "None of them has an outstanding command of the English language," Robbins was quoted as saying. "I don't think they knew what they were getting into."

Michael asked Mica to shut the door. Bad press, he knew, was anathema to stockbrokers who rely on their unblemished reputations to win investors' trust. Everyone in the Drexel branch would be gossiping about this before the day was done. And other local newspapers were now likely to do stories of their own.

Prozumenshikov stabbed his finger onto the printed page before him. "This is a lie," he almost screamed. "And this is a lie, and this." Duncan and Stein were shocked by this uncharacteristic display of anguish. "We could tell right away that it had hurt Michael inside," Stein says. "It was in his eyes." They both tried to soothe Prozumenshikov, but he seemed to need to rage on—to purge himself of his anger and pain. This was his way, Mica had learned by now. He bottled up nothing. "I'll sue *them*," he now began shouting. "I'll sue them for slander."

Soon Prozumenshikov's tantrum subsided and he slumped over his desk with his head in his hands. Mica had been collecting her thoughts, and Michael looked up at her as she began speaking. "Michael," she said, "this is printed here, and you're not ever going to be able to say anything. You can't say *anything*." As much as it might hurt, Duncan said, "You've got to keep your mouth shut and be a man about it."

Mark Stein thought he had a special insight into Michael's predicament, but he kept it to himself. Stein, who was Jewish, knew that the Russian and American Jewish communities overlapped substantially in Minneapolis. Disparaging talk about Prozumenshikov and his family was making the rounds even among people who had never met him. And this newspaper article exposed his previously private feud with fellow Russians for outsiders to see—dignifying the gossip, institutionalizing it. It was an assault on Prozumenshikov's personal integrity before the audience that mattered most to him, the Minnesota business community.

"I think being a Russian Jew, and growing up in Russia and coming over here, his pride was phenomenal in himself and his family," Stein says. "And I think that was what hurt him most. The lawsuit was a big deal to him, but that wasn't the real reason he was angry. They bad-mouthed him, and they were bad-mouthing his parents at the same time. That's what hurt him the most."

Michael, of course, had never hesitated to fire verbal barbs of his own at fellow immigrants. But in the past such discourse had sounded more like a sociology lecture than gossip. Russians were too emotional for the markets, he opined in a detached and superior tone, and they wanted only gains, never losses.

But now it was personal. Michael had begun to receive anonymous death threats on a regular basis. His friends from Leningrad—Val Gilevich, Mark Goldburt, and the others—told him of slurs they were hearing from others in the Russian community. Clearly, he felt, the campaign against him was out of control.

Prozumenshikov jerked open the drawer of his big wooden desk and grabbed the binder that contained his client list. With a flourish, he opened the rings and began yanking out sheets of paper, each bearing the name of a Russian or Ukrainian investor who had managed to survive Black Monday. Finally he finished, returning the now-narrow notebook to the desk drawer. "There are the Russians," he said to Mica Duncan and Mark Stein, gesturing at the pile of paper in front of him. "I will never do business with them again."

For a man who still believed, despite ample evidence to the contrary, that his services were a privilege for his clients, it was the best revenge he could imagine.

For weeks afterward, friends and colleagues noticed a new moodiness in Michael. His outlook was black, his temper short, and his sense of humor buried somewhere beneath a mound of gloom. His general disposition, in contrast to the penitence he had displayed after the stock market crash, was hostile. Any admonition from his boss, Jerry Shaughnessy, drew a defiant response. Whenever a Russian client phoned the office, Michael's upper lip curled in distaste. "I could tell when Michael picked up the phone and it was a Russian," Duncan says. "There were times that he would hang up on them." Other such calls he passed off to Mica, who took messages that Michael refused to answer.

He raved to his remaining Russian friends about the lawsuit—how unfair it was, how soundly Drexel would thrash his antagonists in court. "It drove him nuts," Val Gilevich says. "He was telling me he has so much on those people that he could destroy their lives, how he was never going to lose." Michael persuaded some of his friends to sign statements attesting to his good character, to be used as evidence in court. He asked Mark Tsypin, one of the few Russians who remained on his client list, to testify in court as a character witness, if it came to that.

And to some extent, Michael's friends sympathized with his plight. They felt they had more in common with him than with his Ukrainian adversaries—not only friendship, but the strong bond of their common ancestry in Leningrad. Privately, however, some of them wondered whether the lawsuit might not have merit. Just about everyone in the social circle had lost money on Michael's stock picks at one time or another.

Within the group, Mark Tsypin had lost most, stung by the debacle in Texas Air stock. Tsypin's losses included $2,000 he had invested for his mother-in-law, which he chose to cover himself. After Black Monday, Tsypin had managed to produce the $8,000 Drexel demanded in its margin calls, but he ceased to trust Michael's advice. Tsypin believed that he himself was partially to blame for the losses; he had, after all, authorized Michael to buy the shares. But when Prozumenshikov phoned one afternoon to peddle yet another "can't-miss" stock, Tsypin couldn't help admonishing him.

"Michael," Tsypin said in Russian, "everything is down. Why would I buy anything else? It would go down anyway."

"No, no," Prozumenshikov said excitedly, "it's impossible."

"It's impossible," Tsypin repeated slowly. "When every single stock I bought on your recommendation is down?

"I would understand," Tsypin went on, his tone rising, "if it would be fifty-fifty. But everything? Take a look at my list."

Sensing an unwanted confrontation with a man he regarded as his friend, Prozumenshikov said nothing more about the stock he was trying to sell. "He usually preferred in those cases just to be silent," Tsypin said later. "He was very good at avoiding confrontations." Tsypin didn't say so, but he had been annoyed about his losses for some time. And although he had signed a letter supporting Michael in his legal fight with his former clients, Tsypin had considered suing Michael himself.

Tsypin wasn't the only one in the "Leningrad circle" who was nursing reservations about Prozumenshikov. Perhaps because Val Gilevich had become a stockbroker, he and Michael remained close. "But with the rest of the friends, there was a great tension," Gilevich says. "He was separating himself from everybody else, from the crowd. Everybody was mystified that Michael had begun to turn his back."

Michael Brezman didn't care for Prozumenshikov, but included him in social events out of courtesy and to accomodate his wife, who liked Ellen. Alec and Bella Buzhaker, another couple in the circle, had had frequent run-ins with the broker over stocks he recommended. Mark Goldburt remained loyal to Michael but was put off by his friend's behavior.

It wasn't just that the rumors about Prozumenshikov were so persistent and—as in the cases of elderly immigrants who were said to have lost their retirement savings—so specific. The biggest problem was that Michael, who once had earned less than any of his friends, was now quite arrogant about his success.

Recently, in an offhand remark, Mark Goldburt had referred to Michael's job as "playing" with stocks. Michael's face had reddened and his expression soured. "It's not playing," he said between clenched teeth. "It's investing." Mark tried to turn the matter into a joke, but Michael didn't laugh. For the rest of the evening, he seemed to be sulking.

On another occasion, Prozumenshikov boasted to Goldburt that a big client had just earned hundreds of thousands of dollars on a single takeover-driven stock. Goldburt asked why Michael hadn't told him about the stock. After all, Michael hadn't hesitated to mine Goldburt's contacts in the Soviet Union about products to import and resell in the United States. "Because," Michael said in Russian, his voice suddenly cold, "you are a small chicken. These people invest millions to make hundreds of thousands." Michael hesitated a moment, then finished his thought. "You're afraid," he said.

People in the circle also noticed that Michael was becoming a bit of a glutton. "He could eat like a wild beast," Gilevich says. Michael embarrassed himself at restaurants by ordering too much food—perhaps to demonstrate that money was no object. On his company-sponsored junkets to resorts in Florida, North Carolina, and California, he consumed caviar and and other delicacies at a pace no other broker could match. "He really took advantage," one broker says. "He didn't waste any time."

Michael, Mark Goldburt says, was proud of being among the favored few selected for these perk trips at expensive resorts, and he wanted his friends to know about it. "Of course, it was a different style for us," Goldburt says. "I never went to this kind of hotel."

Other changes in Michael were more subtle. The quality Goldburt liked best, Michael's boyish enthusiasm, now seemed to appear only when he talked about money. Others noticed this as well. These days, "his main subject in conversations was wealth," Val Gilevich says. "We never talked about something else—girls or movies or sports or life—only money." And at one gathering at Michael's home, Gilevich says, Prozumenshikov surprised his male guests by taking them into his study and offering them cocaine—an isolated incident that never repeated itself.

Among themselves, members of the Leningrad circle proffered various theories for Prozumenshikov's new ways. Perhaps his big earnings had swelled his head. "We had become too small for Mike," Mark Goldburt postulated. "Now he was a big boy, and we were just little chickens." Or perhaps he was generalizing his contempt for other immigrants and venting it at his Russian friends. Or, possibly, he wasn't interested in socializing with Russians because he didn't need them as clients anymore. "When he climbed on the ladder," Tsypin said, "we became less and less important as clients, so our social contacts got much less with him. Our accounts are too small to generate any real cash."

Whatever the reason, no one could deny that Michael was becoming distant—and snide. At parties, he often sat silently as the others talked. When they laughed, he rarely joined in, watching instead with what looked like a sneer on his face. Some, no doubt, would have stopped inviting to him to their homes, but for their affection for Ellen. Whatever their feelings about her husband, in fact, everyone liked Ellen. "She's a very nice person," Mark Tsypin said, summing up the feelings of the group. "We felt kind of bad to leave her alone. She needed, more than him, some social life."

That November, a far more pressing concern diverted the group's attention from the problem with Michael: Valery Gilevich was diagnosed with colon cancer. He underwent emergency surgery to remove the tumor and then endured a barrage of chemotherapy. Over a period of months, his friends watched as the color drained from his face and the mischievous twinkle left his eyes.

The illness, Gilevich says, sapped his will to work and interfered with his personal life. "I had some tension in my marriage," he says. "I take the blame. I tried to be a hero, playing, 'We'll overcome.' On a different side of me, I was just totally lost. I was puzzled. I knew that this was the end. I was very withdrawn and lost attention in my family life."

Michael Prozumenshikov was a good friend to Gilevich during this painful period. "He tried to mediate . . . to smooth things," Gilevich says. "He tried to talk to me about how nice my wife was, how much I was wanted at home, and I was making a mistake if I made a decision that would split the family."

In late January, Michael took Val to dinner, just the two of them, at a sushi restaurant they both liked. It was a quiet place in downtown Minneapolis, nestled on the bank of the Mississippi River. As they shuffled through new snow toward the entrance, the two expatriate Russians drew their coats close against a bitter northern wind. They made an odd pair— Michael tall and heavy, his body softened by too much to eat and too little exercise; Val shorter, his frame ravaged by cancer and strange drugs. The Mississippi looked, that night, like the mysterious Neva, flowing beneath vaulted bridges in the classical city of their birth—the city of Lenin, the cradle of the Russian revolution.

Thank God it wasn't the Neva. This city was Minneapolis, U.S.A., and this evening there would be good food and wine aplenty, no bribes to pay, no line outside the restaurant, and no stench of harsh Soviet disinfectants in it. True, Val was ill, but there were blessings to be counted nonetheless. Indeed, that was Prozumenshikov's message once the two men settled at a table and ordered sake, the sweet Japanese rice wine, and an exotic array of sushi and sashimi dishes. Michael had brought Val to this place to inform his friend how much there was to live for.

But he wasn't very good at it. Lacking introspection himself, he couldn't comprehend how the specter of death could make the temporal aspects of life—family, career—seem meaningless. "There was no soul-searching on his part," Gilevich says. "He was not a man who looked into the essential inner part of marriage, but only upon the practical side." How odd, Val thought, that a man as talented at selling as Michael couldn't sell a friend on the most basic commodity of all: life.

What's more, Michael was visibly uncomfortable talking about Val's illness. Soon he changed the subject and rattled on about other matters, including stocks he was researching, rather than discussing the matter on both of their minds. "We just chitted and chatted nonsense," Gilevich says. And to Val, for whom staving off despair required a constant, conscious effort, it was difficult to sustain such mundane banter.

To break the tension, Gilevich looked at the fish-and-rice dainties spread before him and blurted, in English, "Gee, if my oncologist knew what I am eating here, he wouldn't believe it."

At this, an elderly man at another table perked up. "Your oncologist?" the man said. "Who is your oncologist?"

"Dr. Burton Schwartz," Gilevich said. "Do you know him?"

"Well, yeah, sure I know him," the stranger replied. "I used to be an oncologist myself."

To Val's relief, the conversation that ensued lasted throughout dinner, as he and Michael got to know the retired oncologist and his wife. "We started to talk to each other back and forth, back and forth," Gilevich says. "And they were like saviors for me, because this switched my mind, from talking nonsense with Michael to somebody that was very delightful to know." If Prozumenshikov was offended by the diversion, he didn't say so. He actually seemed relieved to be free of the difficult task of confronting Val's cancer.

Despite his misgivings, Gilevich survived the long Minnesota winter. Months passed and warm weather arrived, lifting Val's spirits. With luck and ongoing chemotherapy, his doctors said, he might yet beat the cancer—although they chided Gilevich for refusing to stop smoking.

That summer of 1989, Val's friends staged a surprise party for his forty-fifth birthday. They rented a yacht and lured him to Lake Minnetonka with a ruse about inspecting a small boat that one of his friends was supposedly thinking of buying. "Somehow I didn't suspect anything," Gilevich says. "There was a boat with a 'For Sale' sign, with a capacity of maybe two hundred people . . . a huge boat. I said, 'Boris, you must be out of your mind. We've been talking about a boat that could handle six to eight people.' I walked in, and it was a surprise party."

Prozumenshikov was there—making a nuisance of himself. He had brought a pair of expensive binoculars. And as the boat churned through the bottle-green water of Minnetonka, he collared first one person, then another, exhorting them to peer through his binoculars at the mansions along the shore. "This is Irwin Jacobs's house," he said, his voice brimming with excitement. "And this is the house of my client, a five-million-dollar house." Despite the securities industry recession, Michael had raked in gross commissions of $850,000 in 1988, of which he kept about $350,000 before taxes, and was now planning a $1 million house of his own. Apparently concluding that his friends would be jealous about the project, he chose not to tell them about it.

Michael's antics with the binoculars struck some at the party as pathetic—a subconscious attempt, perhaps, to affirm the legitimacy of his values by placing them in competition with those of his friends. Or maybe he was just trying to remind everyone how successful he was. Whatever, Gilevich was disgusted. "It was just very silly," he said later. "We are grown-up people. The purpose was to go and cruise Lake Minnetonka and have a good time; to celebrate a birthday; to eat good food; to swim. But not to take binoculars and tell everybody this is value; net worth is so much; and this and this and this. I don't know how much of these details he knew, or how much was he was just pretending he knew." Val chose not to make a scene by dressing Michael down at the party. No, he thought, not yet.

Michael continued to drift away from his Russian friends. He seldom saw them, and when he did awkward pauses sometimes punctuated the proceedings. Once or twice, Michael seemed to realize that he was being ostracized by consensus: When he said something his friends found particularly outrageous, he could see them exchanging commiserating glances. Prozumenshikov wrote off this behavior as jealousy—the same emotion he ascribed to his enemies in the Russian and Ukrainian community.

As Drexel's lawyers continued to phone Michael at his office and ask him to respond to this or that allegation in the immigrants' lawsuit, to produce this or that document, the Russian broker's patience grew short. When colleagues asked him about the case, the insults he hurled at the four plaintiffs were often couched in the worst kind of gutter language. Nor did Michael reserve his bad-mouthing for his legal adversaries. He seemed, clients and colleagues say, to have contempt for all Russians.

One of Michael's clients, the well-to-do owner of a chain of print shops, was married to a woman who tutored new Russian immigrants in American language and customs. The client, Jerry Shink, decided to host a dinner for these immigrants and invite Prozumenshikov, whose success, he believed, would be an inspiration to them. "I thought Michael, because he's a countryman, would be very warm and understanding," Shink says. "I mean, they were coming up the way he came up, being janitors and making do with blue-collar jobs."

But Prozumenshikov seemed to lack any sense of noblesse oblige, Shink noted. At the dinner, he was interested only in talking to Shink and his wife. With the immigrants, Shink says, "He was standoffish. He kind of looked down on them, I think because they didn't have any money and they couldn't help his career. That kind of struck me funny."

Little by little, Michael was becoming similarly indifferent to some of his friends from Leningrad. For Ellen Prozumenshikov's benefit, the group might have continued to suffer his impudence—had Michael allowed them to. But he was about to give his friends a taste of his ferocious temper—the payback, perhaps, for real and perceived injustices visited upon him by the Russian community at large. It happened that summer at a birthday party for Michael Brezman's wife, Inna.

In Russian culture, birthdays hold a special place. They are times for ritual and pageantry, for good food and drink and effusive gift-giving. Russian birthday parties are seldom small affairs. Always joyous, occasionally raucous, they are big gatherings of close friends. And Michael's Leningrad circle had a birthday tradition of its own. At each new party, the organizers invented some special way of celebrating—a yacht rental, perhaps, or the surreptitious importation of some far-flung relative, or maybe a creative gag of some kind.

Bella Buzhaker, one of the women in the group, had come up with the gimmick for Inna Brezman's surprise party: The men would drop their trousers and have the words "Happy Birthday" scrawled across their bottoms, a few Russian letters to each man. Michael Brezman was, even now, driving his wife around town on some invented errand. When he brought her home, they would moon Inna and bestow upon her the greeting of the day.

So the men, amid much guffawing and wisecracking, stepped out onto a wooden deck behind the house to have the cyrillic letters inscribed on their backsides. They leaned over a railing, pants around their knees, giggling and smoking cigarettes. Only Prozumenshikov made no move to unbuckle his belt. He stood off to one side, wearing a wary look. And when his turn came to bend over, he refused.

"No," he said. "I will not do this."

"Come on, Michael," Bella Buzhaker said, smiling. "It's your turn. Everybody is doing it."

"I said I won't do it," Prozumenshikov repeated, more forcefully.

From the men, standing bare-bottomed against the rail, came a wave of harangues and cat calls. "Get your ass over here, Michael," one of them said, and they all laughed.

"Michael," Bella chided, "are you chicken?"

To this Prozumenshikov made no reply. Rather, he bolted through a sliding glass door and into the house, with Bella in hot pursuit. "Oh come on Michael," she was saying, "all the boys have some letters, and you've got to have some too." After a brief, seemingly comical chase, she cornered him in the kitchen and continued to tease him as a couple of other women watched. All the men had remained outside on the deck, out of earshot.

Suddenly Michael wheeled on Bella, and the snarl on his face was terrible to behold. His skin color, someone said later, was the vibrant red of a well-ripened apple.

What came out of his mouth was far worse than his expression. At the top of his lungs, Michael screamed insults into Bella's face, treating everyone in the house to a litany of the lowest sexual slurs the Russian language had to offer.

The smile on Bella's face froze, then faded. For a moment, she appeared to be in shock. Then she turned her back and fled, weeping, as Michael continued his tirade behind her. He appeared to have lost all control of himself. "He talked like a pig," says Mark Goldburt, whose wife told him about the outburst later. "They are all the same, these names. They are the same in Russian and English."

When Michael finished, none of the women knew what to say. For a while, only Bella's sobbing broke the silence. "What kind of man are you?" someone finally mumbled. "What kind of man to use such language?"

Prozumenshikov said nothing more. He exchanged a few quiet words with Ellen Prozumenshikov, whose own face was also flushed. And although Michael seemed to have regained his composure, he made no move to apologize.

Within minutes, the Brezmans arrived. Inna Brezman was immediately led out onto the deck, where the men still stood with their pants down. Everyone laughed heartily at the joke. But when they zipped up their trousers and stepped into the living room, still cackling, they could see that something was amiss. Bella's eyes were red and swollen, and Michael was scowling. Tension hung, heavy and palpable, in the air.

The Prozumenshikovs stayed for the buffet-style dinner, but left soon afterward. The moment the door shut behind them, everyone was talking. No one could make any sense of it. How could Michael be so nasty to someone he knew so well? "I use obscene language when I tell jokes," Gilevich muttered. "But I don't say 'Go and fuck yourself' to the wife of my friend." The unanimous opinion was that Michael thought himself too good for the bawdy birthday gag, and, probably, too good for his circle of Russian friends. And no one felt much like partying anymore.

Mark Goldburt was a patient and well-mannered man, both slow to anger and quick to forgive. He laughed freely at his own jokes and those of others—a booming laugh, good to hear, that brought cheer to everyone around him. Yet no one could fail to notice the air of moral authority that Goldburt exuded. As the eldest of the Leningrad group, he often arbitrated disputes among the others. When someone acted up—a child, say, or an inebriated friend—Goldburt's raised eyebrow and quizzical expression was usually sufficient to restore order. "He is very calm," Val Gilevich says. "It has to be something exceptional to provoke him."

As boys, Goldburt and Michael Prozumenshikov had both lived in Leningrad's aged Petrograd district, though they didn't know each other there. An only child like Prozumenshikov, Goldburt had learned to work hard by necessity; since the age of sixteen, it had fallen to him to support his widowed mother. Prozumenshikov, Goldburt knew, also shared his work ethic. And Goldburt had always interpreted this trait as evidence of Michael's good character.

He and Michael had probably passed one another in Petrograd's bustling streets, ridden the same streetcars, drunk watery coffee in the same cafés. Happenstance had carried them around the world to the same American city. And here, drawn together by their common roots, they had forged an alliance. They had helped one another move from tiny rental apartments to their own homes, had painted walls and laid carpet together, had assisted one another in the comforting routine of building their American lives.

Despite all this, Goldburt's bond with Bella Buzhaker and her husband was stronger. Goldburt's wife, Stella, had known Bella for forty years, since they were childhood friends in Leningrad. Bella's husband, Alec, was probably Goldburt's best friend. Now, the pain written on Bella's face after Michael's profane outburst lived inside Mark Goldburt, reddening his own cheeks with empathetic rage and humiliation.

The greedy gleam in Prozumenshikov's eye, the swagger, and the rank materialism, these had been hard enough to swallow. But with his bullying and his filthy language, Michael had gone too far. Goldburt felt he no longer knew his friend, no longer had any confidence in his loyalty or his integrity.

Months passed before Goldburt next saw Prozumenshikov, at a party at Val Gilevich's house. Bella Buzhaker was there, and she and Michael were doing their best to avoid one another. While Bella appeared to be handling the awkward situation with aplomb, Prozumenshikov seemed tense. He paced among the circles of people, eyeing them but not joining in. Then he took up a spot off to the side, standing by himself and picking at a plate of food.

Watching Michael from across the room, Goldburt knew at last what he had to do. He took no pleasure in it. It pained him to rebuke a friend. Yet Mark regarded it as his duty. "The way he handled himself was unacceptable," Goldburt says. "I felt that because I knew him longer—and, again, I am older—I'm entitled at least to tell my opinion."

Goldburt appeared at Prozumenshikov's side and took his friend by the arm. "Come," he said. "I want to talk to you."

Mark led Michael out the front door and into the driveway. It was a cool fall evening, and neither man was wearing a coat. The Prozumenshikovs had driven Ellen's Volvo to the party. Michael suggested that they sit in it, to stay warm.

Mark, after planting himself in the front passenger's seat, got right to the point. He had known Michael for years, he said, and felt that the two of them were close friends. As a friend, he felt obligated to tell Michael his true feelings. "Mike," Goldburt said, "you have become a big snob. You insult people. You lie. And everybody is unhappy with you. I believe the rest of the people feel the same way, but they won't tell this to your face." No one in the circle, Goldburt added, was jealous of Michael; they were offended by his disdain for them.

About halfway through the monologue, Prozumenshikov had begun shaking violently. It was as if, like an unruly child, he had been expecting his punishment for some time and was terrified now that the occasion had finally arrived. Or perhaps his trembling was the result of forced introspection—a painfully deep glimpse of himself through the eyes of a man whose opinion he had once respected.

"I didn't do anything," Michael protested. "I'm the same way I used to be." It was Goldburt and the others, he asserted, who had changed. The space between them—the animosity—was an unavoidable consequence of their diverging financial fortunes.

"Mike," Goldburt said gently, "you're a completely different person. You have become much more successful than all of us, though it doesn't make you any better." In the past, he went on, "I was more successful than you. But I never gave you any indication that I'm higher, I'm better, or I'm smarter. If you don't feel, today, that we are equal to you, you can forget about us. But I don't like to be treated this way, just because you have become knowledgeable about stocks. I don't believe that you're better than me. I don't like the way you talk to me, the way you treat me."

"You're not right," Michael shot back in a wounded tone. "I'm not this person that you describe."

"Maybe," Goldburt said. "But in the way you express yourself, this is the person I see."

As the two of them climbed out of the car and walked toward the house, Michael's face was a mask of resentment. Inside, he drew his wife aside. A few minutes later, Ellen circulated saying her goodbyes, and the couple departed.

With no trace of pride in his voice, Goldburt told the others what he had done. As he did, their heads nodded in approval. Goldburt said it wasn't his intention to break ties with Michael, but rather to tell him honestly about his feelings and the feelings of the group. He remained open to friendship, he said, if Michael mended his ways.

But Goldburt harbored no great hope that Michael would change. The genial and fun-loving young man he befriended in those early days had vanished—if, indeed, he had ever existed at all.

"You have to go to an extreme situation," Goldburt said later, "to see how a person acts: If he is brave, if he is a real friend. When you just meet each other, and talk about nothing, and drink coffee, you will not see his actual qualities."

Perhaps, in his single-minded pursuit of wealth, Prozumenshikov was now revealing his essential character.

"It's very unusual," Goldburt ruminated, "for a person to make this amount of money in this short period of time. Maybe his best side was as a salesman. Or maybe it was inside, and I just didn't have a chance to check."

CHAPTER 12

Until he reached school age in 1987, Daniel Persitz liked to turn the pages of the Dr. Seuss book, *The Cat in the Hat*, while his father, Zachary, read aloud. They had read and reread the little book until the cover's corners dented and cracks softened the spine. Danny, a clever child, tired of the simple story long before his father did.

Privately, Zachary Persitz admired the cat, who invaded children's homes and dreamed up ways to entertain them while their mothers were away. The cat was resourceful and fearless. The cat held aloft a glass bowl containing a frightened goldfish and soothed the creature's needless apprehensions:

> *"Have no fear!" said the cat.*
> *"I will not let you fall.*
> *I will hold you up high*
> *As I stand on a ball.*
> *With a book in one hand!*
> *And a cup on my hat!*
> *But that is not all I can do!"*
> *Said the cat . . .*

And here the book contained an illustration to which Zachary had grown attached. It was of the Cat, balancing the fish in its bowl and the other objects, working hard to please, an affable grin fixed on its face.

This is how Zack Persitz pictured himself. Hydroelectrical engineer, superdad, doting husband, family money manager. Balancing it all and still smiling. And he had managed it well—the work, the family, the money, everything—until he turned over his savings to Michael Prozu-

menshikov, who pledged security but squandered it on a sham called
Texas Air.

Well, it wasn't actually Zachary's money. Most of it was his wife's
car-crash settlement. The rest belonged to his mother, Maria, who had
entrusted it to his care. For his mother's sake, Zachary had forgiven his
grudges against her husband, David Shifrin. And when a stroke debili-
tated Shifrin, Zachary had ceremoniously assumed his stepfather's place
as head of the family. "Don't worry," he said, standing over his old
adversary's hospital bed, looking into the man's strangely fragile eyes.
"Only I can take care of you. Only I can make it better." His mother,
Zack remembered, had smiled. She was proud of him. He had, despite
his inauspicious childhood, grown up solid and dependable. And before
Michael Prozumenshikov frittered away his money, the family had
begun to realize a few of their dreams.

In 1987, not long before the stock market crashed, Persitz and his
wife, Julia, had sold their small home and bought a wooded lot in the
Minneapolis suburb of Minnetonka to build a new one. Zachary asked
Prozumenshikov for $48,000 from the couple's joint account at Drexel
to pay for it. He and Julia were excited about the design for their new
house. It would be spacious and modern, with special touches—a rear
deck looking out onto a wooded hillside and a musical doorbell that Julia
could program to play Mozart, Brahms, or Beethoven.

But Prozumenshikov wasn't eager to supply the money Persitz
demanded, which was tied up in securities. Just a week earlier, Persitz
had withdrawn $13,000 to buy a new car for his mother. To raise the
cash for the lot, Michael was obliged to sell stocks. Those he chose to
liquidate had declined in value since Persitz bought them; thus the trades
produced losses of $14,000.

Though he himself had asked for the money, Persitz was furious.
First he complained that Michael had chosen the wrong stocks to sell.
Then he accused Prozumenshikov of reneging on a promise to select
only stable securities for the account. As patiently as he could, Michael
explained that he had held onto stocks with good prospects and discarded those likely to continue to lose value. One of the stocks Michael
chose to hold was Texas Air—all fifteen hundred shares of it. The Texas
Air shares were then worth $51,000, down sharply from the $70,000
Zack had paid for them just months earlier.

Then came Black Monday. That day, Persitz heard the news on his car radio and wondered, presciently, whether it represented a serious set-back for his account. He tried to reach Prozumenshikov at his office. But Michael, on the phone with someone else, waved off the call. Mica Duncan told Zack he was too busy to talk. In retrospect, the snub roused Zachary's suspicions. Busy indeed, Zack thought—probably busy protecting his own stock holdings while allowing Persitz and other clients to hang.

The crash devastated the Persitz account, the more so because Zack's ill-timed withdrawals of cash had left it heavily leveraged with borrowed margin-account money. But although he was easily angered by trifles, Persitz seemed calm when he and Michael finally discussed the losses—perhaps because he didn't yet comprehend how much he had lost. At the time, he believed Michael's assertions that no loss was final until the shares were sold, that the blows the crash inflicted were merely "paper losses." After all, Zachary had Michael's word of honor that the final product of their financial relationship would be an 18-percent annual return without substantial risk.

But now, the hard truth was that the $70,000 Texas Air investment was worth only $22,500. And in a period of four months, Persitz would receive margin calls demanding $10,000, $8,900, $6,300, and $4,000, all to avoid forced sales of Texas Air and other devalued stocks.

With typical Prozumenshikov optimism, Michael counseled Zachary to pay the margin calls if he could. The crash was only a temporary regression, he said. In coming months, the market was sure to regain its strength. The investors who would do well in 1988, Michael said, were those who avoided having their stakes sold out at crash-influenced prices. Basically, he was right. What Prozumenshikov couldn't know was that Texas Air had reached its high-water mark in early 1987, and now was destined to dribble away to practically nothing.

So Zack and Julia Persitz scraped up the money for the margin calls by draining their small bank savings account and selling some securities in their Drexel retirement accounts. Not long after the crash, Valery Gilevich ran into Julia at Prozumenshikov's office. She was there to pay a margin call. "She was trying not to show her displeasure," Gilevich says. "But you could tell her expression was very angry."

Now Zachary and Julia were laden with leveraged assets, including a heavily mortgaged new home and a portfolio of devalued stocks their broker said they shouldn't sell. Trading stocks with borrowed money had created these problems, Persitz realized. And the way Persitz remembered it, he had never wanted to invest on margin in the first place. So, by his reckoning, the financial pinch was Michael's fault.

In early 1988, Zachary's son was accepted at the Blake School for gifted children. Daniel, now seven, had spent his first-grade year in public school after his father, in his usual thorough fashion, interviewed the teacher and sat in the back of the classroom to watch her in action. But Persitz had since decided that public school wasn't good enough. Danny was displaying high aptitude for science and language, and Zack wanted to be sure his son's mind developed to its full potential.

So Persitz told Prozumenshikov about Danny's acceptance at Blake. The school was offering a half-tuition scholarship based on his son's test scores, Zachary said. But the Persitzes would still need $3,500 a year to pay for the expensive private school. The couple needed money for other things as well, Zack added, including a car for Julia and money to restore the securities in their retirement accounts. He reminded Michael of his promise, over dinner more than a year ago, to provide cash whenever Zack needed it.

Michael was exasperated. Clearly, Persitz didn't understand investing at all. Old agreements, to Michael's way of thinking, were irrelevant in the post-crash world. Investors had just weathered the worst market cataclysm in history. Michael had done what he could to minimize the damage in the Persitz account and position it advantageously for the future. Now he wished Zachary would leave him alone.

Still, Michael had a suggestion. He referred Zachary to a loan officer at the First Bank of Minnesota, who also happened to be one of his clients. Through the bank, Persitz opened a line of credit using the equity in his house as collateral. He immediately spent $16,000 to restore the retirement accounts and $12,000 on a Toyota Camry for Julia—the make and model researched, of course, with his usual zeal. The loan officer who serviced Zachary's credit line remembers him as being "quiet but demanding."

Persitz chose not to tap the credit line for Danny's Blake tuition, opting instead to keep the boy in public school for at least one more year. By then, he hoped, the stocks in his Drexel account would regain their value. And despite his active role in deciding what to do with the credit-line money, Persitz blamed Michael for his inability to send Danny to Blake.

That Michael and Zachary continued to see each other socially made for a complicated mix of emotions. They humored one another solely for the benefit of their children and their wives. And notwithstanding the seemingly placid family dinners and birthday parties for their sons, the long-standing indifference between the two men had evolved into something darker.

Behind Zachary's back, Michael took to deriding him as a nut. During construction of his new house, Prozumenshikov told Mica Duncan, Persitz had skulked around the site with a video camera to gather evidence for a lawsuit if he decided he was being cheated.

What Zachary was actually doing, Julia Persitz says, was making a video of the stages of development of his new home as a curiosity to show friends and relatives when the job was finished. He did, however, take it upon himself to supervise the workers closely and find fault in what they were doing. "He was here every day checking on things, how they were done," Julia says. "And he would be in constant consultation with the builders, changing things at the last minute, adding things. Certain things he did criticize, because he is a civil engineer."

Persitz didn't possess the same expertise in securities brokerage. But as the months passed and his stocks failed to resurge, he treated Prozumenshikov as he treated his contractor: He called Michael constantly to challenge his judgment, to provoke and rebuke him, to hiss at him about his failings. "Their conversations would get very hostile," Mica Duncan says. "Michael would get off the phone and say, 'Zachary is so irrational.' He constantly wanted an accounting of what was going on, because Texas Air was down. There were times when Michael wouldn't talk to him. He would make me talk to him."

At social events with the Prozumenshikovs, Persitz was uncommunicative. His brooding at the dinner table seemed calculated to make Michael feel uncomfortable. Sometimes Michael caught Zachary glaring at him as their wives talked, but his poisonous expression faded when he realized he was being watched. Michael, not a man to be intimidated, was unimpressed.

Indeed, he went out of his way to tease Persitz, as on the occasion he noted that Zachary's constant worrying was giving him gray hair. Persitz said nothing; it was Julia who stepped into the awkward lull that followed the remark. "I like gray-haired men," she said, smiling fondly at her husband.

Later, in the driveway outside the Prozumenshikov home, Michael had another jibe for Zack. "That car is a piece of shit," he said cheerfully, gesturing toward Zack's beat-up old Mazda. "Why don't you buy a new one?"

Persitz stared at Michael in disbelief. He and Julia were swimming in debt as it was. Michael had to know they couldn't afford another new car. Through Zachary's mind, suddenly, flashed a memory of Michael with a leer on his face—a moment, years earlier, when the broker had asked Persitz to guess how much money he was making. Zack, not much interested, said he didn't know. "More than President Reagan," Prozumenshikov crowed, as if supplying the solution to a riddle. "And he makes $250,000 a year."

Zachary's mind snapped back to the present. He wasn't going to give Michael the pleasure of seeing him rise to the taunt. "You're right," he said, glancing down at the Mazda. "I guess I should."

"You son of a bitch," he finished silently.

In 1988, despite Michael's assurances to the contrary, most of the transactions in Zack's Drexel accounts were losers, involving sales of stock weakened by the crash that the broker no longer saw any point in holding. Zondervan, the Michigan bible company, was among those Prozumenshikov dumped. Michael charged Persitz no commission on losing trades, but this was small consolation for Zack when the transaction itself consummated a loss of thousands of dollars.

That October, an article in the *St. Paul Pioneer Press* caught Zachary's eye. It carried the headline, RUSSIAN-IMMIGRANT STOCKBROKER SUED BY FIVE COMPATRIOTS OVER STOCK DEALINGS, and detailed the allegations in the immigrants' lawsuit. Hunched over his desk at the Department of Natural Resources, Persitz read the brief article at least five times, then made a copy to take home to Julia. He placed a phone call to Lucy Dalglish, the *Pioneer Press* reporter, who gave him the name and phone number of the immigrants' attorney. For the moment, Zack decided not to phone the lawyer. First, he would give Michael a chance to explain.

The opportunity arrived on a chilly November night when the Persitz and Prozumenshikov families drove to downtown Minneapolis for dinner together. Throughout the meal, Zachary waited for Michael to say something about the lawsuit. Michael had won control of the Persitz family's savings with an implied pledge of solidarity. "It was loyalty and friendship—us with our wives and children all together," Persitz says.

A friend would tell, Zack told himself as he watched Michael eat. *A friend* would address the issue directly and soothe Zachary's mounting fears. But Michael did not, just as he was failing to make good on his other promises. Perhaps he took Persitz for a patsy—a fool who didn't read the newspapers. But Zachary was no fool.

Finally, as the two couples and their sons took an after-dinner stroll, Persitz could wait no longer. He had read about the lawsuit in the paper, he told Prozumenshikov, his carefully modulated tone betraying little of the resentment he felt. It worried him. What did Michael have to say about it? Were the allegations true?

Michael appeared surprised. For a moment, he continued walking, his eyes on the sidewalk in front of him, saying nothing. Then he dismissed his antagonist with a wave of his hand. No, he said breezily, the charges weren't true. What was more, he added, these people had no evidence. Their lawsuit was sure to be thrown out.

If this was meant to reassure Zachary, it had the opposite effect. "The thought came to my mind that I myself don't have any proof," Persitz says. "Everything was done on a handshake, verbally. I didn't have any agreements in writing."

Michael was still talking, his face now flushed with anger, but Zack could no longer hear what he was saying. If the man had no loyalty or compassion for fellow immigrants, Zachary thought, he must be equally disinterested in the well-being of the Persitz family. Michael's 18-percent guarantee had been a sales pitch, nothing more. The broker might not even manage to replace the huge sum of his wife's and his mother's money the crash had flushed away.

Persitz felt light-headed and, for a moment, nauseated. He wondered if he might faint.

Julia Persitz was also shocked by the self-absorption of Michael's remarks. "It was like he didn't need Russians anymore," she says, "like, you know, this was part of the game. He used them already and now he can go on with his life. I think the drive for money was so strong he just could not see anything else."

Clearly, Zachary decided as he walked, he needed something to give him an edge the other immigrants lacked. There was only one solution. Persitz needed a written, notarized statement of Michael's 18-percent pledge in case it became necessary for him to sue Michael himself. In his anxiety, however, Persitz lost any semblance of tact. Too eagerly, he told Michael he had been thinking about the terms of their original agreement. He wondered whether Michael would mind typing up an agreement that formalized the points they had agreed upon.

Once again, Prozumenshikov waved his hand in the air, as if to brush aside such a silly and unnecessary notion. He and Zachary were friends, he said. "His position was that . . . I should trust him," Persitz said later, "that the agreement I'm talking about is a worthless piece of paper."

Michael's obfuscation was setting off alarms in Zachary's brain, a ringing he could almost hear as his heart pumped blood through his body. At that moment, he decided that he could never rest until he had the document he sought. He would hector Michael about the agreement until he relented, however long it might take.

The following week, Zachary showed up unannounced at Drexel Burnham Lambert. He was shown to Prozumenshikov's office, where he found Michael and Mica Duncan sitting at their desks. Persitz accepted Michael's invitation to take a seat, but perched on the edge of it and declined to remove his brown leather jacket. Ignoring Mica, he began speaking rapidly to Michael in Russian.

Duncan was far from fluent in Prozumenshikov's native language, but she knew enough of it to place the conversation in the context of phone conversations Michael and Zachary had been having lately. The topic for today, as it had been for months, was Texas Air.

Frank Lorenzo's airline enterprise was showing no sign of returning to its former glory. Throughout 1988, it had fluctuated between $9 and $16 a share, less than a third of what Zack paid for it. Persitz had, by now, hatched all manner of conspiracy theories about Michael's original recommendation to buy the stock—one of which was that Michael had sold Zachary shares from his own portfolio to rid it of what the broker knew to be a sure loser.

Now, as Duncan watched, the two men chattered back and forth in Russian. Throughout, Zachary's tone remained unchanged—quiet but intense, its bowstring tightness posing the threat of an explosion that never arrived. "He has such a strange voice," Duncan says. "It's controlled, very soft, kind of piercing." Zachary's expression remained impassive, but Mica could see that his hands were trembling, and the bones in his jaw rotated as he clenched and unclenched his teeth.

So much anger without an outlet, Duncan thought to herself. The man was going to worry himself into an ulcer.

Zachary, it was clear, wasn't getting what he wanted from Michael. Abruptly, and without so much as a glance in Mica's direction, he bolted from his chair and stalked out the door.

Michael waited to be sure he was gone. Then he exhaled audibly. Zachary, he told Mica, was refusing to sell the Texas Air stake for a loss. "My God," Michael said. "I just don't want to deal with this anymore. He thinks it's my fault. I did buy it, and I bought it high, but I tried to tell him to cut his losses. He just won't sell it. He won't take a loss."

For all his impatience with Zachary's emotionalism, Prozumenshikov did feel that the friendship between the families obliged him to do his best to protect the Persitz account. He had tried earnestly to penetrate Zachary's thick hide—to impress upon his client the realities of the market. He now believed that selling the Texas Air stake would be best for everyone.

This Persitz would never do, for reasons Michael knew nothing about. To take a huge loss in Texas Air would be tantamount to admitting that he had failed in his duties as a son and a husband. Planning to surprise his mother with the profits he reaped in the stock market, Zachary had never told her what he had done with her money.

And now he couldn't tell her. Maria Shifrin had once worked for Zina Shirl, one of the plaintiffs in the lawsuit against Michael, and the two women remained close friends. Admitting that he had entrusted his mother's money to the man many Russians were disparaging as a crook would make Zachary look like an idiot. Persitz was so ashamed of his foolishness that he had even stopped discussing the Drexel account with his wife.

Until now, self-respect and control had characterized Zachary's life in America. He had been like the Cat in the Hat, balancing a daunting array of responsibilities. But now the ball was slipping from under his feet and the goldfish bowl was plunging to the floor. And Zachary was helpless to stop it.

Persitz remembered helplessness well. It was the only lasting sensation of his Leningrad childhood, both before and after his mother divorced his natural father.

He seemed to recall his father, Boris Persitz, standing in the hallway outside the communal apartment, pounding and bellowing to be let in. An after-work vodka drinker, Boris Persitz often came home stumbling. When he did, his wife refused to let him in. At first Persitz had indulged her rebuffs and taken shelter elsewhere, but later he had not.

Buried in the boy's brain, somewhere between consciousness and dreams, was the image he had tried so hard to forget: blood splattered on the wallpaper of the apartment. Someone—grandmother?—was running through the hall. She was wailing, and what was it she was saying? Zachary had fled back into his bedroom and covered his head with his pillow, but he couldn't block out the terrible sounds.

Yet Maria Persitz survived, and she left her husband soon afterward. She took to telling Zachary that his father was an alcoholic and a womanizer. "All your father does is whore," she said. "He is not your father." Zachary was inclined to agree. And the boy told Boris so to his face on the rare occasions that he saw him.

When Zachary's mother remarried and moved into a private flat with her new husband, Zachary would have preferred to remain with his maternal grandmother, who cooed to him and fed him good things from the kitchen. But Maria Persitz, Zack recalled later, was angry at her mother and refused to let him stay. She blamed her mother for remaining in Russia in the 1920s when other relatives left for the United States. Zack's grandmother had stayed behind because her husband was an officer in the Red Army. And in 1937, perhaps because so many of his relatives lived in the decadent West, he had been purged from his post, imprisoned and then shot by Stalin.

Zachary anguished over his isolation from his most beloved relative. He took to sitting by himself in a cordoned-off corner or hiding under his bed for hours at a time, hoping secretly that someone would come and find him. No one did, so the little boy resigned himself to solitude, earning the nickname "wolfin," or little wolf.

Young Zack developed other strange habits, such as balancing a chair on the ledge of his fourth-floor window and sitting in it to frighten his mother. Soon Maria Shifrin sent her son to a child psychologist. The doctor said he would grow out of it.

The next year, Maria began having problems of her own. She "felt lonely, couldn't sleep, couldn't eat, and didn't want to talk to anyone," she said later. She underwent psychotherapy and treatment with antidepressant drugs. Her doctors diagnosed her as a neurotic. In those days, in

Russia, clinical depression wasn't acknowledged as mental illness; it was seen as an excuse people used to avoid working. After a few months, Maria appeared to recover and returned to her job as a dental technician.

As Zachary aged, he shed most of his idiosyncracies, just as the psychologist had predicted. Yet he would never be completely "normal" in his family's sight. He was far brighter than the average, for one thing, and his temperament was congenitally morbid. He was given to wistful musing, sometimes about death, other times yearning for order and security in a world where, he knew even as an adolescent, neither was assured.

Winter, for Zachary, was a never-ending night. Leningrad's far-northern latitude, in these bleak months, yielded only a few hours of daylight—a pale, silver mockery of sun that failed to penetrate the fog rolling in from the Gulf of Finland. The pervasive humidity wracked Zachary with sore throats and pneumonia.

Academically, he prospered. After sailing through secondary school and the Leningrad Polytechnic Institute with top marks, he graduated in 1972 with a degree in civil engineering. And soon he landed a coveted supervisory job with the Soviet central construction bureau.

Yet as a young man of twenty-two, Zachary still suffered various physical and emotional maladies. He had recurring headaches—the product, perhaps, of being knocked unconscious twice during hard falls. He was easily fatigued. And he found it difficult to fend off the sense of hopelessness that plagued him after he left the structured environment of school.

Work quickly slipped out of his control. Zachary's skills with people, at this young age, were weak. He didn't project authority, and therefore didn't command the respect of his employees on construction jobs, who were a rough breed of men, the sinewy, hard-drinking denizens of the Soviet working class. Zack quarreled constantly with coworkers and often left before the end of the day. He was so miserable about it that he couldn't sleep at night. He felt that old feeling of helplessness returning, and he could do nothing to stop it.

After spending some time sharing a flat with his brother, Leonard, Zachary moved into a new apartment where his mother, stepfather, and half brother, Alex Shifrin, had taken up residence. It was the Soviet Union's version of a planned suburban community, a passel of new but shoddily built high-rises on the edge of town. All the trees nearby had been cleared. The ten thousand or so people who lived in the complex all used the same public transportation and shopped at the same central clothing and food stores in their district.

One evening, Zack shut himself in the bathroom. Walking past the door, his stepfather thought he heard sobbing from within. David Shifrin knocked, but Zack didn't answer. The man tried the knob and found it locked. To no avail, Shifrin pounded on the door and demanded that Zachary come out. Sensing something wrong, he began heaving his body against the door frame, trying to force the lock. The cheap plywood door gave first, splintering into pieces.

"Zachary was there in the bathroom, at the sink, with warm water and a razor, trying to cut his veins open," says Alex Shifrin. "I think he did cut, but not deep enough. And when dad pulled him out he was crying and saying he's tired of everything—work, you know—and he couldn't deal with people."

It was after this incident that Zachary began visiting a neurologist at the Pavlov Medical Institute. After hearing of Zachary's depression, headaches, and insomnia, the institute's nerve doctor concluded that his problem was more physiological than psychological. Zachary began a program of therapy that included massage, penetrating medicinal baths, and a peculiar nonconvulsive treatment involving wet towels and electric shocks.

Nor was Zachary the only member of his family who had trouble coping with daily life. His mother had suffered a relapse and was back in psychotherapy. She didn't enjoy spending time with her family, she told the doctors, and had considered suicide herself. From 1973 to 1978, she spent time in and out of Soviet mental hospitals. Leonard Persitz, the middle brother, had meanwhile developed his own quirks, such as phoning Zachary at work and claiming that their natural father had died simply to hear how his brother would react.

In 1976, Zachary met Julia Diner. Two years younger than he, Julia was a bright and beautiful young woman with strawberry-blond hair, a warm smile, and preternatural grace. Julia, a violinist, was attending the prestigious Leningrad Conservatory, where the likes of Russian composer Dmitri Shostakovich had preceded her. Introduced by common family friends, Zachary asked her for a date.

During that first afternoon they spent together, the two of them walked through the bustling streets of Leningrad, stopping at a café they found open, passing the palaces and parks. It was spring, and the scent of blooming flowers surrounded them.

Julia, Zachary learned, possessed both a strong will and firmly fixed plans for the future. She had sneaked into Leningrad's only synagogue, though it was forbidden, because she wanted to know what went on there. Influenced by her father, who had huddled over a radio throughout her childhood listening to the faint BBC World Service broadcast, she was planning to leave Russia for the United States. Zachary was entranced. It amazed him that such a woman should be spending time with him.

Yet Zack, tall and lean with his dark hair and eyes, was no less attractive to Julia. He painted, sketched, and wrote poetry. He talked about books emerging from the Russian reform movement. Even when he talked of ordinary things, Zachary sounded as though he were giving a speech. He spoke of his "destiny" and the "drama" of his life to that point. Julia found him a very romantic figure.

The weeks that followed were heady ones for Zachary. He began, for the first time, to understand that life could be a source of pleasure. He and Julia stood in line all night for tickets to the Bolshoi Ballet, which was visiting from Moscow. The cold night air gave Julia bronchitis—she was too sick to see the ballet on the appointed night—and he refused to go without her. Already, he was devoted to her. Hers was the light to illuminate his darkness, the beacon around which he intended to build his life.

But he wouldn't do it in the Soviet Union. Within weeks of their first date, they were making plans to marry and leave Russia together. Having exchanged letters with a great uncle living in New York, Zachary "had heard about the United States and what it was like," Julia says. "It was obvious to us that we had to leave." The two of them were married only two months after they met—he twenty-five, she twenty-three. Alex Shifrin, Zack's half brother, was studying at the Soviet Naval Academy as preparation for a military career and couldn't attend the wedding.

Soon Zack resigned from his job. He told his neurologist that his headaches and insomnia had worsened, hampering his ability to work. The doctor recommended that he be admitted to a clinical branch of the Pavlov Institute for observation and treatment. He consented and on November 1, 1976, he was institutionalized.

By this time, Zachary and Julia had filed for permission to emigrate. She was fired from her job in the Leningrad Conservatory orchestra as soon as her supervisors heard about it. "They consider you an enemy right away," Julia says. "They said I couldn't come near students because I'm a bad influence." It was a frightening time for the newly married couple. They didn't know how long it might take to win a visa—if, indeed, they were lucky enough to leave at all.

Zachary never forgot the institution where he was confined, a dank, centuries-old building with cavernous hallways and soaring ceilings. These had been coated with pale green paint, now faded and peeling along cracks in the plaster. Nurses hurried about leading Down's syndrome patients through the halls and up the central stone staircase. Permeating every corner of the place was the thick, cheesy aroma of the cafeteria, where heavyset women ladled lumps of starchy food onto metal trays.

Later, the question of why Zachary spent time in this grim place would become a matter of considerable controversy in Minneapolis. It was true that he was suffering from chronic headaches and other problems, Julia says. But there was also the risk that he might be assigned to the Soviet equivalent of the Army Corps of Engineers to help build dams in Siberia. Such an assignment would have made it difficult, if not impossible, to leave Russia.

What is clear is that the institute's doctors could find nothing specifically wrong with Zachary. They sought to diagnose him within the theoretical framework mapped out by Ivan Petrovich Pavlov, the Nobel prizewinning physiologist famous for his research on conditioned reflexes in dogs. That is, the doctors tried to establish that Zachary's emotional problems were some kind of learned response to external stimuli, or perhaps related to the head injuries he had suffered. To his regimen of baths, massage, and electrical treatments, they added injections of vitamins and drugs.

While in the institute, Zack's headaches eased, and his sleep normalized. He was diagnosed as having neurasthenia, a type of neurosis characterized by nervousness, irritability, and fatigue, possibly aggravated by a brain injury. In one report, a neurologist noted that he was preoccupied with death.

Within weeks of Zachary's release in December 1976, he and Julia received permission to leave Russia. By happy accident, they had applied for visas at the peak of the late 1970s Jewish emigration, a period when applications were being approved more rapidly than ever before. The couple left Russia in January, traveling by way of Italy and Israel to join Julia's sister, Gina, who had earlier settled in Minneapolis. Zachary's family would follow the couple two years later—including half brother Alex, who was stripped of his military security clearance when his superiors learned he had a brother living in America.

Aside from homesickness, the years that followed had been the richest of Zachary's life. He had quickly landed an engineering job with the state of Minnesota, where his work as a dam inspector highlighted his technical prowess while playing down his lack of interpersonal skills. When Daniel was born, he took to fatherhood with creativity and zest.

He had been, for a long time, genuinely happy.

Happy, Zack Persitz now told himself as he scrutinized the latest account statement from Drexel Burnham Lambert, until Michael Prozumenshikov laid waste to his family's financial security with his lies about conservatism and an 18-percent annual return.

At parties Persitz attended, other immigrants called Prozumenshikov "Michael the Ripper" and openly discussed their hope that he would meet with an accident of some kind. The immigrants' fury was comforting to Zachary. It shielded him from his abiding fear that his problems were his own fault, the result of his gullibility in expecting gains without risk.

Once, someone asked Zack at a party why he remained friends with "that bastard." Having long anticipated the question, Zack had his answer ready. It was impossible to avoid Prozumenshikov, he said. The two families lived near one another, and their children were friends. It was really for the benefit of the children.

This subterfuge disguised Zachary's real motives: Maintaining relations with Michael was part of a secret strategy for recovering his lost savings. He couldn't join the immigrants who were suing Michael; the legal system was corrupt, he decided, and it favored brokers like Prozumenshikov. He must pretend to be friends with Michael and use the friendship to persuade him to guarantee his previous promises in writing. Then, and only then, he could cut ties with Prozumenshikov and file an arbitration claim.

But sticking to the plan wasn't easy. Listening to Michael drone on about his rich American clients now made Persitz physically ill. With his impish face, accented by red hair and that seemingly mocking grin, Michael's features looked demonic to Zachary. "My disappointment with Michael was beginning to change to hatred," he said later. The broker, Persitz had come to believe, was "bleeding me like a leech . . . holding me by the throat like I was dangling and all he needed to do was to let me go."

With appalling ease, Michael had manipulated Zachary with his promise to "make your money work." Michael, Persitz decided, regarded him as a sucker—just another of those naive, spineless Russians. And this notion was more than Persitz could bear.

Old feelings had reawakened in Zachary, the long-buried emotions of a barren childhood. Now, as then, resentment washed over him like a ragged surf, gripping him in its undertow and sweeping him down to deep water where the fish were blind.

There Michael Prozumenshikov waited to devour him. Michael, whom Zack had trusted. Michael, who had promised so much and delivered so little. Zachary Persitz would come to recall the day he turned over his family's money to Prozumenshikov as "my tragic step into the abyss."

CHAPTER 13

Michael Prozumenshikov lowered his deck chair another rung and eased his bulky body backward to expose his face to the generous Hawaiian sun. It was April 1989, and Michael and Ellen had left the waning Minnesota winter far behind. They had been here for two days, at the Mauna Lani Bay Hotel, one of the Big Island's most luxurious resorts, the only one to win the coveted AAA five-diamond award. Their suite, with its private "lanai," or open-sided living room, looked out onto a white-sand beach and the azure water of the Kohala Coast, Hawaii's northwest shore.

They had flown to Hawaii from southern California, where Drexel Burnham Lambert hosted a symposium for its top two hundred stockbrokers at San Diego's LaCosta spa. There the firm had rented an airplane hangar to throw a "Top Gun" party, a motif borrowed from the popular Tom Cruise movie about elite fighter pilots. The brokers and their wives had circulated among the steel-gray jets, sipping champagne and sampling mountains of shrimp, crab claws, and freshly shucked oysters. But as luxurious as the southern California retreat had been, there were also obligatory meetings and seminars, featuring Drexel executives who droned on about the firm's mission in the lean years to come.

For the seventy or so brokers who had achieved Drexel's top sales-incentive level—the firm's true "Top Guns"—the subsequent junket to Hawaii was "pure pleasure," a former executive says. Drexel picked up the $400-a-night tab at the Mauna Lani, a resort shaped like a giant space station and plunked down among golf and tennis courts, hidden waterfalls, and lush tropical vegetation. The brokerage firm also paid for deep-sea fishing, hot-air balloon rides, lavish meals, and any other lark that might strike a broker's fancy.

Now Prozumenshikov, one of only four brokers from the Minneapolis branch to qualify for the trip, relaxed in his deck chair and contemplated his dinner choices. After some consultation with his colleagues from Minnesota—the three-man institutional brokerage team of Steve Lindell, Tom Sullivan, and Michael Larson—Michael opted for reservations at the four-star French restaurant of the nearby Hyatt hotel. For the others, dinner that night was to be a memorable introduction to the legendary Prozumenshikov appetite.

The four brokers and their wives arrived at the Hyatt together and were shown to their table by the maitre d'. "Being from the Midwest," Lindell recalls, "we were all kind of timid about spending other people's money and looking like we're taking advantage of people. But not Michael."

As Prozumenshikov's companions eyed the hors d'oeuvre menu, wondering whether they dared order shrimp cocktail, Michael was loading up on the $65-an-ounce beluga caviar "like it's chips," Lindell says. Warming to the spirit of the evening, someone at the table ordered a bottle of Dom Perignon champagne. Not to be outdone, Michael quickly ordered a bottle of Roederer Cristal, the only selection on the wine list that cost more. Various dishes followed, meat and seafood creations drizzled with complex sauces and arrayed with vegetables like works of mixed-media art, each new course welcomed enthusiastically by the increasingly merry group.

"So we get through this meal, and this bill's up to fifteen hundred dollars," Lindell says. "Then the desserts come out, and of course that's got to be washed down with brandy." In selecting his after-dinner drinks, as in selling stocks to strangers, Prozumenshikov opted for the direct approach. "What's the most expensive after-dinner drink you've got?" he asked the waiter.

"So they came out with this crystal decanter of Louis XIII brandy . . . seventy dollars an ounce," Lindell says. "And he said, 'A round.' I didn't even like it. It was too old for me. But he had his couple of shots—and his $25 cigar that they brought out in a glass case." By the time the four couples finished dinner, the bill was close to $2,000. "We didn't pay for it," Lindell says. "All we did was sign it, and Drexel Burnham, bless their hearts, took care of it."

Thus ensconced in the opulence of Wall Street's most self-indulgent decade, it was easy for Michael Prozumenshikov and the other brokers to believe that Drexel Burnham Lambert's glorious ride would last forever.

The previous December, the firm had shocked its employees by agree-ing to plead guilty to securities crimes stemming from the Securities and Exchange Commission's investigation of insider trading on Wall Street. After refusing throughout the two-year probe to admit any wrongdoing at all, Drexel had suddenly capitulated, agreeing to pay a staggering fine of $650 million. The firm also pledged to cooperate with the government's continuing investigation of its own clients and employees—including Michael Milken, whose allies in the firm had mounted an unsuccessful internal campaign to derail the legal settlement.

Since then, for Drexel's top stockbrokers, the ride had nevertheless continued—the perk trips, the parties, and the lucrative new stock issues underwritten by the firm's well-connected investment bankers. Fred Joseph, chief executive of Drexel, was still giving his cheery pep talks over the internal speaker system. Prosperity was Drexel's birthright, most of its employees believed. Contemplating the end of Drexel was like contemplating the end of the world. "How could we settle when we were right?" says a former executive in the retail brokerage division. "That's how conditioned we were."

By the time the Hawaii trip rolled around, Prozumenshikov was more than ready for it. He needed a break from the growing tension of the Minneapolis branch, a chance to recuperate and reflect on his status at Drexel. For that winter, as the deadly, cold months wore on, all man-ner of problems had plagued him.

First had been the atrophy of Michael's relationship with his new boss, Jerry Shaughnessy. It had begun with the losses resulting from Michael's second bout of hedge-fund trading, which Shaughnessy forced Michael to pay out of his gross commissions. Michael since had become convinced that Shaughnessy gave him no credit for the success of William Humphries, the young broker whose career took off after Michael began giving him pointers.

Most recently, Prozumenshikov had instigated shouting matches with Shaughnessy's deputy manager, who, Michael believed, was taking more than his fair share of the new stock issues the branch received from the underwriters in New York. As the top producer in the branch, Prozu-menshikov felt that he was entitled to the bulk of these new-issue shares of stock, which were easy to sell to clients because they carried no visi-ble commissions. Once or twice a week, Prozumenshikov could be heard bellowing at Shaughnessy's deputy in the hall outside his office. "I am a much bigger producer than you," Michael would scream, not caring who heard him. "You don't mean shit to me."

Even more distressing for Prozumenshikov was a falling out with his best client—Dennis Carlson, the millionaire entrepreneur—just two months before the Hawaii trip.

That February, Carlson told Michael that he was planning a lawsuit over advice he received about a business deal. Carlson's lawyer—the prominent New York attorney Norman Roy Grutman, author of the book *Lawyers and Thieves*—wanted to file the suit in federal court. But to do so, Grutman advised, Carlson needed to shift his legal residence from Minnesota to Arizona, where Carlson also owned a house.

One morning, Prozumenshikov told Mica Duncan that he had a plan to help Carlson make the switch. "I remember, as clear as a bell, walking into the office that morning," Duncan says. "Michael had been out to Denny's house the night before. And he said, 'This is really big news, Mica. Denny wants to sell all of his Minnesota bonds, because he's moving to Arizona. He wants to buy Arizona bonds.'"

In fact, Carlson had given Prozumenshikov no such instruction. But Michael went ahead with the huge transaction anyway, selling $5 million worth of Minnesota municipal bonds—giving up their 8-percent annual yield—and substituting Arizona bonds that paid only 6 percent. Foregoing interest of 2 percent on a $5 million investment meant losing "a lot of money," Carlson says, not to mention Prozumenshikov's big commissions on the trades.

But Michael didn't stop there. "He went on to buy more bonds than he sold," Carlson says. "He had to go deep into the margin account. Now if you borrow money at eleven percent and put it in bonds at six percent, it makes no sense. You're going to lose five percent."

The trades were soon discovered by Carlson's full-time accountant, Brian Bequette, who phoned Mica to inform her that Carlson hadn't authorized them. For Michael, run-ins with his clients' accountants were becoming a habit. While he could often talk his customers themselves into the aggressive trading strategies he favored, he had less success persuading their accountants of the wisdom of his ways.

Carlson immediately sent a registered letter to Drexel, informing the firm that he hadn't authorized the transactions. Then he called a meeting with Michael, the Drexel branch manager, and his own accountant. "I confronted Michael," Carlson says. "I said, 'Why did you do this? Were you authorized?' He said, 'No I wasn't, and I don't know why I did it.' He had done it, and couldn't recall why, and was ashamed that he had done it . . . ashamed and embarrassed."

Carlson was disappointed because he felt that his relationship with Michael transcended business. Much had changed for Carlson in the three years he had known Prozumenshikov—he had, for one thing, gone through a divorce—and he had come to regard Michael as his friend. Over dinner at Michael's house, Carlson had met Michael's charming wife, Ellen, and Michael had taught him the pleasures of drinking frozen vodka. Even now, after Prozumenshikov cost him hundreds of thousands of dollars by swapping the supposedly stable bonds in his account like so many penny stocks, "I could not find it in my heart to get mad at Michael," Carlson says. "Let's just say I believed Michael when he said he didn't know why he did it."

In the end, however, Carlson terminated his relationship with Prozumenshikov and closed his account at Drexel. After haggling with the firm for a year, Carlson would eventually extract $150,000 from Drexel—just over half of what he had lost. And later, to his annoyance, Carlson heard that Prozumenshikov was telling other well-to-do investors that he was still a client.

Michael's adventuring in Dennis Carlson's account was no anomaly. In pursuit of commissions to support his expensive lifestyle, Michael pushed even many of his richest, most prized clients to their breaking points. These were men for whom Michael had genuine respect, entrepreneurs like Dennis Carlson, John Petcoff, and Jerry Shink. Yet Michael harassed each of them in turn, until, in one way or another, they all forced him to stop.

Jerry Shink was careful to maintain accounts at more than one brokerage firm. Shink regarded Michael as ruthless in his quest for commissions, but nevertheless admired the broker's drive to succeed and thought highly of his stock-picking skills. Shink, as part of a comprehensive strategy for managing his own money, had found a place for Prozumenshikov's aggressive approach: He used Michael's skills in options trading and researching speculative growth stocks to augment returns in his six-figure Drexel account. But the bulk of Shink's money was elsewhere, in the hands of a broker considerably more conservative than Michael.

Prozumenshikov knew it, and it bothered him. He had repeatedly asked Shink to entrust him with the rest of his money. Shink had considered it, then decided against it. But Michael wouldn't let the matter drop. He pestered Shink about it at every opportunity, bringing it up during phone conversations three or four times a week.

Finally Shink had enough. "I just told him that I had a comfort level, he was going over that comfort level, and he was going to screw up the relationship," Shink says. At this Prozumenshikov fell silent for a moment, perhaps recalling his break with Dennis Carlson. "I understand," Michael said. After that, Shink says, "He backed off, and he never brought it up again."

But that didn't mean Michael had learned his lesson. He would continue to pressure other clients, in this and other ways, as long as he worked as a broker. Dean Hutton, the Merrill Lynch manager who had given Michael his first big break in the business, thought he knew why. Since Michael left Merrill, Hutton had monitored from afar the progress of his former employee's career. Most brokers who demonstrated the raw selling ability to generate $500,000 in gross commissions during their first full year, as Michael had done, soon became million-dollar producers. Though it might have resulted, in part, from investor wariness during the post-crash recession, the fact that Michael's annual gross remained below $1 million nevertheless spoke volumes to Hutton.

"A lot of his, well, I'd say unethical activities in the business began to catch up with him," Hutton says. "He was probably having problems keeping clients. That's usually the way it works. The person takes off like a rocket and then his customers don't make money, so they leave. That's not the way to build a long-term business." It was Hutton's conviction that Michael could have been even more successful had he been capable of reining in his rambunctious instincts and his compulsive need to spend money on flashy status symbols like jewelry and cars.

Yet brokers with Prozumenshikov's cold-calling and sales-closing skills were rare. And in the stock brokerage business, Dean Hutton suspected, some profit-hungry firm would always be willing to hire a salesman like him.

This theory was about to be put to the test. For Michael, who had worked at three firms in his four-year career, it soon would become necessary to make yet another move.

The end of Drexel Burnham Lambert's romp through the retail brokerage business was abrupt and anticlimactic, like a taxi on an airport dash that stalls a mile from the exit ramp. The wholly unexpected announcement came on April 12, just after Michael returned from Hawaii, in a speech by Chief Executive Fred Joseph over the internal squawk-box system. Drexel was disbanding its entire national brokerage network, Joseph said. It hoped to sell the network as a unit to some other brokerage firm, thereby keeping the Drexel branch offices intact. As Joseph's voice rang, faint and tinny, from the small speaker on Prozumenshikov's desk, Michael and Mica Duncan stared at one another in disbelief. There would be no more trips to tropical resorts on Drexel's tab. The end of the world had come.

The banks that loaned Drexel the millions of dollars it needed each day to process brokers' trades had lost confidence in the firm's ability to function after paying its $650 million fine. So the bankers cut off Drexel's short-term credit. This had the effect of forcing the firm out of the expensive business of selling stocks, while allowing it to continue its investment-banking and mergers-and-acquisitions activities in order to pay outstanding debts.

Few of Drexel's top stockbrokers were willing to stick around and see whether Joseph's efforts to sell the brokerage division would be successful. In a business where sales skills were peddled like stocks and bonds, the brokers quickly hit the streets in search of the highest bidders.

Prozumenshikov was in the thick of it, making phone calls and personal visits to firms he viewed as prospective employers. Michael needed to find a new firm quickly, preferably one that would pay him a big up-front bonus. And the transition from firm to firm had to be seamless, to avoid losing clients. Daniel Prozumenshikov, Michael's eldest son, was enrolled in an expensive private school. Michael now had a second son as well—Ariel, who had just turned one year old. Moreover, Michael carried heavy credit-card debts and was itching to carry through his plan to build a grand new house.

Yet much of the greater Minneapolis brokerage community was wary of the "Mad Russian." There was, for one thing, the still-pending lawsuit filed by Michael's fellow Soviet émigrés, a liability that few firms cared to assume. And because of his clashes with his countrymen, his hedge-fund trading, and his well-known nickname, Michael had a reputation at some firms as "a compliance nightmare," as one local branch manager put it.

Merrill Lynch wanted no part of him. Contemplating working in the wealthy western suburbs, close to where he planned to build his dream home, Michael tried unsuccessfully to sell himself to the Dean Witter Reynolds branch in Wayzata. Also in Wayzata, he went to see Mike Cochrane, the former comanager of Drexel's Minneapolis branch, who now supervised a branch for the brokerage firm of Smith Barney Harris Upham.

Michael sat on a mauve sofa in Cochrane's office and talked about his gross production during the previous twelve months, which had totaled more than $800,000 despite the recession that followed the stock market crash. Michael then "made an attempt to convince me that the difficulties that accompanied him were a thing of the past, trying to get out from underneath the stigma, the stuff that was following him around," Cochrane says.

The Russian broker certainly didn't lack conviction, Cochrane noted, and he was very aware of the negative perceptions he needed to diffuse. Yet as Prozumenshikov spoke, Cochrane couldn't help remembering his own stint as Michael's boss at Drexel, where he had briefly shared supervisory duties with Mort Greenberg. It was all coming back to Cochrane now—worrying about Michael's rapid trades, helping to clean up Michael's messes, "looking over my shoulder, if you will, waiting for something to happen," Cochrane says. "It did not create a huge comfort level."

Cochrane listened politely until Michael finished. Then, just as politely, he declined to make Michael an offer.

Not every firm was leery of Prozumenshikov, however. Thomson McKinnon Securities, a mid-sized company with a strong presence in Minneapolis, expressed interest. So did Shearson Lehman Hutton, the brokerage unit of American Express Company. But the most tantalizing offer came from the Minneapolis branch of Prudential-Bache Securities, the big brokerage firm that the Prudential Insurance Company of America had built. Because of Michael's reputation, "there were a lot of firms that wouldn't talk to him," Mica Duncan says. "Pru-Bache would talk to him, not only talk but they'd pay."

Brad Hudgins, the Minneapolis branch manager of Prudential-Bache, was discussing bringing both Michael and Mica to the firm to continue working as a team. The plan was for the two of them to work for a short time in the Minneapolis branch, and then to move to a new suburban office Pru-Bache planned to open in Wayzata. After a few meetings with Hudgins, Prozumenshikov settled on Pru-Bache as the next—and, he hoped, last—stop on his whirlwind tour of the brokerage industry.

Because Drexel was leaving the retail business completely, it was relatively easy for Michael to move his clients to his new firm. When he moved to Drexel from Merrill Lynch, he had had to contact them one by one and persuade them to shift their accounts with him. But in the move to Pru-Bache, he was able to use a "tape-to-tape transfer" that moved his clients' money en masse. To avoid having their accounts relocated to Pru-Bache, the investors had to request specifically that the money be transferred somewhere else.

"I have had the opportunity to become associated with several other firms," Michael said in an explanatory letter to his clients. "Prudential-Bache Securities is clearly the best choice. Primary among the reasons for joining Prudential-Bache is the high level of service, the tremendous product quality and variety, as well as the research available to me."

Actually, the primary reason was the fat bonus Pru-Bache offered him. Prudential's brokerage arm put a signing bonus of about $240,000 on the table, roughly 30 percent of Michael's gross production during the previous twelve months. He also would receive a large 50 percent share of his gross commissions during his first year at the firm. While Thomson McKinnon's offer to Michael had been in the same ballpark, Thomson McKinnon didn't share Prudential's name recognition. And the other well-known candidate for Michael's services, Shearson Lehman Hutton, hadn't called until the Pru-Bache deal was all but sealed.

Mica Duncan, meanwhile, decided against joining Pru-Bache as Michael's assistant. The reason, she says, was that Pru-Bache's bonus offer to her dropped soon after Michael signed his contract with the firm. Pru-Bache "at the beginning was going to pay me $10,000 to come with Michael," Duncan says. "Then, when Michael signed, it got to be that (they) would pay me $5,000. So there was just no way."

Instead, Duncan took the summer off. She later joined the Minneapolis branch of Kidder, Peabody & Company, Inc., a securities firm, where she found that fellow employees were already aware of her previous association with Prozumenshikov. "When I went to Kidder Peabody, it was constantly, 'Oh you worked with the Russian,'" Duncan says. "It was a very negative connotation." Yet Mica would soon be promoted to the position of compliance manager—riding shotgun over stockbrokers, a job for which her work with "the Russian" had amply prepared her.

As word of Prozumenshikov's Pru-Bache bonanza made the rounds in the brokerage community, some of his Drexel colleagues were stunned. They had expected Michael's past compliance problems—a record that included a total of twenty customer complaints against him during his three years at Drexel, according to a former executive—to damage his marketability.

"He never understood that the rules were supposed to be followed," one former Drexel broker asserts. "He thought the guys that were following them were just crazy. He'd say, 'This is a free country. Why should we have to do these things?' What I can't understand is how an industry that's supposedly so regulated could allow a guy like that to operate as long as it did."

It was not by accident that Prudential-Bache Securities paid Michael Prozumenshikov so much money for his services. In the scramble among securities firms to recruit Drexel Burnham's biggest producers, Prudential was one of the most aggressive players. It bought six of Drexel's soon-to-be-disbanded national branch offices in their entirety, and elsewhere it cherry-picked, recruiting brokers individually.

Prudential hadn't viewed Drexel's Minneapolis branch as a big enough prize to buy the whole office. Drexel's admission of securities crimes had seriously damaged commission revenue at the previously profitable branch; many of its clients in the conservative Minneapolis business community, wary of the taint, had left. But Pru-Bache eagerly pursued certain individual brokers from the branch. It hired six of them, including Prozumenshikov and his friend William Humphries.

Pru-Bache's zeal for this kind of recruiting trickled down from the very top of its corporate hierarchy. Under the leadership of its chairman, George L. Ball, Pru-Bache had probably done more to pioneer the stockbroker star system of the late 1980s than any other firm.

Like the owner of a major league baseball team trying to buy a World Series title with high-priced talent, George Ball had embarked on a sweeping program to lure investment bankers, stock analysts, and big-producing stockbrokers to Pru-Bache. Ball was credited, for instance, with the innovation of doling out brokers' bonuses as loans forgivable over three years, both to shield brokers from a big single-year income tax payout and to commit them to the firm.

Pru-Bache had also broken ground in other ways. In 1981, when the Prudential Insurance Company had bought the Bache Halsey Stuart Shields brokerage group for $385 million, it created what analysts hailed as the nation's first "financial supermarket," linking stock and bond brokerage to sales of insurance and other financial services. Executives at the Prudential parent company talked of "synergy," of merging their company's financial muscle with the Bache group to generate superior profits for both.

Without a doubt, Prudential's purchase of Bache set a precedent for similar acquisitions to follow. Soon after the announcement of the Pru-Bache deal, American Express Company bought Shearson, the country's second-biggest brokerage firm. Then Sears, Roebuck and Company bought Dean Witter, another big securities firm. A wave of smaller transactions followed, including the Kemper Corporation insurance company's acquisition of five regional brokerage firms, which it merged to create its own national securities operation.

At first, George Ball's program of rapid expansion at Pru-Bache drew raves on Wall Street. He quickly beefed up the firm's already imposing retail brokerage empire. The Bache firm's strengths had always been selling stocks to individual investors, not underwriting new stock issues or masterminding corporate takeovers. But in 1986, Ball announced a plan to transform Pru-Bache into an investment-banking powerhouse within three years.

Prudential Insurance poured more than $1 billion into the securities firm to bankroll Ball's ambitious plans. By 1989, the year Michael Prozumenshikov joined it, Pru-Bache had become the nation's fourth-largest brokerage firm, with more than 7,000 stockbrokers and 17,000 employees overall.

Yet the firm hadn't enjoyed the financial success that George Ball predicted. Its financial returns were disappointing throughout the 1980s, including a stunning Wall Street–record loss of $113 million in 1984, the last sluggish year for the Street before the decade's bull market roared into being.

But even later, Pru-Bache had continued to lose money, including a loss of $150 million in 1987. Analysts began to theorize that the concept of selling stocks and insurance under the same roof was flawed. "I think they made a mistake by trying to bring everything under one umbrella," says Perrin Long, a veteran securities-industry analyst. "The Prudential insurance salespeople sold primarily on a fear principal, that you need insurance to protect your loved ones in the event of your demise. The Bache stockbrokers, however, sold enjoyment—the instinct we all have to gamble, to make money. Those are very different motivations, and merging them didn't really work."

Pru-Bache finally got its balance sheet into the black in 1988, with a heartening $80 million profit. But the next year, Pru-Bache's acquisition of the financially troubled Thomson McKinnon securities firm would contribute to a loss of $87 million.

Thus, in the securities industry, the concept of the "financial super-market" was losing its appeal. Now the prevailing opinion was that the blockbuster brokerage acquisitions of the 1980s hadn't done the industry any favors—that the financial backing of deep-pocketed parent corporations had propped up firms that otherwise, like Drexel Burnham Lambert, might have gone out of business.

And in the post-crash recession, the industry was plagued by overcapacity—too many brokers gunning for too few investors, too many investment bankers chasing a winnowing array of deals. Moreover, many in the business were grousing that George Ball's aggressive recruiting program had backfired, keeping pay scales high when the financial realities of the industry called for belt-tightening.

Pru-Bache encountered other problems as well—notably, an inability to prevent serious abuses of its clients by brokers at some of its branch offices. In 1986, the firm had reached a landmark settlement with the hard-nosed Securities and Exchange Commission in a case involving improper trading and fraud at Pru-Bache branch offices in Atlanta and Jacksonville, Florida. The SEC found that Pru-Bache brokers had churned customer accounts and "parked" stock in other accounts, a process of illegally hiding the ownership of stock to avoid rules and disclosure requirements. The SEC, concluding that the abuses demonstrated "deficiencies in Prudential-Bache's supervisory procedures," ordered the firm to scrap its method of overseeing its three hundred branch offices and come up with a new one.

Yet despite this cleanup operation, newspapers would continue to chronicle troubling examples of abuses by Pru-Bache brokers in the years that followed. In May 1993, the *New York Times* would report that Pru-Bache, by then renamed Prudential Securities, Inc., had refused to dismiss a top-producing stockbroker suspected of churning customer accounts, after the firm's lawyer said firing him would taint him as a witness in lawsuits filed by his disgruntled clients.

Two months later, the *Los Angeles Times* ran a two-part series reporting that Pru-Bache customers had lost more than $1 billion investing in ill-conceived oil and gas partnerships, which Pru-Bache had sold during the height of the 1980s' oil-price bust. According to the *Times*, Pru-Bache brokers peddled the energy partnerships in a hard-sales campaign aimed largely at the elderly—in part by comparing the risky partnerships with stable certificates of deposit, or CDs. After the biggest multistate investigation of alleged securities fraud in Wall Street's history, Pru-Bache would agree to pay $371 million in restitution and fines, a penalty second only to Drexel Burnham's $650 million fine in 1989.

Perhaps to compensate for weaknesses in other areas, the firm in the 1980s became a big player in limited partnerships, or shares of businesses that investors could buy. These partnerships ranged from the predictable, such as interests in real estate, to the unconventional, such as oil and gas interests, aircraft leasing, and Arabian horsebreeding. Pru-Bache investors were stung by a badly timed campaign at the firm to mass-market real-estate partnerships shortly before the U.S. real estate market collapsed.

This, then, was the firm that Michael Prozumenshikov joined in late April 1989. It had lost money in two of the previous three years. It was burdened by the heavy spending and grandiose ambitions of its chairman, George Ball. And it was struggling for the limited business of stock investors against formidable competitors such as Merrill Lynch and Shearson Lehman Hutton. Michael, carried away with his usual optimism, described the firm somewhat differently in letters to his clients: "Prudential-Bache is part of the Prudential network, $185 billion strong in assets," he enthused. "You will want to be associated with this rock solid, market wise firm as our valued customer."

Michael Prozumenshikov was to be the centerpiece of Pru-Bache's latest expansion scheme—a push into the affluent bedroom communities west of Minneapolis, the bastion of Minnesota's oldest money. When the Wayzata branch opened in May 1989, Michael was its biggest producer. "It was built around Michael," says William Humphries, who joined the branch at the same time. "He was the one who was going to make it, shake it, bake it."

Jim Tallen, Michael's new boss, was also new to Prudential-Bache. A veteran of the securities business who had worked for such firms as Dean Witter and Merrill Lynch, he came to Pru-Bache that April from a firm called M. H. Novick & Company.

The new Wayzata branch, a Pru-Bache showplace, was on the ground floor of a three-story structure of red brick and polished black stone—the same building, coincidentally, that housed the Wayzata branch of Smith Barney Harris Upham, one of the firms that rejected Michael. It was situated on Wayzata's Lake Street, amid a row of expensive shops and restaurants that faced the picturesque sweep of Lake Minnetonka.

The decor of the branch was a masterpiece of elegant uniformity. Desks, cabinets, and shelves were dark wood, chairs wing-backed leather and tasteful weaves. Individual offices were arranged in a semicircle, around the periphery of a U-shaped corridor. The interior walls of these offices were plate glass, through which similarly dressed brokers could be seen talking on the phone or staring into computer terminals. Even the paintings on the walls were the same. These consisted of nautical prints—renderings of big ships under full sail—and brokers were discouraged from hanging art of their own. This edict had particularly irked one broker who, before moving to the tony Wayzata office, became attached to a stuffed fish. Prozumenshikov's prized map of Leningrad also didn't fit in, so he took it home and displayed it there.

To Michael, who had always hated the commute to downtown Minneapolis, it seemed appropriate that Wayzata should be his professional destination. He enjoyed browsing at the shops on Lake Street and bringing his family to Sunsets, a restaurant with a big lake view.

Comfortable in Wayzata's opulence, he was no longer shy about showing off the symbols of his success. He had once removed his diamond ring and Rolex watch at work to avoid offending middle-income clients, but now he displayed them proudly. He also took to wearing tailored suits and designer ties, toning up his image for the benefit of the rich investors Prudential-Bache had hired him to pursue.

Michael's new sales assistant, Dorene Kainz, was to play an altogether different role than Mica Duncan had at Drexel Burnham. Drexel had paired Mica with Michael in an effort to keep him on the straight and narrow. But Dorene was strictly a sales assistant. Unlike Mica, she had no mandate to try to keep Prozumenshikov under control, or to regularly report what he was doing to his superiors.

The two of them got along well enough, although Dorene found it difficult to get to know her new boss. "He was real aloof," she says. "I would have to ask him pointed questions about how he left the Soviet Union and why. He never said anything to me. I never knew he was Jewish until six months after I worked for him." Michael warmed up a bit when he learned that Dorene's husband was active in national Republican party politics. "As I got to know him, I found out he was very conservative," she says. "He thought Reagan was great."

Michael soon made it clear that he meant for Dorene to share at least one of Mica Duncan's former functions in his professional life: "I basically was the bad-news person," Kainz says. "I'd call if someone was late with money. Or if it was a situation where the stock was really doing badly, I'd try to cushion it before (the client) talked to Michael." Michael, she noticed, always said yes to clients. "I don't ever remember a 'no' coming out of Michael's mouth," Dorene says. "Even if it seemed like an impossible thing to do, he'd say, 'Yes, we can do that for you.'"

On Friday evenings, after the rush of a busy week, Michael still enjoyed sitting and talking with his friend from Drexel, William Humphries. Usually in Michael's office, which had a sidelong view of Lake Minnetonka, the two of them would lean back in their chairs and prop up their feet on Michael's desk. "It is great to be in America," Michael would say, puffing on one of the expensive Cuban cigars he favored. "You just don't understand where I come from."

With Humphries, Michael was remarkably candid. Occasionally, although William knew how much money he made, Michael would indulge himself in poor-mouthing. "I have no money," the Russian broker would say. "I have less money than you." To prove his point, Prozumenshikov whipped out his checkbook and thrust it across his desk at Humphries. Michael, Humphries knew, had received a monthly commission check for $37,000 the week before. But by now, his checking account contained only $900. Michael seemed almost proud to report that he had already spent the rest.

Now and then, the two brokers commiserated about the weaknesses of Pru-Bache's New York stock operations. At Drexel Burnham, an investment bank of the first order, the flow of new stock issues and initial public offerings of stock had been contant and diverse, an edge that Drexel brokers could use to woo investors from other firms. And Drexel's over-the-counter, market-making functions—through which the firm offered its clients hot stocks that weren't available on the New York Stock Exchange—had also been strong.

At Prudential-Bache, Humphries and Prozumenshikov found, the investment banking division was, basically, a George Ball startup that never got started. The Pru-Bache chairman's "Project 89" program to build a competitive investment-banking division within three years clearly wasn't working. Ball had brought plenty of high-priced investment bankers to the firm, but "they weren't producing any business," says Perrin Long, the securities-industry analyst. This confounded Prozumenshikov, who had always counted on selling the investment bankers' new issues to bolster his own commissions. "He thought he was going to see a lot more syndicate issues" at Pru-Bache, says his assistant, Dorene Kainz. "He used to get so frustrated with that, because he always wanted more."

As for Pru-Bache's market-making operation, it wasn't as good as the one at Shearson Lehman Hutton, the other national firm that expressed interest in hiring Prozumenshikov. This meant that the prices Michael offered his clients on over-the-counter issues often weren't as low as those available elsewhere. "He was always bitching about that," says John Kelly, then manager of the Shearson Minneapolis branch. "The fact that he couldn't get the extra grease in there and get his customer a better price."

These weaknesses were a problem for William Humphries as well. But they were nothing, Humphries says, to the predicament he found waiting for him that summer of 1989, when he returned to Pru-Bache after a family vacation in northern Minnesota.

As Humphries sat in his office reviewing his commission report, which was the record of stock trades he had executed for his clients, he saw several trades he hadn't ordered. Baffled, he asked Dorene Kainz where the transactions came from. "She said those were trades that Michael ran through my account because he wasn't licensed in those areas," Humphries says.

When stockbrokers change jobs, securities regulators in states where they do business often take the opportunity to review the brokers' credentials to sell stocks in those states. Occasionally, Humphries knew, a state's regulators would hold up a broker's license while they investigated customer complaints against him.

The practice of allowing an unlicensed broker to continue to do business in the meantime is all too common in the brokerage industry. But it is, nevertheless, illegal. Traditionally, firms that allow it reroute the broker's commissions for these forbidden trades through some other broker's commission report. "You have to be registered, and if you're not, you can't receive compensation," says former Shearson manager John Kelly. "They can't rebate commissions back to you. That's against the law. But, unfortunately, it is done."

The mysterious trades on Humphries' commission journal, he says, had been executed on behalf of Prozumenshikov's clients in South Carolina and Wisconsin, states where Michael wasn't yet registered. In Wisconsin, Humphries learned later, regulators were holding up Prozumenshikov's license while they awaited resolution of the lawsuit filed by Michael's fellow immigrants.

"I went and talked to Michael and said, 'What's this all about?'" Humphries says. "Michael said, 'Hey, it's good. It's good because it will reflect a higher gross for you.'"

Humphries wasn't comfortable with the arrangement, but he told Michael he had another idea. He offered to swap investors temporarily— to let Prozumenshikov do business with some of his own clients, who lived in states where Michael was licensed, while William handled trades for Michael's clients in Wisconsin and South Carolina. This would be a legal way for Michael to maintain his relationships with clients in these states until his credentials were approved.

Prozumenshikov refused. After all, Michael told Humphries, John Petcoff, who lived in Wisconsin, was one of his biggest clients. "I have to do business with this guy," Michael said. "He's very important. I work very hard for him."

For a while, Humphries says, Michael's trades stopped appearing on his commission report. But soon, he says, they began showing up again. Humphries discussed the situation with other brokers in the Pru-Bache branch, who told him that allowing it to continue could cost William his own brokerage license.

When William confronted Michael about it, "He'd say, 'Oh I had to do that; I had to do that trade,'" Humphries says. "I was like, 'No, you didn't.'" Humphries was furious at Michael but felt powerless to do anything about it. Relations cooled between the two men, and their Friday afternoon chats in Michael's office came to a halt.

Finally, William took matters into his own hands, phoning the Wisconsin agency responsible for regulating securities trading in the state. He was a stockbroker in Minnesota, Humphries told the man who answered, without giving his name. He wanted to know whether allowing an unlicensed broker to run trades through his account could result in loss of his own brokerage license. "He said absolutely, yes," Humphries says. "And they wanted to know who it was, how they do it. They wanted to investigate." Quickly, William hung up the phone.

Angry and frightened, Humphries soon began talking to John Kelly at Shearson Lehman Hutton, who had courted him briefly in the past about joining Shearson. At Prudential-Bache, Humphries says, "I felt betrayed. You can't function in an environment where you're not respected."

In January 1990, Humphries left Pru-Bache for Shearson, walking out on a contract under which the firm had agreed to forgive a third of his $28,137 signing bonus during each of his first three years at Pru-Bache. Almost immediately, a letter arrived from a Pru-Bache lawyer demanding that he pay back the bonus, plus interest, and threatening to "entertain all legal remedies" if he didn't. Humphries refused.

Eleven months later, Pru-Bache would file an arbitration claim against Humphries with the National Association of Securities Dealers, seeking to force him to repay the bonus, plus interest and attorneys' fees. Humphries responded by hiring a lawyer to file a counter-claim against Pru-Bache. Humphries' claim accused Prudential-Bache and its Wayzata branch manager, Jim Tallen, of "using William Humphries in an illegal and dishonest scheme to mislead state securities regulators" by using his commission account to process Prozumenshikov's trades.

An attorney for the firm, by then renamed Prudential Securities, Inc., denied the charge. Prudential, the attorney wrote in response to Humphries' claim, "hereby denies these allegations in their entirety." Neither Jim Tallen nor anyone else at the firm, a Pru-Bache lawyer wrote, "knows of nor participated in any 'scheme' to mislead anyone."

Internal Prudential-Bache documents and interviews with John Petcoff, Prozumenshikov's client in Wisconsin, suggest that certain of Michael's trades were, in fact, processed using Humphries' account number. "It's a fact," Petcoff says. "Lots of trades." A document on Prozumenshikov's Pru-Bache letterhead shows that commissions were routed to Michael's account from William's account, and to Michael's account from another unidentified Pru-Bache commission journal. The document, dated July 17, 1989, shows a total of $3,310.74 in transfers to Michael's account, including $727.50 from Humphries' account. Moreover, some of John Petcoff's trade confirmations bear Humphries' name.

Four years after the disputed trades occurred, Humphries would settle with Pru-Bache, agreeing to repay the firm a sum considerably smaller than the $30,000 it originally demanded. As part of the settlement, Prudential's claims against Humphries and Humphries' counterclaim were dropped. At about the same time, Humphries would make another career move, from Shearson to Merrill Lynch, where his Shearson supervisor, John Kelly, had moved before him. And at Merrill, although it took Humphries' Minnesota brokerage license a couple of weeks to clear the state's regulators, his supervisors were adamant that he refrain from trading in the meantime. "They said, 'This is Merrill. We don't need that headache,'" Humphries says.

After months of haggling with Wisconsin's regulators, Dorene Kainz says, she was able to persuade them that the immigrants' lawsuit against Michael, although it technically was still pending, was going nowhere. Finally, Michael's license to trade stocks in the state was approved. And soon thereafter, in April 1990, the lawsuit would be dismissed, eliminating the last painful reminder of Michael's erstwhile business association with his fellow immigrants.

The loss of Dennis Carlson's account and the shortage of new stock issues to sell to his clients had, for a time, diminished Prozumenshikov's commission earnings at Prudential-Bache. Yet Michael found ways to compensate.

As 1989 drew to a close, Michael had more to celebrate than the New Year. A contractor had broken ground on his $800,000 dream house, with a down payment courtesy of Michael's Pru-Bache signing bonus. He had managed to gross $331,000 in commissions before leaving Drexel Burnham that year, despite the firm's image problems. And with the help of a late-year surge in commissions, he had brought in a total of $548,000 during his eight months at Pru-Bache. This placed him on Pru-Bache's President's Council, an honor roll of the company's top two hundred brokers, a distinction made all the more remarkable by the fact that he had switched firms in the middle of the year.

But even as Michael collected accolades for his impressive performance, he was bestowing upon Prudential-Bache legal liabilities that would return to sting the firm later. For Prozumenshikov's earnings that year, and the next, were boosted by some of the most flagrant abuses of his career, his clients say.

As he continued to make enemies, Michael apparently realized that he was treading on dangerous ground. "Some day," he told a colleague, "they might kill me." Prozumenshikov, nothing if not an innovator, had figured out a way to profit even from this worst-case scenario.

He bought life-insurance policies worth more than a million dollars—just in case.

CHAPTER 14

Michael and Ellen Prozumenshikov moved into their new home—a largely self-designed medley of soaring ceilings, picture windows, and hardwood floors—in March of 1990. They had selected the rural lot and the contractor to build it almost a year earlier, soon after Michael joined Prudential-Bache Securities.

Cold-weather construction delays had slowed things down, as had a strange act of vandalism. One weekend, when the workmen were away, the electrical wiring in the half-finished house had been cut. Whoever severed the wires had obviously known what he was doing: The damage was in a hard-to-reach place behind a new wall, forcing the contractor to tear it down and rewire at an extra cost of more than $5,000. Among the extras the workers installed later was the security system that Michael insisted upon.

The finished house, with its modern white facade and $500,000 mortgage, was far grander than the simple split-level home that Prozumenshikov and his family had occupied for the past four years. Still, Michael wasn't completely happy about moving out of the old house. "He had a lot of ambivalent feelings, because it was the (old) house that he had gone through all this change in," says Dorene Kainz. Despite the huge square footage of the new home, Michael told Dorene he didn't plan to buy much new furniture. "The outward structure of the building was the biggest thing," Kainz says. "Outward appearances, to Michael, were very important."

Michael regarded his move into this mansion, like the purchase of his Mercedes-Benz sedan, as symbolic. But the house meant more to him than the car. It represented the fulfillment of his relentless journey into the American Dream—the archetypal vision of an ambitious young immigrant, conceived five years earlier as he gazed at Lake Minnetonka's mansions from the window of his Merrill Lynch office. For a man who had transformed himself again and again, this was to be the last transformation.

And not coincidentally, it resulted in Prozumenshikov's final break with his circle of friends from Leningrad. On the day he was to turn over the keys of his old house to its new owners, Michael phoned Valery Gilevich at home. Gilevich had taken a leave of absence from work because of his ongoing treatment for colon cancer. He hadn't heard from Prozumenshikov in months.

Michael was phoning to ask Gilevich to drive to the old house and pick up a chainsaw he had borrowed from Val a year ago. If Gilevich wanted it, he needed to go get it now, Michael said bluntly. After today, anything left in the house became the property of its new owners. Gilevich peered out the window as he cradled the phone receiver. It was snowing so hard that he couldn't see the trees in his yard. The late-winter blizzard had already dumped six inches of snow on Minneapolis.

"Michael," Gilevich said, "I can't drive. I'm sick. Can you stop on your way home from the office and pick it up?"

Michael said he couldn't. It wasn't on his way, and he had a number of errands to run that afternoon.

"Why didn't you take it with you when you moved out?" Gilevich asked.

"I didn't have a place to store it," Prozumenshikov said.

"Michael," Gilevich groused, "don't shit me. You have all this furniture, and you didn't have a place for a little chainsaw?"

"Well," Michael said impatiently, "I didn't, and now we have to move."

Gilevich, like the other members of the Leningrad group, had only recently learned that Michael was building a new house. No one in the group was really sure whether the Prozumenshikovs fit into their social lives anymore. The women in the group still spoke to Ellen, but the others hadn't seen Michael since that night, the previous autumn, when his friend, Mark Goldburt, had chided him for his rude behavior.

Now Gilevich was furious. Weak and queasy from his latest bout of chemotherapy, he was tired of being cooped up at home, but too ill to go out. On this day, of all days, Gilevich was in no mood for Michael's thoughtlessness.

"Fuck the chainsaw," Gilevich barked into the phone. "Just leave me alone." Then he slammed the receiver down onto its cradle, shattering it.

Most everyone in the Leningrad circle was bemused that Michael had neglected to tell them about his new house—especially Mark Goldburt, who had taken to selling property for a living since being laid off from his engineering job. Goldburt remembered, years earlier, helping Michael sign up clients by throwing a party and asking his friends to move their money to Michael's firm. Hard words had passed between them since then, it was true, but Goldburt still felt that Michael should have offered to let Mark sell his old house. Their friendship, Goldburt decided, was finished. It was like "a broken glass," he said, whose razor-edged shards could never be reassembled.

As for Valery Gilevich, he would see Prozumenshikov only a few more times—enough to realize that whatever rapport he had once shared with Michael had also faded. "I have no idea what made him withdraw himself," Gilevich says. "Just gradually, you know, it was all over."

Prozumenshikov's dream home, nestled in its wooded glen at the end of a row of well-kept houses, wasn't far from the Prudential-Bache office in Wayzata. And after years of jockeying through heavy rush-hour traffic to downtown Minneapolis, Michael relished the bucolic country drive.

At 6:30 A.M., when his Mercedes rolled down the ramp from its heated garage, it was still dark outside. As Michael navigated the curves of Ringer Road, he could see lights twinkling in the kitchen windows and, on some mornings, pick out a dark shape in the broad meadow to the west, where deer grazed. At Crosby Avenue, he turned left toward the expressway, now passing houses obsured by groves of tall pine and oak trees.

To his inevitable pleasure, Prozumenshikov ignored the highway entrance ramp when he reached it, and instead turned left onto Wayzata Boulevard, a frontage road that ran parallel to the expressway. This quiet two-lane road carried his Mercedes down a hill and into the village of Wayzata, with its art and curio shops, interior decorators, brokerage branch offices, and restaurants. As Michael cruised along Lake Street toward the Pru-Bache branch, the advancing dawn was visible as a pale blue glow in the sky, off across the lake in the general direction from which he had come.

At Pru-Bache, coffee and computer updates awaited, followed by phone calls to his biggest clients. By now, Michael had about five hundred customers, not all of whom he spoke to regularly. Many of the accounts were inactive IRAs, and many others belonged to very small investors, who rarely traded stocks, although Michael still phoned them frequently with ideas. The handful of Russians who remained on his client list, including Zachary Persitz and Mark Tsypin, the last holdover from the Leningrad group, now did very little trading.

Perhaps fifty of Michael's clients bought or sold something as often as once or twice a week. And about twenty more clients were Michael's true cash cows—the aggressive investors to whom he spoke every morning and whose active accounts generated the bulk of his commissions. Some of these investors were wealthy businessmen, well-seasoned in the vagaries of the stock market.

And for those moneyed few not accustomed to aggressive trading, Michael had a proven technique for bringing them around to his way of doing business. He beseeched them to visit the Pru-Bache Wayzata branch, which in itself rarely failed to impress. Once he had a client in his office, he used his very best hook: a high-tech computer terminal called a "Shark" machine.

The Shark provided moment-to-moment reports on stock trades by the huge institutional investors that dominated the market—pension funds, mutual funds, money managers. It detailed the buying or selling recommendations of the most influential Wall Street brokerage houses. And it provided highly accurate analysis of stock-options volatility, which was useful in determining whether the prices being quoted for stock options at exchanges in Chicago and New York were favorable. The Shark was so sophisticated and expensive that few retail brokerage firms had one; Michael's terminal was one of only four or five in the greater Minneapolis area.

Until he got the Shark, Michael had never understood how far down the food chain retail stockbrokers and their clients really were. They were bait fish, he realized now, skimming the surface of the ocean, easy prey for the institutional traders who prowled the deep water. Now he could track these behemoths as they executed their giant trades. And he was able to make money for his more adventurous clients by following them, picking up the scraps they left behind as they churned through the markets. Time after time, Michael had watched his clients' faces light up as they peered into the computer screen and slowly grasped the power that the Shark machine offered them.

"If you saw a stock that normally averaged three hundred–share trades, and if, all of a sudden, you saw two or three five thousand–share trades come across, each one higher than the last, you didn't have to be too smart to know that something was going on," says one of Michael's former colleagues. "You could make money by jumping in and buying something. Michael did some of that. He watched it a lot."

One investor whom Michael impressed with the Shark was Roy Vinkemeier, a college finance teacher and well-connected local venture capitalist. Vinkemeier often put together deals involving start-up businesses on behalf of his friends in the Minneapolis business community whose ranks included a number of famous professional athletes.

Vinkemeier was very high on Prozumenshikov. "I've dealt personally with a couple of hundred stockbrokers, and he was far and away the best," Vinkemeier would tell *Minneapolis/St. Paul* magazine in 1992. "He never took notes and he never forgot anything. A month later he would remember what you'd said to him. He had three computers going in his room, and he knew when someone was filing to get rid (of assets) before they did. The second a stock was sold, he could tell you who sold it, where it was sold, and for what price."

Through Vinkemeier, Michael met such local celebrities as former Minnesota Vikings players Scott Studwell, Tommy Kramer, and Jim Gustafson. His first introduction was to Studwell, the former all-pro linebacker, a tall and imposing man with close-cropped blond hair, a fearsome handshake, and vivid blue eyes. During his playing days, these eyes had often been seen on national television, gleaming behind a face-mask when the camera panned him after one of his ferocious tackles. Now Studwell was working as a player liaison for the Vikings at their practice facility in Winter Park, Minnesota.

Studwell was looking for help in selling the thinly traded stock of a small local company called Action Card Express, Inc., which, among other things, printed business cards. Studwell had invested $25,000 in the company, a start-up venture involving both Vinkemeier and a former Vikings teammate. In return, Studwell had received the shares of stock that he was holding. "I basically went with Michael on a trial basis and gave him this issue to see if he could sell it," Studwell says. "It wasn't the easiest stock to sell, but he eventually pushed it through."

Studwell never knew it, but Michael had accomplished the sale by dumping it on other clients he valued less. One of them was Galen

Honn, a retired paint and hardware merchant. Michael sold Honn the stock by telling him that executives at Action Card Express were going to use the company to take over a local orange-juice company called O-Jay Foods. Prozumenshikov told Honn that Prudential-Bache was offering the stock for $2.80 a share, though it was publicly listed at $3.00 a share, because Pru-Bache "had bought a whole block of stock at a reasonable price," Honn says. After the takeover, Prozumenshikov assured Honn, Action Card "was going to be a $5 or $6 stock right away." Impressed, Honn bought 10,000 shares for $28,000, plus a $2,000 commission.

Action Card's acquisition of O-Jay Foods went forward as planned. But rather than doubling as Michael had predicted, the stock's price fell. Much later, Honn would sell it for a loss of about $18,000.

Scott Studwell, meanwhile, earned a tidy $15,000 profit when Michael sold his Action Card stake. The former football star soon transferred his $1.3 million account from another broker to Prozumenshikov at Prudential-Bache. "What I was impressed with, more than anything, was that he was almost always the first one in the office and the last one to leave, and he was very conscientious," Studwell says. "I talked to him more in the course of probably six or seven months than I'd talked to any broker for fifteen years." Studwell introduced Michael to his friend, Tommy Kramer, the recently retired quarterback of the Vikings, who opened a $500,000 account at Pru-Bache. Soon Michael was also pursuing Hershel Walker, the Vikings' star running back, recently acquired from the Dallas Cowboys.

Now, in addition to seeking referrals to other Minnesota Vikings, Michael began trying in earnest to consummate his plan to sell products to and from the former Soviet Union. He had incorporated a company for this purpose; he called it Danar, Inc., a moniker derived from the first names of his two sons, Daniel and Ariel. Michael wasn't particular about what he would trade with his native country. But the project, despite the daily hoopla in the newspapers about the opening of Russia to Western commerce, had proved more difficult than Michael imagined. He had arranged a deal to sell Russian military clothing to a department store in New York, which collapsed when the sellers in Russia unexpectedly raised their asking price.

After a great deal of effort, Prozumenshikov managed to set up a second tentative deal, selling a new wound-closing surgical product to the agency that bought goods for Russian hospitals. The product was manufactured by a Minnesota company in which Michael himself owned stock, called Osmed, Inc. Because Russian currency had no value in the West, it was unclear how the buyers would pay. Michael hoped to extract payment from Russia's reserves of gold and silver, says Dorene Kainz.

One December afternoon, Michael's friend Stuart Kloner, the man who had sold him his Mercedes, visited the office. Michael handed Kloner an invitation from the Moscow Medical Institute to travel to Russia and discuss importation of the U.S.–made surgical product. As a former Soviet citizen, Michael was afraid of being detained if he went to Russia himself, he told Kloner. He wondered if Stuart wanted to become a partner in the deal and visit Russia on his behalf.

Kloner agreed. After some hasty preparations, Stuart left for Moscow in January 1990, taking along a Soviet immigrant named Zayla Berler as his guide and translator.

When Kloner returned, he was full of horror stories about Russia. "When they got to the hotel, Stuart in his wildest dreams, I don't think, ever imagined it being that bad," Dorene Kainz says. "There was no heat, and it was freezing, and there was only one blanket on the bed. He didn't sleep the whole time he was there. There was no soap, so Stuart walked to the street corner thinking he was going to buy some soap, and that's just not the way it works. They had lost their luggage, too. I guess that's kind of notorious: When you go to the Soviet Union your luggage never follows you. By the time they got their luggage it had been picked through and stripped of anything that was worth anything."

Neither these travails nor the fact that the deal later fell through damaged Kloner's relationship with Prozumenshikov. "There were very few people," says Dorene Kainz, "that I can say were Michael's really close friends, because there was a part of him that he would not release. I think he and Stuart hit it off real well. Stuart was intrigued by Michael."

It was important to Prozumenshikov to make his import-export idea work, in part because of the faltering fortunes of the securities industry. Each day, the *Wall Street Journal* carried some gloomy new headline about the prospects of Michael's chosen vocation. In the first quarter of 1990, the New York Stock Exchange traded an average of only 161 million shares of stock a day, well below the volume before the crash; by September, the Exchange's daily volume would tumble to an anemic 142 million shares.

The reticence of small investors to trade stocks was now accompanied by a downturn in Wall Street's previously lucrative investment-banking businesses. And with the collapse of the junk-bond market backed by Drexel Burnham that financed so many corporate takeovers in the 1980s, revenue from mergers and acquisitions was also on the skids.

Analysts estimated that 40,000 jobs had been lost in the securities industry since the crash. And although the entry-level clerks and superfluous administrators had long since been weeded out, another wave of layoffs was beginning on Wall Street. These cuts would target the cream of the Street, fifty-year-old investment bankers and managing directors who had spent their entire careers at firms that were now turning their backs on them. That March, Robert C. Winters, chairman of Prudential Insurance, Prudential-Bache's parent company, said 1990 would be "a tough time for owners of securities firms," although he didn't hint at the painful changes to come at Pru-Bache later in the year.

As always, the financial problems facing New York securities firms also plagued their representatives in branch offices across the country. "My income for the first seven months of the year was about ten grand a month," says one of Prozumenshikov's Pru-Bache colleagues. "And all of a sudden it crashed down to about two grand a month. That's a lot; it's a change of lifestyle."

Locked into a huge new mortgage and credit-card debt of about $150,000, Prozumenshikov couldn't afford such a change. The refusal of Drexel Burnham Lambert to pay Michael for his 2,060 shares of non-marketable Drexel stock had hurt him financially, depriving him of $93,000 the firm owed him. Michael had sued Drexel for the money that February of 1990. But later that month, when Drexel filed for bankruptcy protection and closed its doors, Michael had become just another of the firm's many creditors.

Prozumenshikov's monthly mortgage payment was $4,600, plus property taxes. The credi-card bills were accruing thousands more per month in finance charges. The tuition for Daniel's private school cost thousands a year. The Prozumenshikovs had plenty of assets—the house, cars, jewelry, fine art, IRAs, and college accounts for their children—but these were mostly illiquid. Even accounting for Michael's big commission earnings, his bills were becoming burdensome.

Yet Michael's self-image was geared to constant upward mobility. To a man who had grown up with nothing, the idea of scaling back his lifestyle, of accepting austerity as his lot, was repugnant. On his desk, as his new motivational tool, he now displayed a photo of an oceanfront condominium in Boca Raton, Florida, where he hoped to retire. He also was lusting for a new top-of-the-line Rolex watch he saw in a catalog, which was made of pure gold and encrusted with diamonds, Dorene Kainz says. It was a matter of some discomfort to Michael to defray the purchase of the new Rolex, even temporarily.

William Humphries, whose relations with Michael had improved since Humphries left Prudential-Bache for Shearson, chided Michael during phone conversations about his compulsive spending. Inexplicably, Michael defended himself by implying that he lived high because it was expected of him as a top producer for his brokerage firm.

"They make me do this," Michael said.

"Who are 'they?'" Humphries asked.

"Prudential," Michael said.

"They didn't make you buy that house," Humphries scoffed. "They didn't make you buy that car. You're doing it to yourself. You want to live like a king, and you can't afford it."

In some of Michael's client accounts, things were getting worse than even William knew.

It started in the account of Laron Honn, the elder brother of Michael's client Galen Honn. Galen, whom Dennis Carlson had referred to Prozumenshikov when Michael was at Drexel, now maintained accounts at Prudential-Bache for himself and five of his relatives. In all, these accounts were worth about $2 million. For a while, Galen's relationship with Michael had been good. Honn and his wife had been out to dinner with the Prozumenshikovs on two occasions. For someone born in a Communist country, Honn was inclined to remark, Michael had surprisingly deep knowledge of the stock market.

Yet since Prozumenshikov moved to Pru-Bache, Galen Honn says, the commissions for the stock trades Michael executed had often been higher than the discounted rate on which he and Honn had agreed. As this problem repeated itself, Galen's opinion of Michael changed. "When I got to know him better," Honn says, "I found out that he was just in it for one thing, and that was to make money for himself. His customers came second."

And while inflated commissions might have been an accident, what happened in the account of Honn's brother, Laron, obviously wasn't.

The accountant who handled tax matters for both Honn brothers discovered that Michael had—for more than a year, at both Prudential-Bache and, to a lesser extent, at Drexel—been brazenly churning the securities in Laron Honn's account.

In September 1990, Laron Honn filed an arbitration claim against Michael and Pru-Bache that read like a textbook on statutory churning, or trading stocks merely to generate commissions. The claim said Prozumenshikov had executed 173 transactions in Laron Honn's Prudential-Bache account during five months in 1989—most of them without Honn's knowledge, some of them after Honn had demanded that all trading in the account cease.

This activity, the claim alleged, produced an annualized "turnover ratio" of about 12.0—twice the level that most regulators acknowledge as proof positive that an account has been churned. Just to break even, after the excessive trading and the margin-account interest, the stocks in the account would have had to appreciate at a rate of 29 percent a year, the claim said. Wall Street's best and brightest, the elite mutual-fund managers to whom investors flock to turn over their money, rarely were able to generate returns that good.

And Michael hadn't come close. In fact, the arbitration claim said, Laron Honn had suffered $125,000 in trading losses and paid $75,000 in commissions during his seventeen-month association with Prozumenshikov—this despite the fact that Michael frequently assured Honn he was making money, according to the claim. Almost as an afterthought, the claim alleged that Michael had violated a Minnesota fraud statute by guaranteeing that Honn would lose no money, and lied to Prudential-Bache by reporting that Honn had thirty years of experience investing in stocks and bonds. The claim demanded $200,000 in restitution and $200,000 more in punitive damages.

At firms such as Merrill Lynch, allegations of this severity against a stockbroker, if found to be correct, would be grounds for immediate dismissal. Instead, Prudential-Bache would soon send Michael on an expense-paid ocean cruise to Europe and—despite his fears of being detained there—Russia. The trip was a reward for Prozumenshikov's big production of commissions.

Laron Honn's lawyer sent a copy of the arbitration claim to Mica Duncan and later phoned to ask her to act as a witness for Honn when the matter went before an arbitration panel. Duncan declined out of loyalty to Michael, she says, although she knew that Honn's lawyer could compel her to appear at the hearing by having her subpoenaed.

As Michael's former assistant and now compliance manager for the Minneapolis branch of Kidder Peabody, Mica Duncan had special insight into the merits of the Honn claim. Flipping through the allegations, she knew instantly that this claim was different than the lawsuit Michael's immigrant clients had filed in 1988. "He was doing something he shouldn't do," she says. He was doing something [at Prudential-Bache], and he was doing something as an agent for them. It was their responsibility to put an end to it."

William Humphries had a simpler way of explaining what Michael had done in Laron Honn's account. "He used to trade Laron with reckless abandon," Humphries says. "He was churning people, buying and selling quickly for no reason. Change the story, you know, buy, hold it two days, and sell it out. He was lying to people, just to do more business."

In 1991, a lawyer representing Ellen Prozumenshikov would phone Mica Duncan and ask her opinion about whether he ought to fight the Honn claim or pay money to settle it. "You should settle it," she told him. Mica had, by then, been subpoenaed as a hostile witness. If the case went to arbitration, Duncan told Ellen's lawyer, "You aren't going to like my answers." Eventually the case would be settled, with Ellen Prozumenshikov and Pru-Bache, together, paying Laron Honn an award that totaled about $100,000, Galen Honn says.

Furious about what had happened in his brother's account, Galen Honn closed his accounts at Prudential-Bache in 1990. But before turning over Honn's money to him, he says, Pru-Bache took it upon itself to deduct $1,400. Earlier, the firm had refunded this sum to Galen when he complained that he had been overcharged on a stock trade. Honn says Jim Tallen, Michael's boss, told him that because he was closing his accounts, he was no longer entitled to the discounted commission rate he had previously enjoyed. Later, a representative for the firm wrote Honn to say that Tallen's decision to deduct the money was justified. "We trust that this has clarified our position on this matter for you," the Pru-Bache letter said.

Prozumenshikov, apparently having learned little from the Laron Honn debacle, was now testing the patience of another of his longtime clients, John Petcoff, Milwaukee's "Tire and Battery King."

Though undeniably rich, Petcoff was also low-key, a man of plain talk and plain tastes who lived in a modest suburban home and was as comfortable in a hamburger joint as a four-star restaurant. He had made his money with street smarts and hard work, and had begun dabbling in the stock market late in his business career. "I was always a very optimistic fellow," Petcoff says. "I feel that you need to be optimistic to be successful. I can see now that it's easy to sell a person who wants to be successful."

With Petcoff's assent, Prozumenshikov had always kept Petcoff's big margin account loaded with stocks, a habit that cost his client as much as $50,000 a year in interest payments. Only lately had Petcoff come to the conclusion that his stock holdings were generating insufficient returns to compensate for these finance charges. And, lately, Prozumenshikov's stock recommendations seemed to have little rhyme or reason. "He was shooting in ten different directions like buckshot, hoping that something would stick," Petcoff says. "He would just throw anything at you, and you'd tell him no, and an hour later he'd come back with something else."

Even now, however, Michael retained the trait that made him such a good salesman, his fierce and unwavering conviction. "He did it in such an intelligent, enthusiastic, depth-of-knowledge type thing that, man, when he spoke, it was like the Gospel," Petcoff says. "I think he thought he was God."

It was, once again, an accountant who alerted Petcoff to the fact that his account was probably too active. That year, 1990, the accountant's bill for preparing Petcoff's income tax return was $1,500 higher than usual. The reason, the accountant said, was that his staff had been obliged to cull a stack of Prudential-Bache trade confirmations that was eight inches high, Petcoff says. "My accountant was screaming at me because the trades were just getting ridiculous," Petcoff says. Prozumenshikov, he says, "was churning the account."

Like others of Michael's clients, Petcoff often traded stock-options contracts, financial instruments that allow investors to control big stock positions for relatively little money. Basically, these options entitle investors to buy or sell stock in the future for a prespecified price. They can be used in many ways—either to speculate in the market or in conservative strategies designed to lock in stock market profits. Many of the investors and stockbrokers who use options don't fully understand them.

A single, overly aggressive options-selling strategy popular in the mid-1980s, for instance, had wiped out an entire generation of naive investors when the market crashed.

Michael had taught himself about options while working at Drexel Burnham Lambert. He had help from Drexel's New York–based chief options strategist, a patient, low-key math wizard named Harrison Roth. Unfortunately, Roth says, Michael had used his new skills with inordinate zeal—encouraging clients to try the riskiest trading strategies in perilously large volume. "I told him he was doing it in excessive size," Roth says. "Mostly what he learned from me was not to do dangerous things, and he didn't always listen to me. He was in over his head."

Since then, at Prudential-Bache, Prozumenshikov had taught himself more new tricks for trading options, much to the chagrin of his client John Petcoff. One morning in September 1990, Michael phoned Petcoff and urged him to try one of these strategies. He wanted Petcoff to buy $37,000 worth of options and hold them for only two hours. These options were nearing expiration, Michael said, and were likely to surge suddenly in value.

Petcoff declined. He had to leave for a business meeting, he said, and didn't have time to learn about some new options trading strategy. But Prozumenshikov, he says, wouldn't take no for an answer. "He was trying to tell me he could trade the options at ten or eleven in the morning and get out by noon or 1 P.M.," Petcoff says. "He said we could make $30,000 to $40,000 in an hour."

What followed, as Petcoff tried to get off the phone so he could leave for his meeting, was a frenetic forty-five-second conversation, which Petcoff remembers like this:

"Do you want to do this?" Michael asked. "I can guarantee double what you invest."

"No," Petcoff said. "That's gambling. I don't want to do it."

"Well, I did it," Michael said. "I made $30,000."

"I don't understand it," Petcoff said. "It's dangerous."

"No, no, no, no," Michael said. "I watch. If we make a mistake, I can cancel."

"Michael," Petcoff said, "I don't want it."

"No, no, no," Prozumenshikov pleaded. "Listen to me."

"I don't want it," Petcoff repeated. Then he hung up the phone and walked out of his office.

Petcoff learned later, he says, that Michael had bought the options for him anyway. His Prudential-Bache account statement shows that the trade—a September 21, 1990, purchase of one hundred options contracts based on a popular index of blue-chip stocks—cost $37,602. But rather than appreciating, the options' value rapidly plunged. Michael sold them later that day for $7,060. In a matter of hours, Petcoff had lost more than $30,000.

Prozumenshikov may well have intended for Petcoff to earn money on the trade, but the odds of success were astronomically remote, says Harrison Roth, Drexel's former options strategist. "He was gambling on a big, sharp, and sudden decline in the stock market," Roth says. "If he got it, there would have been a big leveraged profit. That's the usual dumb thing, betting against the trend. It's very dangerous."

Petcoff was livid. He complained to Michael's manager, Jim Tallen, that Michael had executed the trade without authorization. Tallen, he says, told him that Michael's sales assistant had overheard Petcoff agreeing to the trade. Petcoff then wrote a letter to Prudential-Bache, asking that the trade be reversed and his account credited for the amount he had lost. "It came back a couple of weeks later," he says, "saying they're not going to honor it, that it was a legitimate trade."

After this episode, Petcoff says, he made an effort to slow the pace of his trading with Michael—although, strangely, Petcoff still found it difficult to resist Michael's advances.

In addition to Prozumenshikov's adventures with stock options, some of his clients say, the broker had fallen into another dubious habit: reporting that certain of the stock trades he recommended had been his clients' ideas, rather than his own. Melvin Brisse, a retiree who lost thousands of dollars trading stocks with Michael, says he learned about this problem only after closing his account at Prudential-Bache.

Brisse consulted a securities lawyer about filing an arbitration claim against Michael and his firm. After reviewing his account statements, Brisse says, the lawyer told him it would be useless to file such a claim, although the account had certainly been very active. The lawyer pointed to notations on the statements, printed alongside the stock transactions. There, in small print, the word "unsolicited" appeared, again and again.

"What does that mean?" Brisse asked.

"It means you asked for the stock instead of him recommending it," the lawyer said.

"Nothing could be farther from the truth," Brisse said.

"Nevertheless," the lawyer said, "it's on every sheet. We don't want to take the case, because we think it would be hard to win."

After being singed by customer complaints at Drexel Burnham Lambert, Michael had apparently learned to record some stock trades he recommended as unsolicited, to protect himself from legal liability. Brisse complained about his trading losses to Jim Tallen, to no avail. "He said, 'Where are you coming from? You asked for these trades,'" Brisse says.

John Petcoff and Galen Honn both noticed similar "unsolicited" notations on their account statements. In a letter to Prudential-Bache Chairman George Ball about another matter, Honn made note of the problem: "Mr. Prozumenshikov called me to purchase Action Card!" Honn's letter said. "This trade was solicited by a Prudential-Bache broker, and was knowingly marked unsolicited."

What Jim Tallen and his superiors at Prudential-Bache did about the various allegations against Prozumenshikov isn't clear.

But Tallen privately admonished Michael for his aggressive trading, says William Humphries. Both Humphries and Dorene Kainz recall that Tallen, on at least one occasion, forced Michael to pay a trading loss out of his gross commissions. This, Humphries says, embittered Michael toward his boss. Prozumenshikov "didn't like Tallen," Humphries says, "contrary to what Tallen thought." John Kelly, then manager of Shearson Lehman Brothers' Minneapolis branch, says Michael complained that Tallen "didn't support him" within the firm.

In late 1990, the sea changed at Prudential-Bache Securities. Under pressure from the Prudential parent company, George Ball began to disassemble the pieces of his firm's failed forays into investment-banking and other financial specialties. In November, Ball announced that the firm would scale back its money-losing investment-banking division, laying off 120 of its 130 investment bankers. A month later, Pru-Bache shut down its risk-arbitrage department, which previously had traded takeover stocks for the firm's own account. It also closed its Canadian brokerage operations and cut back its international stock-trading operation.

The changes, Prudential Insurance executives said, reflected a desire for a new focus at Prudential-Bache: a return to the Bache group's core business of selling stocks to individual investors. "Given the losses we have been sustaining recently in (the investment banking) business, and the prospect for greatly reduced investment-banking opportunities over the next few years, it's clear that continuing to pursue our original strategy no longer makes sense," Prudential Insurance Chairman Robert C. Winters said at the time. Soon, as part of the effort to set a new direction for the firm, Prudential-Bache would shorten its name to Prudential Securities Inc.

It would have been hard enough on Prudential-Bache stockbrokers like Michael Prozumenshikov if the financial press had confined itself to reporting the firm's retreat from the businesses it had tried to build in the 1980s. The *Wall Street Journal* also frequently reminded its readers that Prudential was likely to lose as much as $100 million in 1990—an estimate, it turned out, that fell substantially short of the firm's actual loss of $242 million.

But the *Journal* went further than that, quoting analysts who predicted that Prudential Insurance executives would soon rid themselves of George Ball, or possibly sell Prudential-Bache to one of its competitors. The *Journal*'s pièce de résistance was a front-page feature article mocking George Ball's habit of mass-mailing his employees odd memos. According to the article, Ball had begun a recent memo on the firm's investment-banking layoffs like this: "My daughter has a pimple on her chin, and she's unhappy. She's 18. I have a pimple on my chin, and I'm happy. I'm 52. It's called perspective." The *Journal* article went on to detail many other passages of Ball's strange communiqués.

The article did nothing to improve the image of a firm that Wall Street already viewed as floundering. Three months later, George Ball would resign, divulging his departure in another of his memos, entitled "All Good Things."

Michael Prozumenshikov thought he had escaped the consequences of bad publicity by leaving beleaguered Drexel Burnham Lambert. He complained to William Humphries that Prudential's image problems were damaging his business. "Pru was falling to pieces right under his nose," Humphries says. "It's hard to do business with people. Your clients question you too much."

It was at this time that Prozumenshikov began to seriously consider leaving Prudential-Bache for Shearson Lehman Brothers, a firm whose local manager had been courting Michael for some time. For the past year, in fact, Michael had been pursued by John Kelly, a charming and articulate manager who, Michael felt, would appreciate his talents.

Kelly was a man who trusted his own instincts. Earlier, when Kelly was deciding which brokers to recruit from Drexel's Minneapolis branch, Prozumenshikov's name was on a list of bad apples that Kelly had compiled by talking to brokers at his firm. In the notes he made of one conversation with a former Drexel broker, Kelly had written: "Michael . . . Russian . . . avoid."

But he had reckoned without Michael's personal charm, selling skills, and earnest enthusiasm, not to mention his $800,000-a-year in gross commissions. On the number of occasions that Kelly had taken Prozumenshikov to dinner, Michael was invariably engaging, warm, and witty. A crack salesman himself and a good teacher of salespeople, Kelly knew a natural when he saw one. "Michael and I just really hit it off," Kelly says. "We really liked each other as people."

Kelly could see that Michael was aggressive to the extreme, but he felt he could manage it. Kelly was confident he could control him and channel his selling talent into a wholesome approach to the business. He had, after all, tamed the lions of Drexel before; six former Drexel brokers, including former branch manager Bill Krebs, were now working for him. "I felt comfortable that he'd respect me," Kelly says. "I'd go to bat for him and if I said 'No, you can't do this,' I'd give him a valid reason." Still, Kelly asserts, Michael's "rock-and-roll style" would have been curtailed at Shearson.

Kelly had noticed a change in Michael after the Russian broker's Prudential-sponsored trip to his native city of Leningrad—a change Kelly liked. When the two of them got together for dinner soon after Michael returned, the Russian broker was more subdued and contemplative than Kelly had known him to be in the past.

"His mind seemed to be elsewhere," Kelly says. "There wasn't this fire that I had noticed. It gave me a different sense of him. I sensed that maybe the rah-rah days were over . . . maybe he was looking to get his business really going and not be so rambunctious about it." About Russia itself, Michael said little. "He said, 'Man it was great to get back in the United States. I just don't have any desire whatsoever to live back there.'"

Soon Kelly and Prozumenshikov got down to talking money. Kelly was proposing a package that would pay Michael a total of $800,000 in incentives, he says, including $300,000 in advance.

The only question was whether Michael's disciplinary history would pass muster at Shearson. For some reason, Michael had been coy about granting Kelly permission to review his disciplinary file at the National Association of Securities Dealers, known in the industry as a "U-4."

Kelly remembers one final conversation with Michael Prozumenshikov that January of 1991, over dinner at Sasha's, a Wayzata restaurant that looked out onto Lake Minnetonka.

Michael was in a good mood, having shed the reserve Kelly noticed after the trip to Russia. He was distinctly upbeat, more like his ebullient former self. He was hatching a plan to sell bonds to the national bank of Russia—huge trades, Michael gushed, that would rake in incredible commissions. He wanted to know what Shearson could do to facilitate the deal, whether it could offer better prices for the bonds than Prudential could.

As the two men leaned back in their chairs after dinner, Kelly handed Michael a form that would authorize Shearson to review his U-4 file. "We're getting down to the nitty-gritty here," Kelly said. "Now, Michael, the ball is finally in your court. I've got to get this document back before we can go any further." Major customer complaints on the U-4, Kelly knew, would scuttle the deal. From looking at the U-4, Kelly says, "I'd have known in five seconds" whether Shearson could hire him.

Cheerfully, with a wave of his fleshy hand, Michael promised to fill out the form and mail it to Kelly soon—before he left, the following week, for yet another Prudential-Bache perk trip, this one to Santa Barbara, California.

He never got the chance.

CHAPTER 15

Later, even under intense questioning, Rudy Lekhter couldn't be sure of the precise moment when his friend, Zack Persitz, first expressed an interest in firing one of Lekhter's handguns. He did, however, remember being surprised by it. Zack was a quiet man who had never shared Rudy's zest for firearms, and Rudy knew that Zack's wife, Julia, absolutely abhorred them. The Persitzes had made it a point never to buy violent toys for their son, Danny.

It was, therefore, fascinating to Lekhter to watch Persitz squeeze off shots with both hands wrapped, police-style, around the weapon as though he had been doing it all his life.

Now Zack began again, extending his arms in front of him and squinting over the top of the .357 magnum revolver. Ever so gently, he squeezed the trigger, as Rudy had taught him to do. A violent recoil whipped his hands backward. The concussion, muffled by the headphones the two men were wearing, was a dull thump.

They were standing in a narrow bay with pale green walls, one of sixteen such compartments lined up side by side. Extending south from the row of bays was a large, low room, which ended twenty-five yards away in a wall of gray steel. The wall was fixed at a forty-five-degree angle, to guide bullets harmlessly into an aperture above. Nicks and blemishes from errant shots scarred a concrete column in the center of the room.

In each of the sixteen bays, people stood loading, aiming, and firing handguns. Every few seconds, a thump sounded as someone squeezed off a shot. Sometimes the thumps came in irregular bursts, like popcorn popping, as three or four people fired more or less simultaneously. Business at Bill's Gun Range, a sound-insulated chamber in the basement of a suburban shopping plaza, was brisk that Sunday afternoon. Persitz and

Lekhter had waited about twenty minutes to rent their stall. They had
taken target practice here, together, for two Sundays in a row and on this,
the second Sunday, Zack's accuracy had improved markedly.

Rudy Lekhter, a short, rotund man who played violin for a living,
loved guns. A National Rifle Association member, he had amassed a collection of sixteen firearms—pistols, rifles, and shotguns, which he
stowed in various rooms of his house. Rudy's affection for guns, Persitz
knew, dated to the old days in the Soviet Union, before Lekhter immigrated to the Unites States.

Lekhter's wife, Margarita, had belonged to a high school shooting
team in the couple's native city of Odessa, and Rudy had occasionally
fired guns with the team. A jolly man with twinkling eyes and a clever
wit, Lekhter sometimes became grave and spoke earnestly of the right to
bear arms, a privilege he deemed as basic to his new life as an American
as his freedom of speech.

Julia Persitz had never quite understood why Lekhter dabbled with
firearms. Lekhter was an immensely gifted musician, the Minnesota
Symphony's first-chair violinist. To Julia, also a musician, it seemed
senseless for Rudy to take chances with his hands. What if the barrel
jammed, as sometimes happened, and the pistol blew up?

Despite Julia's almost pathological fear of guns, Zachary had
recently told Rudy that he was considering buying a revolver to keep
around the house. He was often away overnight, inspecting dams in
remote areas of the state, and he worried about his wife's safety while he
was gone. He planned, he said, to try to talk her into learning to use a
gun to defend herself, if necessary.

Once, while at Lekhter's home for dinner, Persitz had asked to see
some of the pistols in Rudy's collection. He questioned Lekhter method-
ically about various types of guns—which of them Rudy preferred and
why. Since then, Rudy had invited Zack to tag along when he went to
gun shows at the Minneapolis convention center.

Now, suspended before Zachary Persitz hung a caricature of Iraqi
president Saddam Hussein. A bull's-eye superimposed over Hussein's
chest awarded six points for a flesh wound and ten for a shot through the
heart. These targets had been hot sellers at Bill's Gun Range since the
U.S. and European air bombardment of Iraq began earlier that month.

Persitz inspected the big Smith & Wesson revolver. The barrel was
long and thick, molded of gleaming stainless steel. Pins fastened a

wooden butt to the pistol's metal frame. The cylinder of the firing chamber now contained five .38 caliber bullets. A versatile weapon, the .357 magnum would fire either .38 or larger .357 slugs. It was heavy enough that Persitz's arm tired after only a few seconds of holding it aloft. His hands were thin, but his fingers were long, which helped in grasping the weapon.

Persitz leveled it at the target, stiffening the muscles in his forearms. He took careful aim, then squeezed the trigger again.

Thump. He felt the kick, and saw the paper ripple. He had hit Saddam squarely in the chest.

Later, as Persitz and Lekhter left the range and climbed into Zack's small Mazda, the two men discussed which of the various guns they had fired might be most appropriate for Julia. After some debate, they settled on the .357 magnum. It was a revolver, with a six-shot cylinder, like guns in the movies, and it packed sufficient force that one well-placed shot was likely to stop an intruder.

The Mazda emerged from the underground parking garage adjoining the range, into the fading light of a cold January afternoon. Cars whizzed by on Broadway, the busiest street in the working-class Minneapolis suburb of Robbinsdale. It was still snowing. During the drive back to Lekhter's house, Persitz fell silent. He was driving fast, Lekhter noticed. The streets were slick, and Rudy wished he would slow down.

It was snowing harder as the car rolled to a stop in Lekhter's driveway and the two men got out. Lekhter waited as Persitz unlocked the trunk. Inside lay the gun cases, alongside some toys they had packed earlier—a rocking horse and a brightly-colored locomotive with wheels and handles for a small child to ride. Persitz was taking the toys, which Lekhter's daughter had outgrown, to the younger of his two sons, Jonathan, who wasn't quite two years old.

Now, as Persitz removed the case containing the .357, he made his pitch. "Look," Zachary said, "would you mind if I show this to Julia to try out, to hold, and see what she feels? Maybe we should buy something like this."

For a few seconds, Lekhter said nothing. It wasn't like loaning Zack his lawnmower or a set of wrenches. He had known Persitz for twelve years and had always thought him insular and reserved. He was dimly aware that Zack had been institutionalized in the Soviet Union, for reasons that were unclear. Yet these were not the factors that prompted

Rudy to balk at Zachary's request. He simply felt uncomfortable loaning out a handgun to anyone, even a family friend.

On the other hand, Lekhter liked Persitz, and he had no reason not to trust him. What's more, it would be awkward to say no.

"Okay," Lekhter said finally. "But bring it back soon."

Lekhter checked the revolver, twice, to be sure it wasn't loaded. Then he returned it to its case and lay the case in the trunk. Just before Persitz slammed the trunk door shut, Lekhter noticed that thick snowflakes already were collecting on the toy horse and train and on the black vinyl of the revolver's case.

Zachary Persitz had always known that his heart held many secrets he couldn't share with others. Julia, his wife, understood, and she accepted it. He needed, occasionally, to withdraw from those around him, to isolate himself even from his wife and young sons.

"He would have this calm time sometimes, where he would be very quiet," Julia says. "I don't know if it was depression. It was his way." It was, perhaps, a purging process that relieved Zachary's daily stress and the many wounds left over from his childhood—the "disturbing, long-standing, intense feelings of loneliness," as a psychologist would later put it.

Thus, hiding his feelings about Michael Prozumenshikov—the paralyzing rage and shame over his stock-trading losses—came naturally to Zachary Persitz. And it was necessary, if he was ever to recover his family's money.

Almost two years earlier, a letter had arrived from Prozumenshikov asking Persitz to acquiesce in the transfer of his family's brokerage accounts to Michael's new firm, Prudential-Bache Securities. "Thank you for your continued support," Michael's letter said, "and most of all, thank you for your confidence."

But Persitz had no confidence in Prozumenshikov. By the time Michael left Drexel, he and Zachary were speaking to one another only when they had to—as on the occasions their wives made arrangements for the families to get together. "When I stopped working with Michael, he and Zachary never spoke," Mica Duncan says. "I mean, they didn't do anything in the account. They did not have a warm business relationship, not at all."

The bulk of Zachary's remaining money was tied up in his fifteen hundred-share stake of Texas Air Corporation. And the reason he had allowed his accounts to be moved to Prudential-Bache was another of Zachary's secrets: Until he had an agreement guaranteeing Michael's promise to make Zachary's original investment of $100,000 grow at a rate of 18 percent a year, Persitz felt that his life was inextricably linked to Prozumenshikov's.

The previous March, with Texas Air's Eastern Airlines subsidiary grounded by a strike, its chairman, Frank Lorenzo, had taken Eastern into bankruptcy proceedings in an attempt to break the union. Since then, rumors had circulated that Lorenzo planned to sell Texas Air's other big subsidiary, Continental Airlines—an idea Wall Street liked. From June 1989 to August of the same year, Texas Air's stock price had climbed from $13.50 a share to $22 a share. At the latter price, Zachary's fifteen hundred shares were worth $33,000. Though the sum was still less than half of the $70,000 Persitz had sunk into Texas Air, this was the best chance he would ever have to cut his losses by selling out.

Persitz visited the Prudential-Bache Wayzata branch at that time, apparently to discuss the Texas Air stake. "They spoke Russian," says Dorene Kainz, "so I don't know what they talked about. But they didn't appear to be mad. Later Michael said, 'That was Zachary Persitz.' It left no impression on me at all."

Ellen Prozumenshikov says Michael urged Zachary to sell the Texas Air stock. Julia Persitz has a different recollection—that Michael never recommended selling the stock until much later, when it reached its very bottom. "We wanted to sell it . . . when it did go up for a while," Julia says. "Michael said, 'Oh no, it's going to go even higher.'"

Yet by year's end Frank Lorenzo had cut no deal to sell Continental Airlines, and Texas Air's stock price resumed its skid. For the year, Lorenzo announced, the once-mighty airline conglomerate had suffered a record loss of $886 million. This time, Texas Air's destination was oblivion. There would be no more rallies, no more opportunities for Zachary to cut his losses.

As he examined the business section of his newspaper, the *St. Paul Pioneer Press*, on New Year's Day 1990, Zachary noted that the stock had given back all the previous summer's gains—and more. Texas Air was now trading for $11.75 a share, and Zachary's stake was worth just $17,625.

He said nothing to anyone about it. By then, the disintegration of Zachary Persitz had begun.

That spring, Zachary's six-feet-two frame dropped 20 pounds, to 165 from his usual 185. He suffered from abdominal pain and wondered whether he might be getting an ulcer, although a trip to the doctor revealed no organic damage. He had many aches and pains, in fact, each of which he interpreted as a symptom of some grave illness, perhaps cancer.

Never a sound sleeper in the past, he now suffered from chronic insomnia. Night after night, as he retired with Julia, he nurtured the hope that, finally, his mounting exhaustion would force him to sleep until morning. But it never happened. At the slightest noise, he awoke with a start, then lay there, his mind racing, until no reclining position could make him comfortable. Many were the nights that Julia found him downstairs, reading, or simply staring into space, as dawn approached, his hand resting on the family dog for comfort.

Zachary's moodiness and lack of communication were creating tension in the marriage. He had lost interest in sex. And since the birth of the Persitzes' second child, Jonathan, in April 1989, Zachary had begun to complain regularly about the burden Julia's evening work schedule placed on him. Julia had always felt that she understood her husband better than other people, but lately he was a mystery even to her. "He's the kind of person who has (hidden) feelings inside of him," she says. "There are two there."

Julia's schedule called for rehearsing in the evenings with her chamber orchestra, which obliged Zachary to take charge of picking up Daniel and caring for both children in the evenings. "We both were busy with our own lives, and our lives were quite different," Julia says. "He wanted me to be there. Physically and emotionally, it was hard on him."

Julia had been sympathetic, until her husband began to suggest that she quit her job. At this, Julia balked. When the two of them quarreled, she says, "I would be the one who would shout and he would just close up for a while." Zachary found it difficult to remain aloof when Julia was angry at him, however. He was the one who sought to make up— usually too quickly, before his wife had cooled down, she says.

Nagging Julia about changing her schedule to spend more time with him and the children became a habit for Zachary. Finally, Julia decided that he had pushed her too far. "This is what I do," she told her husband. "When you married me I was a musician. You knew that. I have to work. I can't imagine life without working."

For a time, the couple considered divorce, Julia says, although they never lived separately. Soon, though, Zachary decided that divorce wasn't what he wanted, and he told Julia so. "She had a big heart," he said later. "She was kind. She kept me on line . . . like a good parent. Nobody had loved me before her."

And in any case, Zachary knew well enough the real source of his discomfiture wasn't Julia's schedule. His problems, he felt, all emanated from a palatial country home barely three miles from Zachary's own house, where a heavyset man named Michael Prozumenshikov resided.

In May, Persitz learned that the lawsuit filed by Prozumenshikov's émigré clients had been dismissed. This confirmed, for Zachary, what he had feared for years. The lawsuit had been doomed from the start, he thought, because Michael "was very shrewd and clever and they could not prove that he had made certain promises to them when taking their money."

In a sense, Persitz decided, Michael's ability to mislead Soviet investors was a function of the way things worked in the old country. There, the government inevitably betrayed its citizens; the only people a man could trust were his closest friends. Transplanted to the United States, Zachary felt, Michael's Russian clients had brought this bias with them. They had trusted Michael—he himself had trusted Michael—because of the Soviet predisposition to stick with one's own kind.

In his newspaper, Zachary read that a bankruptcy judge had wrested control of Eastern Airlines from Texas Air and appointed a trustee to run Eastern. The judge's decision was a major setback for Frank Lorenzo, one that marked the failure of his strategy to use bankruptcy proceedings to reduce Eastern's labor costs. The defeat reflected itself in Texas Air's stock, which was now languishing at a pitiful price of $7 a share. At this level, Zachary's stake was worth about 15 percent of what he had paid for it. He noted the development with grim resignation. It was, by his way of thinking, all Prozumenshikov's fault. "I was very angry at Michael," he said later, "but I wouldn't show it."

Unlike most of Prozumenshikov's former friends from Leningrad, Zachary visited Michael's grand new house—for a housewarming party, dinners, and other events. Always, he noted, Michael entertained with conspicuous extravagance. As Prozumenshikov made a point of telling him at one such function in June 1990, Persitz didn't look good. His cheekbones protruded sharply from his face, and his clothes seemed to hang from his lanky frame. His skin was even paler than usual, and his eyes were rimmed with red.

At this party, Persitz asked Prozumenshikov to step into his study and talk for a moment. There, Zachary's careful reserve evaporated. Plaintively, he pleaded with Michael to give him an agreement formalizing the broker's previous promises. What Zachary was asking for, he said, was short and simple—something like this: "I, Michael Prozumenshikov, have received from Mr. Zachary Persitz an initial investment of $100,000 as of October 1986, and I guarantee to treat it as my own money with a guaranteed return of 18 percent." It was no more, Zachary asserted, than Michael had promised at the time.

As Persitz remembers it, Michael finally assented to the request, promising to mail him such an agreement the following Monday. But the document never arrived. "He said that he would give it," Persitz said later in his heavily accented English, "but he (was) always finding different kinds of excuses not to give it to me."

Financially, ends had ceased to meet for the Persitz household. Zachary earned take-home pay of $550 a week, Julia about $200. Their mortgage payment was $1,500, plus roughly $400 a month in property taxes. And soon, the payment on the adjustable-rate mortgage would rise by $200 a month.

Zachary and Julia no longer had any cash savings, only devalued stocks in their Prudential-Bache accounts. The equity in their home had, in effect, been drained by their credit line with the First Bank of Minnesota—the one that Michael advised Zachary to open. And unlike Prozumenshikov, with his perk trips to sumptuous resorts, the Persitzes had not been able to afford even a modest vacation for the past two years. When people asked why they didn't take holidays, Zack lied, saying his work schedule didn't allow it.

By now, Zack was using the First Bank credit line and his Visa cards to pay the family's bills. Because he balanced the checkbook, he was, for a long time, able to hide the gravity of the family's financial problems from his wife.

Similarly, although he loathed pretending that the $33,000 his mother had entrusted to him was still intact, Persitz refused to tell her that most of it was gone. When his mother asked him for money for a vacation she was planning, he took more cash advances on his credit cards. Soon his outstanding Visa balances topped $10,000, in addition to the First Bank credit-line debt of $40,000.

For a time, the credit line had allowed him to make only small payments that covered the interest charges accruing on the debt. But in the fall of 1990, when Zachary missed a payment to the bank, a loan officer threatened to change the status of the loan to a less favorable arrangement, he says. And in November, First Bank forbade Zachary to take additional advances on his credit line. The Persitz family's debt-to-equity ratio was becoming too high, a letter from the bank informed him.

By now, the family's Prudential-Bache accounts were worth only a small fraction of what Zachary had invested with Michael in 1986. There were Julia's and Zachary's retirement accounts, together worth about $11,000; Daniel's custodial account, which held about $6,000; and the joint account that contained the Texas Air stock, now worth a total of less than $15,000. Persitz could no longer bear to keep tabs on the stocks he owned. "I stopped reading business sections of newspapers because it was making me sick," he says.

To Zachary's eternal shame, he had even taken $1,000 from the money his elder son was saving to buy a computer. "It was getting real bad," he says. "I just didn't know what to do." With his family income likely to remain more or less constant until he and Julia retired, there seemed to be no prospect that things would ever improve.

Now, with every check he wrote, Zachary blamed Michael Prozumenshikov. He regarded his enormous debts as Michael's, rather than his own. And he was terrified, he says, by the control the broker still had over his family's remaining assets. But if Persitz closed his accounts at Prudential-Bache, he feared, Michael would certainly disparage him to other people, as the broker had bad-mouthed other of his former Russian clients.

The hopelessness of Zachary's financial prospects now provoked, in the man who seldom showed his feelings, uncharacteristic displays of an explosive temper. Some years before, when his mother moved out of a condominium she owned, Zachary had assumed ownership of the unit. After renting it out for a while, he had arranged to sell it. The buyer, a man named Jerry Ackerman, was required as part of the transaction to make a series of monthly payments to Persitz.

On one occasion, when Ackerman was late with a payment, Persitz went berzerk, screaming into the telephone so loudly that Ackerman had to hold the receiver away from his ear. A couple of days later, Zachary and Julia stopped by the condo together to collect the payment. When Ackerman told Zachary that he couldn't produce the money that month, Persitz appeared to lose control of himself, raving about fiscal responsibility to a man he barely knew.

Julia stared at Zachary as he bellowed at the startled Ackerman. This wasn't like her husband at all.

At home, it seemed to Julia during that winter of 1990 that Zachary became more quiet and contemplative than ever. Anticipating his fortieth birthday, which was in February, he spoke often of unfulfilled goals and, a little morbidly, of things he wanted to do before he died. He wanted to sculpt and paint more, he said, and to write more poetry.

Daniel Persitz complained that his father spent less time with him than he once had—and that his driving, when the two of them traveled in Zachary's Mazda together, had become reckless. After a couple of traffic accidents, Zachary was inclined to agree. Preoccupied constantly by his worrying, he felt that he was becoming "a menace to my children," he says.

At about this time, Persitz began writing and illustrating a children's book, which he called *Pinky Bananga*. He planned to use it to teach his younger son to read.

The book was about a race of people living on a planet called Chunga, where reading was forbidden and books were ground up as mulch. The protagonist, a boy named Pinky Bananga, finds a book left by a previous civilization, which contains the key to curing a mysterious illness that is sweeping the planet of Chunga.

The story line, displaying influences as diverse as Ray Bradbury's *Farenheit 451* and Dr. Seuss, was so compelling that Julia had recommended Zack try to find a publisher for it. Its theme, a heartfelt one for Zachary, was the importance of reading.

The book was colorful, illustrated by hand in bright yellows and pinks, cheery hues that represented a brief escapist fantasy for Zachary Persitz. For in his real life, black and gray were the only colors he could see.

Still unable to sleep at night, Persitz roamed the house or puttered in the garage, often imagining that he heard prowlers outside. He took his dog for walks in the middle of the night. At times, Zachary thought he saw shadows moving in the woods behind the house, near the wooden fort he had built for Daniel.

Zachary's self-image as capable and devoted family man was in tatters. He felt like a failure, he says, "as a parent, as a spouse, and as a son." Lately, he had even taken to refusing to answer the phone when he was home alone; it might be his mother, asking for some of her money. For this, he said later, "I hated myself."

During working hours at the state Department of Natural Resources, Persitz was always exhausted. "I would come to work and I would just sit in my chair in my office in a stupor for an hour," he says. "Then slowly I would start doing something, doing my work." Zachary liked getting out of the the office for his occasional inspections of Minnesota's many dams; the country drives and the comforting inspection routine suppressed, for a while, the worrisome buzz in his brain.

Inevitably, however, as Persitz found himself sitting alone in his house, facing another sleepless night, his thoughts turned to Michael Prozumenshikov. Michael, for Zachary, had become "the paramount of all evil. He pretended to be my friend but destroyed me and mocked me."

Persitz had taken to filling the time by conducting imaginary conversations with his nemesis. "I was almost constantly talking to Michael, just in my head, trying to reason with him," Persitz says. Occasionally, he imagined he saw Michael crouching in the corner of the living room. "Mike would laugh at me," he says. "He looked like a devil, red hair, mocking me." When Zachary did manage to slip off to sleep, he often would dream of begging Michael, unsuccessfully, to give back his money.

It happened that Jonathan Persitz had been born only three months after the Prozumenshikovs' second son, Ariel. The two families' elder sons were also the same age, bore the same first name, and were close friends. The two older boys, as toddlers, had both attended the same nursery school. And these were just a few of uncanny parallels running between the two families. The Persitzes and Prozumenshikovs had emigrated from the same Russian city. By accident, they had wound up in the same American city. And their family finances were linked, at least in Zachary's mind, by the business relationship between him and Prozumenshikov.

But here the parallels ended. Upon reaching school age, the families' elder sons had gone in different directions. While the Persitz boy attended public school, Daniel Prozumenshikov had been enrolled in the private Montessori school.

The most painful stroke, for Zachary, had come the previous fall, when Michael's son transferred to the Blake School—Minnesota's best private learning facility, the school Persitz had wanted his own son to attend. By now, it was obvious that the Persitzes would never be able to pay the Blake tuition. Prozumenshikov, Persitz told himself, was using the commissions he had made by squandering the Persitz family's money to give his son opportunities that Zachary's son would never have.

That January of 1991, Zachary and Julia attended a birthday party at Michael's house for his youngest child, Ariel. The party was really for adults, who celebrated the birthdays of their children together as a matter of Russian custom. There, Zachary learned for the first time that the Prozumenshikovs had hired a nanny to care for Ariel while his parents were working. Childcare had long been a worry for Zachary and Julia; Julia's mother was obliged to live with the family five days a week to care for Jonathan.

Persitz watched as Prozumenshikov circulated among the guests. When he saw the chance, he drew Michael aside. For what seemed like the hundredth time, he asked Michael for an agreement formalizing his financial commitment to the Persitz family. "I said, 'Let's go to your office so that you can write it and give it to me. It will take us five minutes,'" Persitz says. "He said, 'No, I can't. I'm with my guests. I'll mail it to you in a couple of days.'"

When Ellen Prozumenshikov entertained, she typically asked guests to step into the garage if they wished to smoke. But Zachary didn't smoke, she knew, and his allergies tended to flare up when he was around people who did. So she was surprised to find Persitz in the garage four or five times that night, mingling with the smokers. Later, it occurred to Ellen that Zachary might have been examining the control panel of the Prozumenshikovs' security system.

At work the following week, Persitz did everything he could to avoid leaving his office, anticipating that Michael might call about the agreement. Each day at 5 P.M., he hurried home to check his mail. By Friday, no agreement had arrived, and Zachary knew at last what he had to do. Cool reason replaced the confusion in his brain. And although his thinking had long since crossed socially accepted boundaries, it remained orderly and precise.

For months, Zachary Persitz had traveled from darkness into still deeper night. But now, as if by magic, the darkness broke.

The following Monday, January 28, was a gloomy day, the sky heavily overcast and the temperature never far above zero. It had snowed, on and off, all day. Zachary's last assignment was to inspect the Gray's Bay dam on Lake Minnetonka. As the sun sank, the temperature dropped. It would be well below zero by midnight.

When Persitz finished at Gray's Bay, he drove to Wayzata. Inside the storefronts of a few of Lake Street's shops, Christmas lights still twinkled. Zachary guided his small car along Lake Street, stopping here and there for the people who hurried, breathing steam from their mouths, to their parked cars.

At Lake Street's intersection with Minnetonka Avenue, Persitz turned right. There, visible through the window of his ground-floor office at Prudential-Bache Securities, was Michael Prozumenshikov. Behind the three-story building was a parking lot. It was for customers, mainly; employees used the heated underground garage. Near the battleship-gray garage door, Persitz parked his old brown Mazda.

Hunched over the heater in his tiny car, he waited. He hoped Michael didn't have one of the guns he owned with him.

At about 6:30 P.M., the garage door opened. As Michael's Mercedes inched up the ramp, Persitz opened his car door and stepped out. With one foot in the car and one in the snow of the street, he hailed Prozumenshikov with a wave of his hand.

Michael stopped his car and rolled down his window. Zachary hollered out to him, asking whether they could talk.

"Sure," Michael said, looking a little confused.

Prozumenshikov watched as Persitz climbed back into his car, then followed the Mazda across Lake Street to a parking lot just west of Sasha's, Michael's favorite lakefront restaurant. There Michael parked his prized Mercedes-Benz and stepped out of the car, leaving his wallet in a briefcase on the front seat.

The door of the compact car was standing open. And Michael climbed inside.

CHAPTER 16

It was shortly after noon when Captain Dale Fuerstenberg, chief of the Washington County sheriff's office investigations unit, felt the pager on his belt go off. A deluxe model, the pager could be set to beep or vibrate. Fuerstenberg chose the latter setting. He joked to his detectives that he did it for the thrill.

Fuerstenberg was in his county car, an unmarked Mercury Cougar, having just left a meeting at the state Bureau of Criminal Apprehension in St. Paul. He had driven there from Stillwater, the quiet riverfront town where the sheriff's headquarters were, to try to breathe life into an unsolved murder case. One day in 1979, an eighteen-year-old girl named Marlys Wohlenhaus had come home from school and surprised an intruder, who bludgeoned her savagely with some kind of blunt instrument. She was still drawing breath when they found her, but her brain was dead. With her family's consent, doctors removed the girl from the respirator and let her slip away.

Police had questioned a couple of suspects at the time, but found insufficient evidence to charge anyone with the crime. Now, Fuerstenberg felt that the available leads—including grisly photos of the crime scene—warranted another look. Crime lab capabilities had improved drastically since 1979. Fuerstenberg had deposited the evidence at the BCA, hoping the agency's technicians could tell him something useful.

Fuerstenberg never knew the dead girl, so his motives in reopening the case were strictly professional. Yet on several occasions, as the captain sat at his desk peering at homicide file photos of a vibrant high-school senior who never reached graduation, his eyes had strayed to the bulletin board above his desk where he displayed a photo of his own teenage daughter.

Now Fuerstenberg stopped at a convenience store to use the pay phone. He was a tall man, with the blond hair and mustache of his German ancestry. His manner was laconic, his voice tinged with rural Minnesota's northern twang. Today, because of his meeting, he was wearing a suit and topcoat that offered insufficient protection from the bitter January wind.

On the police radio, Fuerstenberg had heard something about detectives leaving headquarters to investigate a crime scene. The dispatchers avoided discussing specifics on the police radio, which was monitored by newspaper and television reporters. But because it seemed to involve more than two detectives, it was probably something major.

When Fuerstenberg phoned in, the dispatcher told him that all available detectives had scrambled to the composting and water treatment facility at the riverside hamlet of Marine-on-St. Croix. Apparently, the dispatcher said, a maintenance man there had found a piece of a human body.

Fuerstenberg jerked his car into gear and barreled east toward the St. Croix River, Minnesota's border with Wisconsin. Just before he reached it, he turned onto the two-lane stretch of Minnesota Route 95, passing back through Stillwater. The Cougar flashed past snowcapped pine trees, farm entrances, and homemade signs advertising fresh eggs, firewood, and sides of beef—a landscape worthy of a Currier and Ives print, and an unlikely setting for a dismemberment murder.

Fuerstenberg slowed to make the left at the compost-site entrance, then coaxed his car up a steep grade to the top of the hill. There, as he rolled to a stop and climbed out, the captain saw a half-dozen vehicles, mostly unmarked squads.

A group of people was standing around a large brush pile to the west—four or five detectives, a uniformed sheriff's deputy, and a short man in an insulated bodysuit, who was probably the maintenance worker who had reported the crime. As Fuerstenberg approached, Sergeant Investigator Jay Kimble was taking photos of something wedged into the side of the brush pile.

Kneeling with the others, Fuerstenberg could see the severed hip joint of a human leg. Protruding from a black-and-green garbage bag, it was a frozen, bloody mess. The hip socket was visible in the center of grotesquely shredded muscle tissue. There was blood on the branches nearby; it had probably been wedged there while still warm.

Jay Kimble, five-feet-ten and trim, rose to his feet and greeted Fuerstenberg with a grin. Quickly, he filled the captain in. Someone had rammed the gate below. After fixing it, Jack Turner—and here Kimble gestured toward the maintenance man—had seen crows on the brush pile and began poking around. It was Turner who found the leg.

Kimble spoke rapidly and well. As he did, his hands were constantly moving, his eyes darting from side to side and alighting on various people and objects around him. He had a reputation as the best talker in the department and was often the one Fuerstenberg chose to testify when cases went to trial.

Like Fuerstenberg and many other police officers, Kimble had a tendency to chuckle when describing the mayhem he had seen. This was a learned response—a defense mechanism. "When you deal with dead bodies, particularly something that's dismembered or the typical shotgun-to-the-head suicide, you have to deal with your own mortality," Kimble says. "So there's morgue humor, if you will. You have to cope at a level where you can remain professional regardless of the carnage you see."

No one had to tell Jay Kimble or the other detectives the basic axiom of murder-scene investigations. It was simply this: Anything, no matter how small or seemingly inconsequential, might have value in finding the killer. Therefore, detectives were trained to think comprehensively—to find and preserve anything at all the killer may have left behind.

Kimble showed Fuerstenberg three or four red spots in the snow near the brush pile—the stains that Jack Turner had initially thought were deer blood.

Next the detective pointed out the tire tracks that criss-crossed the parking area east of the pile. Kimble had measured the tires of Jack Turner's pickup truck and the squad car that responded to his call, he said. Here, off to the right, were tracks that were too narrow for the truck or the squad. They were the tires of a compact car, Kimble said, possibly the killer's vehicle. He had knelt and blown on them to remove new snow, and then photographed them.

Now, gingerly, the detectives removed the leg from its resting place. It was frozen solid and extended straight, bent only slightly at the knee. It had been inserted foot first into the garbage bag. Big and heavy, covered with reddish-brown hair, it was apparently the leg of a large man.

Fuerstenberg and his men circled the brush pile, searching for more body parts, as Kimble videotaped the proceedings. Visible everywhere in the snow were the three-pronged footprints of crows—the crows Jack Turner had seen, the crows that unwittingly led human beings to this body.

It was Fuerstenberg himself who discovered the second leg, as he climbed to the top the brush pile. Wedged between a couple of logs, it was resting in an identical black-and-green garbage bag. Unlike the other leg, this one was doubled over at the knee. At first, Fuerstenberg thought it was an arm. Nearby, he noticed, were remnants of tinsel from someone's discarded Christmas tree.

A half-hour or more passed before the detectives found anything else. Unlike Fuerstenberg, most of the detectives were wearing heavy coats and hats. Dressed in his suit, light coat, and standard black shoes, Fuerstenberg could feel the wind cutting through him.

Over to the side, north of the main brush pile, Fuerstenberg noticed a smaller pile of tree branches. He turned to Jack Turner, who was standing a few yards away, watching the detectives work.

"Is this the brush from where you were digging out the leg?" he asked.

"No," Turner said.

"I think I know where the rest of him is," Fuerstenberg said.

Fuerstenberg knelt and began pawing through the branches and snow. He, like the others, was wearing latex surgical gloves. Not only did the gloves fail to offer protection from the searing cold; they caused Fuerstenberg's hands to sweat. The sweat froze next to his skin, producing a sensation not unlike placing his hands in a freezer and leaving them there, resting on the frozen metal.

Now Fuerstenberg's fingers reached a hard surface. Its color was beige. As he continued to dig, feeling for the edges of the object, he uncovered the outline of a naked human torso, resting, chest down, in the snow. The neck had been severed just above the shoulders—the legs, just below the buttocks. The arms were still attached, but the forearms had been cut above the wrists. The head and hands were nowhere to be found.

The torso was big and unwieldy, difficult even for several strong men to move. After photographing it, they wrestled it off to one side and lay it beside the legs they had found. Later, a hearse would transport the body parts to the county medical examiner's office.

For hours, the detectives continued to paw through the snow with their latex-gloved hands in a futile search for the head and hands. They took turns, searching for a few minutes, then sitting in one of the cars and thawing their hands by the heater.

Kimble, meanwhile, produced a rake and began dragging it across the red stains in the snow. As he did, the size of the stains seemed to expand. Other detectives approached and stood around Kimble in a half-circle. As Kimble scraped at the red snow, the metallic scent of blood, obscured throughout much of this grisly process by sheer cold, rose to the investigators' nostrils.

In the light of the waning sun, Kimble saw a glint of metal. He dropped to his knees. There he found the gold bridgework of two human teeth, which were still attached to a piece of jawbone. Looking closer, Kimble found the small white buttons of a dress shirt, pieces of what looked like skin and muscle tissue, and a severed fingertip. Each of these, in turn, Kimble picked up gingerly and deposited with his shaking hands into its own plastic bag.

Kimble looked at the men standing above him. This, obviously, was where the dismemberment had taken place, almost certainly while the body was still warm. Eyes met as the detectives pondered the imponderable. They had no way of knowing whether the victim was alive when the dismemberment began.

For a moment, silence hung in the frigid Minnesota twilight.

"Jesus Christ," someone finally said. "What a mess."

Ellen Prozumenshikov was frantic about her husband's disappearance, but she had handled the police interviews with grace and precision. Most of her contact was with Tom Lucas and Jim Decowski, two detectives from the Hennepin County sheriff's office, which was handling the investigation in Minneapolis. They had both been very kind throughout the difficult period.

Ellen wanted, of course, what the detectives couldn't yet give her—answers, an end to the agonizing uncertainty.

It had been two days since Michael disappeared, without any word from kidnappers or anyone else about his whereabouts. Ellen had reported her husband missing the previous Monday night, after his series of mysterious phone calls to her, to his boss, and to some of his clients. He had said that he was trying to raise $200,000 for a client, whose name he wouldn't divulge. He had been speaking in Russian, something he never did in the presence of American clients. He hadn't come home that night. And that was all anyone knew.

It was Jim Tallen, Michael's boss, who suggested that Ellen phone the police, after she called Tallen in a panic at 3 A.M. to report that Michael still wasn't home. The children were in bed, but Ellen had been up all night, waiting by the phone.

At 6:15, Tallen had picked up Ellen at her house. As instructed by the police, they drove to Prudential-Bache to look at Michael's office. Nothing was out of place. There, beside Michael's phone and his computers, was a legal pad with his list of things to do that day. The two of them phoned the police and told the officers they saw nothing suspicious.

Since then, Ellen's house had been swamped with people, police officers, relatives, and others; the phone and doorbell ringing constantly. The phone company had been out to place a trace on the line, in case Michael had been kidnapped and the kidnappers called the house.

The police had found Michael's car in a parking lot abutting Lake Minnetonka's Wayzata Bay, near Sasha's restaurant. In the summertime, boaters used this lot to gain access to a boat ramp; in winter, ice fishermen used it to drive their pickup trucks out onto the lake's frozen surface. Michael's wallet and briefcase were inside the car. Ellen told the police that Michael, when he could help it, never parked his car outdoors.

The next day, Wednesday, Michael's disappearance had been reported in the newspapers and on television. Ellen's house was still populated by well-wishers and relatives, including, at various times, Michael's friend Stuart Kloner and his wife, other friends, Ellen's relatives, and Michael's parents. All day they waited, people scurrying to the kitchen to fetch whatever Ellen and the elderly relatives needed, the nanny helping to watch the children.

At about 6 P.M., the phone rang. When Ellen picked it up, Detective Decowski was on the line. Quietly, in a practiced monotone, Decowski told her that police in Washington County, east of Minneapolis, had found a body. They didn't know whether it was Michael's, he said. Decowski asked where the police could find her husband's medical and dental records. He also wanted to know whether Michael had any scars or other distinguishing marks on his body.

"I told him that he had two scars, one scar he had on the right arm and another one is on his right lower-side abdomen from the appendec-tomy," Ellen said later.

Ellen Prozumenshikov hung up the telephone. Slowly, she turned to face the people gathered in her house.

Susan Roe, a woman in her mid-thirties with sandy-blond hair pulled back in a ponytail, fastened a surgical mask over her face, slipped on a pair of rubber gloves, and approached the autopsy table. Upon the stain-less steel surface lay a vinyl body bag, through which the outline of the irregularly shaped objects inside were vaguely distinguishable. Susan Roe's job, as a forensic pathologist, was death—or, rather, diagnosing its causes. She had learned her craft during a residency at Indiana Univer-sity, where she had followed her husband after medical school in Texas.

The autopsy procedure has two basic components, and on this Thursday morning, Roe was to be relieved of one of them. Typically, the pathologist first made a chest incision, removing and inspecting the internal organs. The second step was an incision from ear to ear and removal of part of the skull, to permit examination of the brain. Today, however, there was no brain available to examine.

All business, Roe unzipped the body bag and pulled it open with her hands. She had examined the body parts briefly yesterday evening when the hearse driver brought them in, the legs still wrapped in their black-and-green garbage bags. They were frozen at the time, but not com-pletely, which told Roe the body had been outside for less than two days before it was found. Because performing an autopsy on frozen flesh was impossible, Roe had left the body parts out, overnight, to thaw.

Now, she noticed, they were still cool to the touch, but pliable enough to begin the procedure. The ragged remains of skin and tissue along the neck, buttocks, and forearms were ghastly in the extreme, but—for the moment, at least—Susan Roe scarcely noticed them.

Roe lay the torso out flat on the table and took a chest X ray. Next she used a circular saw to make a long, vertical incision through the chest and rib cage. The internal organs, she found, were in reasonably good shape, with the exception of the liver, which showed a bit of fatty change. The heart was a little larger than normal, but the arteries around it were not substantially clogged. A great deal of blood remained in the heart, which was fortunate, because blood was needed to perform vari-ous chemical tests.

The internal organs weren't especially pale, so Roe determined quickly that the victim had not bled to death. She also was heartened to see that the soft muscle tissue of the legs and torso contained no excess blood. This, thankfully, meant that the dismemberment had occurred after the victim was dead.

Two stab wounds were visible, one on the right arm and another on the left side of the back. Because these wounds also showed no sign of hemorrhaging, Roe ruled them out as the cause of death. More likely, they occurred by accident, as the killer was hacking up the body. Judging by the lack of chest trauma, the cause of death had probably been a blow or shot to the head.

Now Roe examined the dismemberment sites themselves. The area below the left buttock showed some evidence of regularity, suggesting the use of a heavy blade—for instance, that of an axe or hatchet. Elsewhere the tissue was torn, apparently by the jagged edge of a saw. Roe had seen tears like this before; in one such case, the killer had used an electric circular saw to dismember the body.

The skin of the right side of the torso had taken on a pinkish-purple color. This lividity, which was also visible on the legs, meant that the body had lain on its right side for at least eight hours before the dismemberment occurred.

Later, after washing up, Susan Roe stood before a lighted panel and compared the X ray of the torso to another, older chest X ray obtained by Hennepin County detectives. She was looking for inconsistencies, evidence of physical injuries or degenerative diseases that might have proven that the two X rays were of different people. There were none.

Roe had, earlier, examined the torso for scars. And there they were, in the places Detective Decowski had advised her to look—the appendectomy scar on the abdomen and another jagged scar on the right arm.

The X rays, the scars, the hair color, and body weight—all this left no doubt whatsoever in Susan Roe's mind. This, indeed, was the body of the missing Russian stockbroker, Michael Prozumenshikov.

In the greater Minneapolis brokerage community, in which gossip was a tool of the trade, all manner of rumors and cruel jokes had begun to make the rounds. Michael Prozumenshikov's body had been found, headless, handless, and frozen stiff in a hilltop meadow forty-five miles east of Minneapolis. The brokers who had worked with him at Drexel

Burnham Lambert were suddenly in high demand, called upon by colleagues to recount the stories of his run-ins with clients and to speculate freely about who might have killed him.

One story had it that Michael had led a double life as a gunrunner and that his murder was somehow connected to the Mossad, the Israeli secret service. Another was that he had been executed by the Russian Mafia, for whom he had supposedly been laundering money. This mob group's method of choice for murder was—incorrectly—said to be dismemberment by chainsaw. Among former Drexel brokers, a rumor got around that someone was murdering all the former top producers of Drexel's Minneapolis branch. Yet another tale had it that Michael had been smuggling live sables into the country to make fur coats, and had been murdered after stiffing his suppliers.

At the Minneapolis branch of Kidder Peabody, Mica Duncan's emotions ranged from anguish to anger—the latter directed at both Michael's murderer and the brokers in her branch who were now joking about the state of Michael's body when it was found. "There were a couple of people in here," she says, "that were either insensitive, or they didn't realize how much I cared about Michael, who said some things. You know, you just don't even forgive anybody for something like that."

John Kelly, who had tried to recruit Michael for Shearson Lehman Brothers, was visiting Shearson's Midwest headquarters in Kansas City when he heard, from brokers in Minneapolis, that Michael was dead. Kelly had tried to phone Michael at Prudential-Bache the previous Tuesday, but had been told that he was out. On Wednesday, a police officer had phoned Kelly in Kansas City, asking why Kelly's name was on a pad in Prozumenshikov's house, but refusing to answer any questions in return. Kelly, when he heard what had happened, was shocked and saddened. "This was a nice guy," he says. "I mean, I knew he was aggressive, but I like those kinds of people." Still, Kelly couldn't help being relieved that he had been so cautious about hiring Michael. "Because," he said later, "when you go out and hire somebody, you're saying, 'I vouch for this person.'"

Mike Cochrane, manager of the Smith Barney, Harris Upham Wayzata branch that had rejected Michael, felt similar emotions. "You kind of just thank God for it not happening here," Cochrane says. "It goes through your mind. I think that's natural."

In the sleepy village of Wayzata, Michael's murder was the first anyone could recall for years. For a time, it was the dominant topic of conversation in the shops and restaurants, a tale repeated and embellished incessantly for months afterward. Police visited every company doing business in the three-story Wayzata building that housed Michael's Prudential-Bache Securities branch. The murder had terrorized the people who worked there, because it was apparent from the news accounts that Michael had been abducted immediately after leaving work. And the killer, everyone knew, was still at large. The building's managers changed the after-hours electronic entry system and posted an armed guard in the lobby.

As for Prudential-Bache Securities itself, Michael's murder had come at an unfortunate time—amid the firm's retreat from its bloated 1980s persona, just two weeks before the resignation of its chairman, George Ball. And while the company could have done without another negative story in the newspapers, reporters were everywhere, trying to interview Pru-Bache brokers, Pru-Bache clients, and Jim Tallen, the Wayzata branch manager.

Other than cursory responses to such basic questions as Michael's age and length of tenure at the firm, Prudential's public stance on the murder of Michael Prozumenshikov was silence. Stockbrokers in the Wayzata branch were forbidden to discuss the case with reporters. One such broker phoned William Humphries at Shearson Lehman Brothers to gripe about the lack of trust Prudential was demonstrating in its employees. "Anybody who talks about it loses his job," the broker said.

When a *Wall Street Journal* reporter phoned Jim Tallen asking about Michael's career as a stockbroker, Tallen would say only: "He was a wonderful guy. We're very, very sad about this. It's an awful thing. We have no indication that this has anything to do with any of his dealings here." Tallen then directed the call to a company spokeswoman in New York who had never met Michael and knew nothing about his Russian roots or his rise from poverty.

Many of Michael's clients learned about his murder through the rumor mill or the newspapers. Scott Studwell, for instance, had phoned Michael's office on Tuesday, the morning after he disappeared. "They told me that he wasn't in today, and they didn't know if he was going to be in today," Studwell says. "It was unusual, because he was always there." That night, a friend called Studwell and told him Michael had disappeared. "All of a sudden an alarm went off, and I told my wife, and she was like, 'Oh God, he ran off with all our money,' and this and that. It's just a natural reaction. I didn't feel like that had happened. But at the same time you can't help but wonder where the hell he went." The next day, Studwell phoned Tallen directly, who confirmed that Michael had vanished.

Among Michael's former friends from Leningrad, the reaction to his disappearance testified to the depth of their alienation from him. When Mark Goldburt arrived home from his new job as an engineer one evening, his wife, Stella, was waiting for him.

"Did you know Mike is gone?" she asked in Russian.

"What do you mean 'gone'?" Goldburt said.

"He disappeared," she said.

"What do you mean 'disappeared'?" Goldburt asked, more baffled than before.

"Somebody just called me and said that Mike's disappeared," Stella said. "He didn't show up for a few days at home."

Mark Goldburt stood for a moment in silent contemplation.

"He probably grabbed some money and ran," he said.

The next day, Goldburt's morning newspaper carried a brief news item reporting that a dismembered body had been found in Washington County. It was said to be the body of a heavyset white man, although it hadn't yet been identified as Michael. "I said that this is probably Mike," Goldburt says. "I was not sure, but I suspected that maybe he is involved in something which is not very legal." Goldburt was sad, he says, but not terribly surprised. The prevailing opinion among members of the old Leningrad circle, Goldburt says, was that Michael had gotten involved with the Mafia.

The fire that burned within Captain Brent Running, head of investigations for the Hennepin County sheriff's office in Minneapolis, was visible to others only in the wry smile that played around his lips when he heard a good one. Running's graying hair and slow drawl belied the workings of an agile mind, well-seasoned in the subtleties of evidence and alibis, expert in practical human psychology.

Running was in charge of the massive investigation of Michael Prozumenshikov's murder, an effort in which a half-dozen law enforcement agencies, including the FBI, were assisting. The body had been found in rural Washington County, but Prozumenshikov had apparently been abducted from Wayzata, which was in Hennepin County. So, although the Washington County sheriff's men were helping out, the case was really Running's.

It wasn't every day that the cream of the Wayzata business community wound up dead and dismembered on a compost heap, so the case carried a high profile. It had found its way onto the evening newscasts every night that week. The *Minneapolis Star Tribune*—dubbed "The Red Star" by Running's detectives for its liberal editorial policies—had run it on the front page for two consecutive days.

Under pressure to make an arrest, the detectives were working overtime. Using Prudential-Bache client lists and other names found on legal pads at Michael's home and office, they were phoning literally dozens of his clients and acquaintances all over Minnesota.

There were a number of unique aspects to the case, a couple of which were Prozumenshikov's exotic ethnic background and his remarkable professional success. Only seven years earlier, Running's detectives learned, the man had been working as a janitor. Now he was living in an $800,000 house in one the region's swankiest suburbs. He drove a Mercedes-Benz and had been carrying fifteen credit cards in his wallet at the time of his death. Prozumenshikov apparently had been a devoted family man.

Another extraordinary twist was the number of people with plausible motives for the crime: the unabashed hatred for the man among people in his own immigrant community. Many of Prozumenshikov's former clients told police they had lost money investing with him. Four of his countrymen had sued him unsuccessfully for restitution of trading losses. To Running, what was most astonishing was the number of people who said openly that they weren't sorry he was dead.

Clement Seifert, the old man who had lost his life savings by investing with Michael, had shocked the detective who visited his house by saying that he knew his grievances against Prozumenshikov made him a suspect in the murder. When the detective assured Seifert to the contrary, Seifert had added something: He wanted to testify in defense of the murderer, if and when he was caught. "It's not that I condone murder," Seifert said calmly. "It's just that you should understand how badly this guy treated people."

Running's detectives had heard every rumor—from the Russian Mafia tale to the multiple revenge slaying scenario, in which a group of angry people with motives to kill Prozumenshikov were said to have teamed up to do the deed, as in the Agatha Christie novel, *Murder on the Orient Express*.

Running himself didn't give much credence to these stories, though they were getting plenty of play among Prozumenshikov's stockbroker colleagues. The Russian Mafia theory was out because this clearly wasn't a professional hit. It was too sloppy. Just up the road from the compost site, a passerby had found the murderer's bloody hatchet. At Taylor's Falls, Minnesota, on a bridge leading across the St. Croix River to Wisconsin, someone had found Prozumenshikov's $16,000 gold Rolex watch.

It was Running's feeling that whoever cut up the body had been operating in a state of high panic. This is how Running pieced it together: The killer, probably someone Prozumenshikov knew, had abducted him as he left his office Monday evening. Possibly at gunpoint, the killer had forced Prozumenshikov to make a series of phone calls, trying to raise $200,000.

After failing at this, the stockbroker was murdered a few hours after his abduction, probably by a blow or a shot to the head. Early the next morning, the killer drove to the compost site, where he dismembered the body using a hatchet and a hand saw. Running tried to imagine the killer's frantic emotions as he drove north on Route 95, stopping every few miles to hurl evidence from his car. Divers had been up and down the icy stretch of the St. Croix River beneath the Taylor's Falls bridge, searching without success for Prozumenshikov's head and hands. Possibly, these body parts were in Wisconsin somewhere, lying in the woods.

Most likely was the possibility that some disgruntled former client had killed Michael. But where to start? The detectives had located a dozen angry people in only the first day of phoning around.

Although Ellen Prozumenshikov didn't know it, she was not the only woman living in the western suburbs of Minneapolis who had reported her husband missing the previous Monday night. That night, when Zachary Persitz failed to show up at home by nine o'clock, his wife, Julia, had made a series of phone calls to friends and relatives trying to find him. It was very unlike Zack to come home late, and even more unusual for him not to call.

Julia had phoned Zachary's boss at the Department of Natural

Resources, Craig Regalia, who told her that Zack had said something about inspecting the Gray's Bay dam on Lake Minnetonka. This sent Julia into a panic. She knew how thorough her husband was in his inspections. Maybe he had walked out onto the ice to get a better look, and fallen through it into the icy water of the lake.

Julia phoned Alex Shifrin, Zack's half brother, and asked him to call the Minnetonka Police Department. Sensing the edge in Julia's voice, Alex obliged. Within an hour, a squad car for the state highway patrol rolled past Gray's Bay dam looking for Persitz. The trooper saw nothing amiss.

Julia phoned Rudy Lekhter's house and spoke to Rudy's wife, Margarita. Margarita said she hadn't heard from Zachary, but would have Rudy stop by the house and wait with Julia until Zack arrived. Alex Shifrin also volunteered to come over and wait, though his wife was expecting a baby at any moment.

When Zachary's Mazda finally eased up the driveway of his house at 11:30 P.M., both Julia and Rudy were waiting for him. As her husband stepped out of the car, Julia flew into a rage, her cheeks stained with tears. "I was shouting," Julia says. "I didn't want to hear anything. I just wanted to let it out."

Uncomfortable in the middle of a family fight, Lekhter said his good-byes and departed. Only minutes after Rudy left, Alex Shifrin showed up. Julia, Alex says, was still crying and demanding to know why Zachary hadn't called. Zack, Alex says, mumbled something about working late and held up a file folder full of papers. Eager to get back to his pregnant wife, Alex stayed for only a few minutes.

Julia, finished with her outburst but still furious, turned her back on Zachary, fetched some blankets and pillows, and arranged a makeshift bed on the living-room sofa. When she retired there, he didn't try to dissuade her. Her husband, as far as she knew, went to bed in the couple's upstairs bedroom. At about midnight, Zachary phoned Regalia to tell his boss that he was home. He was sorry his wife had bothered him earlier, he said, and he would see Regalia the next day at the office.

Since that night, fear had come upon Julia Persitz in a silent wave. Michael, she learned the next day, had also failed to come home after work. The coincidence of Zack's absence and Michael's disappearance that night "absolutely terrified" Julia, though she didn't confront Zachary about it.

By Thursday, the positive identification of Michael's body was in the newspapers and on television. On that day, Julia phoned Ellen Prozumenshikov to offer her condolences. She was so sorry, she said. She wanted to know what she could do to help.

Ellen's son, Daniel, had been invited to a birthday party Saturday for Daniel Persitz. Now, Julia offered to care for Danny Prozumenshikov throughout the weekend, if it would make things easier for Ellen. After asking her son whether he wanted to go early to the Persitzes, Ellen agreed. The Prozumenshikov boy would spend two nights and three days at the Persitz home.

At one point, Ellen Prozumenshikov phoned the house to ask how Danny was doing. Ellen heard ringing on the line, then two voices saying hello, as Zachary and Julia picked up separate phones simultaneously.

"Zack," Julia said sharply, "put the phone down."

Zachary, to Ellen Prozumenshikov's amazement, hadn't called to express his sorrow about Michael's death. Now, given the opportunity to speak to her, he simply hung up.

"It was strange," Ellen said later. "I thought he has a heart for this kind of situation."

On Monday morning, one week after Michael Prozumenshikov's disappearance, two detectives from the Washington County sheriff's office, Jack Nelson and Ted Preisler, drove to Minneapolis. There, they sat down over Styrofoam cups of coffee with their counterparts at the Hennepin County sheriff's office, Al Anderson and Bob Salitros. Over the weekend, Nelson said, a telephone tip had come in. Maybe it was something, or maybe it was nothing.

An employee of a St. Paul car wash had phoned the Washington County switchboard over the weekend. He reported that a man had come to the car wash the previous Tuesday morning, demanding that the staff help him clean his trunk. When the staff moved to oblige, they could see that the carpeted interior of the trunk was matted with a thick red liquid that looked like blood. At first, the man had denied it was blood. Then he had said it was deer blood.

As this suspicious figure left the car wash, someone had thought to take down his license-plate number. Everyone had forgotten about the episode until they saw a report about a dismemberment murder on the evening news.

The car wash employee didn't remember much about the man, only that he was tall, thin, and unshaven, and he had a temper. Visibly agitated while he waited for the staff to help him, he had snapped at them for working too slowly. Then he had pitched in himself, using his bare hands to pull out big chunks of frozen blood and dropping them by a drain to melt.

There was one other thing, the employee said. The man had a thick foreign accent of some kind.

By the next morning, the brokerage community's rumor mill was buzzing with new information. The police were said to have arrested a suspect in Prozumenshikov's murder.

Mica Duncan heard it, as did many of the stockbrokers who had worked with Michael at Drexel Burnham Lambert. Reports on the local all-news radio station confirmed the rumor: Hennepin County Sheriff Don Omodt had scheduled a 1 P.M. press conference to announce an arrest and to release the suspect's name.

Shortly before the appointed hour, Duncan phoned her friend Mark Stein, the young stockbroker with whom she and Michael Prozumenshikov had briefly shared their office at Drexel. Stein was now working at Shearson Lehman Brothers, whose Minneapolis branch was in the same downtown skyscraper as Mica's Kidder Peabody branch. Duncan had heard from a friend, she told Stein, that the killer's last name began with the letter P.

The two of them tuned their radios to the news station, chatting as they awaited the beginning of the news conference. As they talked, Duncan hauled out her old Drexel Burnham rolodex.

Now she began flipping through the "P" file, reading off names to Stein on the phone. They discussed each of Michael's former clients in turn, debating whether it was possible that this or that investor had committed the appalling crime.

After ruling out a half-dozen potential suspects, Mica's fingers came to rest on one especially dog-eared card. In clear, penciled letters, it bore the name Zachary Persitz.

Even Mark Stein remembered Persitz—the cold stares and icy

reproach during Zachary's occasional quarrels with Michael. He was wound tight, all right. Maybe he was the guy.

Duncan considered the idea for a moment, then discarded it.

"It couldn't be him," she retorted, her fingers resuming their stroll through the rolodex. "He's too much of a pussy."

CHAPTER 17

The day of Michael Prozumenshikov's funeral was unseasonably warm for early February, though a gentle rain fell steadily outside the Temple Israel synagogue. More than 150 came to pay their respects, a mix of Prozumenshikov's relatives, colleagues, clients, and former friends from Leningrad. The rabbi's service was brief but eloquent—a tribute to Michael's professional achievements and his devotion to his family. Much of it was addressed directly to Daniel Prozumenshikov, Michael's son.

There were three personal eulogies, each delivered by a non-Russian friend of the deceased. Stuart Kloner, the one-time Mercedes-Benz salesman, began by describing Michael's pleasure in purchasing his sedan four years earlier. Kloner's description of the transaction raised eyebrows among some of the Russians present. Michael had told these people he bought the car used, for a bargain price, from a man in Chicago; Kloner, apparently unaware of the lie, divulged that Michael had bought the car new.

Next were talks by Steve Engler, a friend from Michael's Drexel Burnham days, and Michael's last boss, Jim Tallen. "The message I got," a former colleague said, "was that nobody knew the guy. Nobody had any idea what was going on, really, with him. He was a mystery to everyone. The only stuff they could talk about was how successful he'd been."

Later, the long line of automobiles in the funeral cortege rolled slowly down Third Avenue and turned into the Temple Israel Memorial Park. The cemetery was a large plot of land on a hillside, dotted with markers and tall oak trees. Michael's grave lay beneath a smaller maple tree, a sapling that, as it grew, would shade the grassy spot for many summers to come. A bench was provided for the Prozumenshikov family, beneath a small tent to shelter them from the drizzle.

As the coffin was lowered into the grave and the rabbi spoke final funeral rites, Joseph Prozumenshikov, Michael's father, rose from his seat. The elderly man raised a clenched fist into the air, weeping disconsolately and wailing in both Russian and English. "My son," he cried, his voice resounding above the hushed congregation. "They have taken my only son."

For Joseph Prozumenshikov and the rest of Michael's immediate family, the funeral date—February 7, 1991—would be enshrined forever in tribute and remembrance.

And for Zachary Persitz, confined in a narrow cell at the Hennepin County courthouse, the day was no less significant. Julia Persitz marked the occasion by bringing Zachary's children to visit him in jail. Quietly, peering through a thick glass panel and speaking into a telephone receiver, ten-year-old Daniel Persitz wished his father a happy fortieth birthday.

Of all the works of men, murder is the loneliest. Whether for the thrill, for money, or for revenge, the act transports its practitioner to a space only he can occupy, isolating him from family, friends, and his most basic nature.

Zachary Persitz sat alone in his cell and agonized silently over his mistakes. He could see now that he had made many of them in his blinding panic and haste. Torturing himself with the details did no good, but Persitz couldn't help it.

Zachary's thoughts returned to the small, sterile motel room in Rochester, Minnesota, seventy miles southeast of Minneapolis. He and his boss, Craig Regalia, had inspected a dam together that afternoon, and they had more to visit the next day. The two of them checked in at Rochester's Best Western Inn, sharing a room to save money for the state.

They had been there no more than fifteen minutes when the pounding came at the door. Zachary was the one who opened it. On the doorstep of the second-floor balcony stood a group of four stern-faced men, one of whom held up a badge and identified himself as James Decowski, a detective for the Hennepin County sheriff's office. The others rattled off their names as well.

As from a great distance, Persitz heard himself agreeing to answer some questions, even as he watched two of the police officers lead Regalia out of the room. That, Zachary realized now, had been a mistake. He should have refused to talk.

The pair of them started in, asking him where he had spent the previous Monday night and Tuesday morning.

These were questions Persitz had anticipated, though not nearly so soon, and the answers came out easily. After work, he said, he had gone to see the movie *Green Card* at the Shelard Cinema. After the movie, he had driven home and remained there all night. The next morning, he had arrived at the office at 9 A.M. and worked through the day, eating lunch in the canteen.

Pressed for details by Decowski, Persitz added that on his way to the movie he had stopped at Children's Palace, a toy store, to look at a bike for his son. Asked about the car he had been driving, Zachary mentioned his brown Mazda sedan.

Much of what happened next had become a haze in Zachary's mind. For as Decowski's mouth continued to move, a vortex had opened beneath Zachary's feet and he had seemed to plunge into it, as in a dream of falling, the room spiraling around him as he fell. When he landed, he was still in the motel room, staring into Decowski's face.

"When did you last wash your car?" Decowski demanded. It was the second time he had asked the question.

Zachary said nothing. And now Decowski's lips were moving again, advising that Persitz should think carefully before answering because his response was very important.

Three weeks ago, Zachary finally blurted. His wife, Julia, had washed it.

Rapidly, the detectives charged on through their questions. Had he ever taken a vacation with Michael Prozumenshikov? He had. Had he been Prozumenshikov's brokerage client? Yes. Was he satisfied with the service he received? He was.

Decowski now informed Persitz he could place him at a car wash within blocks of his office on the previous Tuesday. Why hadn't Persitz mentioned this before?

They knew, Zachary realized suddenly. They knew it all, and they were trying to hound him into confessing. He wouldn't give them the pleasure.

"I forgot," was all he said.

The air in the small motel room was too hot to breathe. Persitz was licking his lips with a dry tongue. His eyes were blinking rapidly. He asked for a glass of water, and one of the detectives got up to fetch it for him.

The questioning went on for an hour before the two detectives finally got to the point. They didn't believe his story. They believed that he was the man who killed Michael Prozumenshikov.

After more questions—Zachary barely remembered what they were—the detectives had placed him under arrest and read him his rights, including his right to remain silent. But it was much too late for that. Persitz had long since incriminated himself by agreeing to answer questions without being arrested.

"This is really . . . this is a misunderstanding," Persitz sputtered. "If, you know, you'd let me talk to my wife, I could clear this misunderstanding up."

Ignoring his request, they handcuffed him, hands behind his back, and led him down to the street. He rode to Minneapolis in the back of an unmarked police car. Later, a man had come to take samples of his blood, saliva, and hair, including pubic hair.

Zachary Persitz had not seen his boss again that night, but Craig Regalia had nevertheless been busy. Until 4 A.M., when Regalia finally drove home to his wife, the detectives peppered him with questions about work schedules, state-owned hatchets, and rubber suits.

Julia Persitz had relied, since this waking nightmare began, on her considerable reserve of inner strength and her sense of loyalty to the man with whom she had shared her life for fifteen years. She took comfort in one basic conviction: Despite the unexplained circumstances of her husband's absence on the evening of January 28, she simply refused to believe that the gentle father of her two children could possibly have done anything like this.

Just days earlier, Julia had phoned Ellen Prozumenshikov to ask about Danny Prozumenshikov's first day back at school after the murder. Fifteen minutes later, the doorbell rang—the musical doorbell that Zachary specially installed for Julia when the house was built. The men waiting outside bore grim news.

Now Julia Persitz was looking for the best lawyer money could buy, though she had little of her own to pay him. After interviewing a series of the most famous trial attorneys in the state, Julia settled on Joe Friedberg, a short, pear-shaped, former encyclopedia salesman. Friedberg, after a series of splashy murder acquittals and other courtroom coups, had acquired a reputation as Minnesota's smartest criminal lawyer.

There was, for instance, the 1974 case of Ammanuel Ambaye, an African exchange student who admitted killing his roommate, disemboweling him, and draping his intestines throughout their apartment. For him, Friedberg had won an acquittal on grounds of insanity. A string of long-odds victories followed, prompting one prosecutor Friedberg bested to declare him a miracle worker. Once, the *Minneapolis Star Tribune* reported, Friedberg had slapped down a pair of $100 bills before the start of a trial in which he was the defense attorney and said to the prosecutor, "Two hundred dollars says I'll kick your ass." Less sensationally, Friedberg had also won groundbreaking awards for women whose bodies he claimed had been damaged by the Dalkon shield birth control device.

Friedberg operated his own firm and had no partners, so that no judge could force him to hand off a case to another attorney if he was busy with something else. In his office hung a photo of an old-style electric chair, with its metal cap and leather restraining straps. It symbolized Friedberg's heartfelt opposition to capital punishment. He was gratified that Minnesota had no death penalty.

On another wall was a photo of his first racehorse, Shared Reflections. Near it he displayed a unique collection of coffee mugs, including one that said "WARREN BURGER EATS QUICHE." Another bore the caption "HUNG JURY," beneath a drawing of twelve well-endowed male jurors.

For his services to the Persitz family, Friedberg charged a flat fee of $150,000, which covered everything except the appeal—if Persitz was found guilty. Relatives pooled their resources to help Julia come up with $65,000, and Friedberg agreed to accept the rest when Julia sold her home, which she immediately put on the market.

To compensate for his lack of partners, Friedberg often contracted out legal work to other firms. His cocounsel in the Persitz case was to be a young criminal lawyer named Paul Engh—a tall, lanky man who guarded his emotions carefully, Friedberg's opposite in both appearance and temperament.

The final member of the Persitz defense team was Bill O'Keefe, a private investigator Friedberg had used often in the past. O'Keefe, the son of a newspaper reporter, worked exclusively for lawyers, helping them to construct their defenses. He was a seasoned professional, good at his job, a man hardened by years of grueling leg work.

The prosecutor in the case was Kevin Johnson, a successful and politically ambitious assistant county attorney. Johnson, a Republican, had recently lost a statewide election for attorney general to the latest incarnation of Minnesota's most prominent political family, the Humphreys, of Hubert Humphrey fame. He was a member of the Hennepin County attorney's three-man special prosecutions unit that handled most of the murders and sensational drug and sex crimes.

Kevin Johnson had a strong case against Zachary Persitz, the result of terrific police work by Hennepin and Washington County detectives. It was the strongest case, in fact, that either Johnson or Joe Friedberg had seen in some time.

For starters, three employees of the Downtowner Car Wash in St. Paul had identified Persitz as the man who instructed them to clean blood out of his car trunk on the morning of Tuesday, January 29.

In Zachary's house, police had found records attesting to the sorry state of his family finances at the time of the murder. They also found a receipt for a pair of handcuffs, purchased a month before the murder at a police supply store.

In Zack's appointment calendar, along with his notes to himself about an upcoming math test his son was to take, police found a number of notations about handguns. On his desk at the Department of Natural Resources, the page of the yellow pages reserved for gun stores also showed some notations—"9 mm luger" read one black-inked scrawl; ".357" read another.

When detectives impounded Zachary's car, it was in bad shape. The hood was scratched and dented, and technicians found traces of red paint in the abrasions that matched the red paint of the compost-site gate. Moreover, a triangular piece of bronze plastic found at the compost site appeared to fit a similarly shaped hole in the grill of Zachary's car.

Inside, the car reeked of urine, an indication that Prozumenshikov's dead body might have voided itself there. The driver's seat had been cut out and replaced with a boat cushion. On the ceiling, floor, and rear-view mirror were droplets of blood which a crime-lab technician said were consistent with the blowback splatter pattern common in close-range gunshot wounds to the head.

An attendant at the Washington County compost site had identified Zack as having visited the site the summer before the murder. Persitz, she said, had been asking a lot of questions about what happened to the brush pile there, including when and how often they burned it. She said she had seen the official seal of the Department of Natural Resources on the side of the car he was driving.

A coworker at Zachary's office had told detectives that during the week before the murder, Persitz had been asking where he could find a rubberized suit to avoid getting wet when he inspected a dam. A bloody hatchet had been found near the compost site that matched one missing from Persitz's locker at work. The police had even obtained a search warrant to clip hair from the Persitz family's dog, to see if it matched hair stuck to a blood-smeared plastic tarp found at the compost site.

And the briefcase Zack had with him when he was arrested contained a copy of the local movie listings, opened to a page advertising the movie, *Green Card*, the one he told police he had attended on the night of Michael's murder.

It was an avalanche of evidence, Joe Friedberg told Paul Engh and Bill O'Keefe as the three of them sat discussing the case in Friedberg's office. It suggested an obvious pattern of premeditation, which was necessary for the prosecution to prove murder in the first degree. Friedberg would have to try to dispel the impression in court: Zack, coolly planning the murder for weeks or even months in advance. Michael, sitting in the driver's seat of Zachary's car, his hands cuffed, possibly behind his back. Michael, unable to raise the $200,000 Zack demanded. Michael, helpless and prone, shot in the head, execution-style, at point-blank range. Zachary, having prepared in advance to cut up Michael's body by obtaining a rubber suit.

From Friedberg's point of view, the clumsy disposal of the body wasn't surprising. In the real world, he knew, instances of murdered people "vanishing without a trace" were rare. Never having been in such a position, most people failed to grasp the problems associated with disposing of a body. Even the most isolated hiding place could, and probably would, be found.

Still, police had never found the head and hands of Michael Prozumenshikov. More significantly for the prosecution, the murder weapon itself was also missing.

And even in the face of all this evidence, Zachary doggedly denied killing Michael. He told his defense team a complicated story about being duped by a hit man for the Italian Mafia into helping with the murder of Prozumenshikov. Meeting with Bill O'Keefe five times a week, Persitz had supplied the private investigator with exhaustive, vivid details, including the color and model of the car the man had driven and the fact, Zachary said, that the man let slip that he had flown in from Nevada. Persitz had even supplied O'Keefe with a sketch of a heavyset, bearded suspect.

At first, no one on the defense team believed him. But as the days passed and he stuck to his story, O'Keefe decided to look into some of the details. Amazingly, the investigator's efforts met with considerable success. He actually found a suspect with an Italian name who more or less matched up to Zachary's description of the hit man. He had flown into Minneapolis from Reno just before Michael's murder and flown back just after it. In Minneapolis, he had rented a car similar to the one Zack described. The man was said by people to whom O'Keefe spoke in Reno to resemble the sketch Zack had helped to prepare.

One by one, Bill O'Keefe, Paul Engh, and Friedberg's wife and personal assistant, Carolyn Friedberg, came around to the opinion that Zack might be telling the truth. Joe Friedberg himself still didn't buy it. By mid-March, Joe was taking a lot of grief from the others about his stubbornness. As a final test, Friedberg asked Zack to submit to a polygraph test, administered by a former FBI polygraph expert. Zack agreed and passed the test with flying colors. Finally, Friedberg himself reluctantly conceded that Persitz might be telling the truth.

Then, one morning, O'Keefe received an urgent phone call from Carolyn Friedberg, who told him the police apparently had made some kind of a breakthrough in the case. O'Keefe had better get down to the county attorney's office right away, she said.

When O'Keefe arrived, Kevin Johnson informed him that detectives had found the murder weapon at Rudy Lekhter's house, a .357 magnum revolver that conclusively linked Persitz to the killing. In an interview with detectives, Lekhter, a friend of Zack's, had admitted that he and Zack had fired weapons at a gun range on the day before Michael's murder and that Zack had borrowed a gun from Rudy at that time. Though his expression remained impassive, O'Keefe was furious. In an instant, all his hard work for these past two months had been rendered worthless.

Fuming, O'Keefe rode the elevator down to the street and strode two hundred yards to the county courthouse where Persitz was incarcerated. Friedberg had obtained a court order allowing O'Keefe and Persitz to have face-to-face "contact visits" the police couldn't overhear.

Finally, after clearing the security checks, O'Keefe was alone with Persitz. The old story was out the window, he said bluntly. The police had found the murder weapon. And that meant all the work O'Keefe and Friedberg had done chasing Zack's phony tale was wasted. Now, O'Keefe said, he wanted to know the truth. Zack's only chance of avoiding the minimum sentence of thirty hard years in prison, he said, was to trust the legal team Julia was paying so much money to try to help him.

Persitz showed no emotion, but neither did he immediately answer O'Keefe's question. Instead, he began asking O'Keefe a series of questions of his own. He wanted to know the details Rudy had told the police. What had Rudy divulged about the gun range, for instance?

"Enough," O'Keefe snapped. "I'm not going to answer your questions so that you can bullshit me and tell me a creative lie. I want to know what really happened."

Suddenly, the wall came down. Zachary's tale began spilling out. Persitz roamed freely through the years, chronicling Michael's taunts and his own bitterness over the broker's handling of his family's money. Persitz raged for more than an hour, almost oblivious to O'Keefe, letting out the storm of emotions he had been containing for so long.

The climax was a harrowing account of what happened on the night of January 28, to which O'Keefe listened in stunned silence. For the first time, O'Keefe says, he understood the depth of Zachary's hatred for Michael Prozumenshikov.

That night, O'Keefe and Joe Friedberg met with Julia Persitz at Friedberg's sumptuous suburban home. There they pressed Julia harder than they had in the past. The old defense, based on trying to prove

Zack's innocence, was finished, they said. Now they were going to have to devise a completely new strategy. Again and again, the two of them hammered home the point that whatever happened, Zack's life would never be the same. Both Julia and her husband had to learn to trust their defense team implicitly and tell them everything they knew if any kind of effective defense was to be devised.

Julia continued to protest that she knew nothing, only that Zack had come home late that night and asked her to meet him at the YMCA the next day with a change of clothes. Both O'Keefe and Friedberg, they say, could see that she was telling the truth.

This left only one conclusion: Zack's antipathy for Michael was a cancer that had grown quietly inside him for years. It was an aspect of Zack's secret life, the side he showed to no one, not even his wife.

It was after the police found the .357 magnum that Joe Friedberg began seriously to consider the seldom-used mental illness defense. As Friedberg knew, demonstrating that a given defendant meets the so-called McLaughlin standard of psychological disturbance—basically, an inability to distinguish right from wrong—is exceedingly difficult.

There was some history of mental illness in the Persitz family, including stays at a Russian mental institution by both Zachary and his mother, Maria Shifrin. Zack's brother Leonard had been diagnosed as a manic depressive and hospitalized, off and on, at a local psychiatric facility. In court, it might be effective to place Leonard on the witness stand and have him describe incidents such as the occasion on which he stood on the median of an interstate highway and removed his clothes, trying to give them to passing motorists, Friedberg thought. The insanity plea was the defense of last resort, but now the last resort was all Friedberg had left.

In the past fifty years in Hennepin County, there had been only two insanity acquittals. But Joe Friedberg was willing to take the chance because—as it happened—he had won both of them.

Ellen Prozumenshikov was growing tired of the excuses and the interminable delays. More than a year had passed since Michael's murder, and still the case went nowhere.

Financially, Ellen's future was secure. Because of her husband's forethought in providing his family with high-yield life insurance policies, Ellen told Mica Duncan she was going to be able to keep the house she had shared with Michael. She sold his Mercedes to her brother, Duncan says, but kept many of their mutual possessions, including the artwork Michael had loved so much. Still, Ellen told the prosecutor, Kevin Johnson, she felt she couldn't rest until Persitz was permanently behind bars.

Ellen called Johnson weekly to check on the progress of the case. At the beginning, she had called nearly every day, asking for updates or informing the prosecutor of anything she felt was pertinent. The insanity defense of Persitz, when Friedberg divulged it during a court hearing, seemed to worry Ellen. She had seen an article in the *Star Tribune* in which Joe Friedberg told a reporter he had obtained records of Zachary's stay in a Leningrad mental institution. It was Ellen's contention that Persitz had entered the institution solely to avoid military service, Johnson says.

"You have to understand what these people are like," Ellen told Johnson. "In Russia you learn every day how to try to defeat the system. Persitz was very good at that." Moreover, she said, the records of the institutionalization were suspect. With the former Soviet Union now mired in political chaos, any kind of document could be had there for the right price.

On another day, Ellen phoned Johnson after reading a news story about the Jeffrey Dahmer dismemberment-murder case being tried in Milwaukee. The article reported that Dahmer theoretically could be freed within a year if found not guilty by reason of insanity. She wondered if the same were true for Zachary. Technically, yes, Johnson admitted. But it never worked out that way. Even if acquitted on the grounds of mental illness, he said, Persitz was likely to spend most of his life confined in an institution.

Trial dates had repeatedly been scheduled and scrapped as Joe Friedberg tried to obtain additional medical records from Russia. Soon, though, Johnson was able to call Ellen with heartening news about the insanity plea. An employee at the Department of Natural Resources had come forward, the prosecutor said, to report that Zack told coworkers he had avoided the draft in Russia by feigning mental illness.

As the latest trial date, August 1992, approached, Ellen phoned Johnson to express her concern "that her husband's reputation would be sullied during the trial," Johnson says. He told her he would make an attempt to have any evidence about Michael's career or dealings with other clients than Persitz excluded as irrelevant.

By August, the defense still wasn't ready. Hennepin County Judge Robert Schiefelbein, who would be presiding over the case when it finally went to trial, granted another continuance. Schiefelbein had a good reason for being so lenient about the trial dates: He wanted all conceivable evidence to be present at the trial so he wouldn't have to retry the case later if new evidence was found. The judge set a new trial date of January 11, 1993, but that too, would be abandoned in its turn. It would be June 1993, more than two years after Michael's death, before the trial actually began.

Ellen Prozumenshikov had not seen Julia Persitz since the day in February 1991 when Ellen picked up her son after his weekend at the Persitz household. They themselves had not built the wall that stood between them, but they both acknowledged its presence. Once the best of friends, sharing their mutual experiences of marriage, career, and childbirth, they would never speak to one another again.

For Julia Persitz, life had become a daily struggle. Her house had remained on the market for months without selling. When she finally closed a deal in September 1992, Julia felt she was getting less than it was worth—about $250,000. She kept nothing from the sale; paying off the mortgage accounted for most of the proceeds, and the rest went to Joe Friedberg. With her two children, she moved into a much smaller townhouse in the nearby suburb of Plymouth.

At the beginning, Julia had declined interviews with journalists, although one local television reporter had managed to capture her on tape by speaking to her at her door while a cameraman photographed the conversation using a telephoto lens. Later, Friedberg encouraged Julia to cooperate with the media. It would help, he said, in getting out Zachary's side of the story.

A contingent of the Russian community, including some of Michael Prozumenshikov's disgruntled clients, had emerged as Julia's supporters. They helped out in any way they could, as did members of Julia's orchestra. A group of fellow musicians had even offered to play a concert to raise money for Zachary's defense, but Friedberg advised against it. The musicians might not like it, the lawyer suggested, when her husband admitted the gruesome crime in court.

As for Zachary, seeing him was a source of endless heartache for Julia. His eyes were pale and lifeless, rimmed by dark circles, and he had put on a paunch. Unlike O'Keefe, Julia was allowed no "contact visits." When she saw Zachary, it was always through a glass wall. She nevertheless took the children to see their father often. "He tried to cover the pain he had, and it was very hard for him, especially when the kids were there," she says.

Despite her misfortunes, Julia refused to pity herself. She took comfort, she says, from her children—especially her elder son, Daniel, who was handling the situation better than anyone could have expected.

"I think I'm lucky," Julia said. "Daniel is such a good kid."

By now, Zachary Persitz was an old hand at legal limbo. He understood that Friedberg was in no hurry to try the case, and also grasped his attorney's reasons. In addition to the very real efforts to obtain officially authorized records of his stay at Leningrad's Pavlov Medical Institute, Friedberg felt it would be best to let the publicity die down. The case would fall out of the community's consciousness, and any popular sentiment for retribution would fade away in procedural delays.

But that didn't make his life any easier. The sensation that his imprisonment was a dream from which he would awake had long since passed. With it had gone most of Zachary's hope for an improvement of his lot. Yet the strong sense of unreality, of dreamlike disbelief, remained.

Jail was an utterly dehumanizing experience. In his cell, a video camera monitored Zachary's every move, including his use of the small toilet. There were many squabbles in jail, usually about what the prisoners would watch on television. In one such confrontation, Persitz had broken his hand. The small lockup at the Hennepin County courthouse, where Persitz spent more than two years, had a reputation as an especially hard place to do time because it lacked the outdoor exercize and work facilities of a larger prison.

But from Zachary's point of view, the daily monotony of cell block 7-E was his ally. "He didn't want to go to the gym, or drink coffee," says a fellow prisoner. "He didn't want his mind activated. He wanted to dull, kill his mind because if he started to think of his situation he'd get depressed."

Zack filled some of his time by writing poems and making collages for his children, cutting out pictures from the magazines available in the jail. "He said his children, and watching them grow up, was the only thing that kept him going," the fellow inmate says. One disturbing collage he chose not to give to his two sons juxtaposed photos of smiling children against cautionary snippets of the ditty, "Don't Sit Under the Apple Tree (With Anyone Else But Me)." At the bottom was a picture of a violin, beside a few bars of another song, "I Don't Care What Becomes of Me."

Occasionally, Joe Friedberg approached Kevin Johnson about the possibility of a plea bargain, with Zack agreeing to plead guilty to a lesser crime than first-degree murder. Johnson rebuffed these appeals, both because of the strength of his case and the fact that Ellen Prozumenshikov was dead-set against it. "Even though Persitz had zero criminal background and probably wouldn't murder again," Johnson said, "he committed a first-degree murder, and it was my obligation to convict him of what he was guilty of."

Persitz had undergone a series of interviews with psychiatrists and taken tests designed to determine whether he was, now or in the past, mentally ill. The prosecution's psychiatrist, Carl Malmquist, concluded that Zack's personality was obsessive-compulsive, but said he wasn't legally insane. Other psychiatrists retained by Friedberg painted a bleaker picture; they said Zack was compulsive with paranoid and psychotic features.

In interviews with these mental health professionals, Persitz described the events of the night of Michael's murder. It was Paul Engh, the lawyer assisting Friedberg, who noted that listening to Zachary talk about that night was like watching him describe a movie he had seen—as if his truest self had been off to the side, watching as some other phantom committed acts of unspeakable barbarism.

While in jail that fall of 1992, Zack spent much of his time with a Minneapolis millionaire named Russell Lund, heir to the local Lunds grocery-store chain. Lund was accused of murdering his estranged wife and her boyfriend. Persitz and Lund found they had things in common. Both had been indicted on first-degree murder charges, and both were represented by defense attorney Joe Friedberg. The two of them holed up together whenever possible, speaking earnestly and quietly for long periods.

In November, Russell Lund was transferred to the psychiatric unit of a local hospital. Within days, reports came back to the jail that Lund had suffocated himself by securing a plastic garbage bag over his head. Persitz was impressed, he later told a psychiatrist. He added that he thought he heard Lund speaking to him from the grave. "Come join me buddy," Persitz said Lund beseeched him. "We'll be together again like we were before."

Four days later, Zachary cut the bottom out of a garbage bag in a jail common area. He removed his pants, placed the bag over his head, and tried to secure the plastic around his neck by knotting his pants leg. Within moments, a jail guard had spotted the suicide attempt and was pulling the bag from his head. As a result, Persitz was transferred to a locked psychiatric unit of the Hennepin County Medical Center for observation and treatment, under the fictitious name of David Hammerstein.

In the cell, Zachary left a rambling, handwritten suicide note, begging forgiveness from his wife and children, his mother and brothers, and Ellen Prozumenshikov and her children. "There is only so much grief and pain that a human could take," the note read. "Even animals (such as elephants) die out of grief, even wild beasts that are very strong and so full of life die in captivity.

"I have to perform a surgery—to cut off the infected appendix from the healthy body of my family. It will be painful, but quick. I have to have courage to do it!

"Death is the greatest of life's teachers. It is only the ignorant and those who are afraid to live who fear it. The wise accept Death as their intimate friend and most gracious teacher. To be fully active and fully functioning as a person, we must make death a lifelong friend! What else is to say? There is nothing left! My life, my dreams, my fairy-tales are finished. I am leaving quietly, 'English-style,' without slamming the doors."

Zachary concluded his note with a rhyme from his favorite Dr. Seuss book, which he recalled from memory.

Then we saw him pick up
all the things that were down.

He picked up the cake,
and the rake, and the gown.
And the milk, and the strings,
and the books, and the dish,
and the fan, and the cup,
and the ship, and the fish.
And he put them away.
Then he said, "That is that."
And then he was gone
with the (sic) tip of his hat.

And here the note contained a sketch of the Cat in the Hat himself—smiling as he poised gracefully atop a ball, balancing a book, an umbrella, a fishbowl, and a cup.

Zachary Persitz now became utterly passive as the trial approached. For one thing, he had undergone a series of electroshock treatments, despite fears that the therapy might damage his memory and make him incompetent for trial. For another, he at last understood that even an insanity acquittal didn't mean he would go free. Zachary's only sentiment as the attorneys prepared for trial, Paul Engh says, was "a vague hope that things might get better for him."

On each day of the trial, the Prozumenshikov and Persitz families arrayed themselves on opposite sides of the spectators' gallery. To impartial observers, they resembled guests at a wedding, bride's side to the left and groom's side to the right. But despite the awkward intimacy of the thirty-six-seat gallery, the two sides never spoke. And neither Ellen Prozumenshikov nor Julia Persitz, though their paths crossed often during the four weeks of the trial, so much as nodded at one another.

In the mornings, before things got started, a stifling silence prevailed, punctuated only by occasional whispers and the arraignment proceedings of suspects unrelated to the Persitz case. Drawn to this narrow chamber by loyalty and the most extreme personal anguish of their lives, the Persitz and Prozumenshikov families were obliged to watch a procession of wife beaters and drug dealers go before the bench of Judge Robert Schiefelbein.

The Persitz case was being tried in two parts—the first to establish whether Zachary was guilty of premeditated murder, the second to determine whether he was sane at the time. If the jury acquitted Persitz in the first phase, the second would be unnecessary. Facing overwhelming evidence of premeditation, Joe Friedberg was less than sanguine about this prospect.

Each day at 9:30 A.M., the jury of nine women and three men filed into the courtroom, followed by Schiefelbein, whose lanky frame, white hair, and customary black robe made him a study in ascetism. When everyone was settled, two guards led Zachary himself into the courtroom through a rear door to the table he shared with Friedberg and Engh.

The first week of the trial featured a devastating presentation of the state's evidence against Persitz. Kevin Johnson sought to prove that Zack had planned the crime in advance; Friedberg, to demonstrate that it was a spontaneous crime of passion.

Ellen and Julia sat quietly throughout the testimony, even when witnesses described finding the body parts. Most of this the two women already knew. Only when the guards wheeled out a slide projector and pulled down the silver screen facing the jury box did Ellen and Julia both rise, with most of their friends and family, and file silently out of the courtroom. Michael's mother, Ida, remained. From the hallway, people could hear her wailing as the first of the slides of her son's dismembered body flashed onto the screen.

But as damning as the prosecution's evidence was, it was merely a prelude to the most important single component of the trial: Zachary's testimony in his own defense, which began on Monday, June 21, 1993.

As his name was called, Persitz rose from his seat and plodded, in his ill-fitting gray suit, to the witness stand. His eyes were rheumy and vacant. It surprised no one to learn that Zachary had been under the influence of tranquilizers throughout the trial.

He raised his right hand to take the oath, and then Friedberg began, leading him, as planned, through an account of his immigration and early life in the United States. The two of them moved quickly through the years, as Persitz described his first meeting with Michael Prozumenshikov. He told how Michael had aggressively pursued him as a client, disputing Ellen Prozumenshikov's earlier testimony that her husband had been reluctant to mix business and friendship. He described Michael's guarantee to make his money grow at a rate of 18 percent a year without substantial risk. He told of the shame of his financial ruin.

This was the easy part, merely the buildup, but it served to calm Persitz on the stand. Now he continued as Friedberg prompted him through to the evening of January 28, 1991. Zachary's account was slow and methodical, as if speaking required a prodigious effort.

Michael had accompanied him willingly into his car that night, he said. There Zachary asserted that Michael owed him a total of $200,000, based on the stockbroker's pledge of an 18 percent annual return. Zachary wanted Michael to sign an agreement promising to pay him that sum.

It been Prozumenshikov's idea, Persitz testified, to try to raise the $200,000 that night. The two of them had been at this for hours, phoning Michael's clients and his boss, Jim Tallen, from a drive-up pay phone at a nearby shopping mall. At one point they bought fast food at a McDonalds drive-through and ate it in the car, Persitz said. Finally, giving up on the futile quest for $200,000, they drove back to the lot where Michael's car was parked. When they got there, Persitz stepped down on the accelerator, raced through the lot and drove straight out onto the frozen surface of Lake Minnetonka. That was the moment, Persitz said, that he produced the .357 magnum revolver.

Speaking as evenly as when he described his immigration to the United States, Persitz admitted brandishing the gun and forcing Prozumenshikov to put on a pair of handcuffs. The real trouble, Zachary said, had begun after Michael asked to have the handcuffs removed because he couldn't sign an agreement while wearing them. And at that point, rather than signing the agreement Persitz had prepared, Prozumenshikov declared that he had to "take a piss," Zachary testified.

The two of them had climbed out of the car and urinated, not far from one another, on the frozen lake, he said. They could see lights in the windows of the mansions lining Lake Minnetonka—the mansions that had so inspired Michael Prozumenshikov as a young stockbroker just starting out. At the moment, Persitz said, the gun was in his coat pocket. Suddenly, he said, Michael began walking quickly toward his car, which was parked about three hundred yards away. Persitz jumped back into his own car and wheeled around to intercept Prozumenshikov. Michael couldn't run in his flat-soled leather shoes. "He was like a duck on the ice," Persitz said in his monotone.

Standing only a few yards apart, the two men began shouting at one another, Zachary went on. "I was calling him a crook, different names," he said. "He was calling me a dirty Russian immigrant, you know, the same like everybody else, something like that. And he was shouting at me that I am just jealous of his success and stuff. And I told him that this is all bullshit because I never was jealous of him, I never would want to work like him, to do to people what he does. Anyway, the arguments were getting hotter and hotter. I sent him to hell; he sent me to hell."

As Persitz spoke, the weeping of Michael Prozumenshikov's mother became audible from the spectators' gallery. Near her mother-in-law, Ellen Prozumenshikov sat watching Persitz, her arms crossed in front of her. She looked very tired, as though she had been crying recently, but there were no tears on her face.

"We were shouting for another few minutes," Zachary continued, "and then at the very end he shout at me in Russian. He shouted at me—" Here Persitz broke off his testimony and, much louder, spoke a phrase in Russian. "It means," he continued in English, "I fuck you and fuck your family.

"And then what happened is that I was looking at him, I saw his lips moving and he was close, but I couldn't hear what he was saying. Everything was very quiet around me, and then I was feeling that my head hurts from the cold.

"I looked around me and I didn't see Michael. I looked down and he was laying on the snow. And I had gun in my right hand, so I couldn't believe it. I bent down on my knees, and his body was all limp. He didn't breathe. And I was in such a rage for what he made me do, so I pulled him into the car onto the driver's seat, which was—the car was parked—pull him on the driver's side, and I shot him a second time."

Now, from the spectators' gallery, moans and exaggerated scoffs were heard. To Kevin Johnson, as he sat at the prosecution table, it seemed obvious that Persitz was lying—crafting his story to fit the evidence the police had found, including the blood and urine in his car.

"The only rational explanation that I see," Persitz continued, heedless of the noise from the gallery, "is that I was very mad at him for what he was trying to do—what he was doing to me. Then I didn't know what to do with his body. I sat there, I cried, then I drove home." Prompted by

Friedberg, Persitz added, "I moved him from the driver's seat into the passenger's seat."

When he arrived at home, Persitz said, he saw Rudy Lehkter's car. So he turned around and drove back in the direction from which he had come. He stopped at a nearby park and left Prozumenshikov's body there, he said. Then he returned to his house.

After quarreling with Julia, Zachary spent most of the night in the garage, he testified, wondering what he ought to do. At about 5 A.M., he left the house. "I went to Meadow Park to see if the body is still there," he said. "I had terrible dreams. I mean, I was wondering if it happened. So I went to see the body, and picked it up and I decided to bury him."

Persitz heaved Michael's corpse into the trunk of his car, he testified, and drove east on Highway 94 toward Wisconsin. "In my head I had this silly commercial, 'Escape to Wisconsin,' somehow. And I thought, well, that's where I'm going to escape to." Instead, he wound up in rural Washington County, just inside the Minnesota state line. "I had lots of thoughts, not very coherent thoughts," he said. "It was like I didn't believe it was happening. I was just driving like a robot."

Persitz saw a sign for a compost disposal site. He crashed through the steel gate, he said, because he couldn't see it in the dark. "I was planning to dig a grave and put the body there in the grave," he said. "I had shovel from my garage along with me, and I tried to dig a hole in the ground. I couldn't, because it was all frozen solid." He said he tried digging with a hatchet as well, but it didn't work.

Now, in the front row of the spectators' gallery, Ellen Prozumenshikov looked down at the floor. A group of newspaper reporters, who had been scribbling frantically throughout Zachary's narrative, now stopped and looked up as Persitz described what happened next.

"I had a big fear," Persitz went on, "that Michael would be coming back to haunt me. I decided that I should separate parts of his body so that he wouldn't be able to come together again and haunt me. So that's why I separated his legs and put them into this pile of brush that was at the site there. And I put them separately, too, one in the top, one in the middle. And I buried his body in the snow down there."

In response to a question from Friedberg, Persitz said he cut off Michael's head and hands with the hatchet because he didn't want the body to be identified.

"I was crying," Persitz continued, stammering now, "and I was shivering like I'd never been before in my life, and I was imagining that I'm just cutting . . . cutting a piece of wood, and I just. . . . It was making me sick, the smell and the view of the body."

Now, in the gallery, Ellen Prozumenshikov's lifted her gaze from the floor and stared straight at Zachary Persitz. Her expression was pure fury. Michael's mother, Ida, glanced at Ellen and shook her head in commiseration.

Winding down now, exhaling audibly, Persitz described leaving the compost site and driving north, hurling his hatchet and other tools from the car as he went. At Taylor's Falls, he said, he dumped Michael's head and hands into the St. Croix River, and tried to do the same with the broker's Rolex watch. Despite the fierce wind and subzero temperature, he was driving with his windows open, because of the stench of urine in the car. Even so, said, he gagged several times and had to stop to relieve himself by eating snow.

When Friedberg finished with Persitz, Kevin Johnson rose to begin his cross-examination. His mission, in addition to hammering the weak points in Zachary's account of the killing, was to eliminate any sense of sympathy the jury might have for the defendant.

"Mr. Persitz," Johnson said, "correct me if I'm wrong, but from the way you just testified, you believe you're the real victim in this case, don't you?"

"In a way," Persitz said, "yes."

"Now, you're fairly intelligent, well educated, is that correct?"

"Yes."

"You have a degree in engineering?"

"Yes."

"Speak three languages?"

"Yeah."

"And as a matter of fact, you've been preparing yourself for your testimony today for over two years, haven't you?"

"Not really," Persitz said. "I was just trying to have this trial as quick as possible. I wasn't waiting for this amount of time."

"Now as part of the discovery process in this case," Johnson went on, seemingly oblivious to Zachary's protestations, "all the police reports, grand jury transcripts, all this has been made available to you, hasn't it?"

Here Joe Friedberg objected, but the damage was done. Simply but effectively, Johnson had sketched out his own skepticism about Zachary's account of the killing. Next, the prosecutor got Persitz to admit that he had asked the police officers who arrested him about the penalties for various homicide charges—and that Zachary had prepared for trial by reading the grand jury testimony of police and others that led to his indictment.

Next, turning his own assertions into questions, Johnson suggested that Persitz had intended to kill Prozumenshikov from the moment he accosted him and that he had been holding a gun to Michael's head as the stockbroker phoned his wife and clients. Otherwise, Johnson asked Persitz, why didn't Michael tell Ellen he was with Zachary when he called?

"Michael probably felt embarrassed because of my financial situation," Zachary responded. "And every time when he was embarrassed by his clients, at least Russian clients, he would tell different stories to his wife."

For more than an hour, Johnson grilled Persitz about the details of killing Michael and cutting up his body. He asked what tools Zachary used to dismember the corpse. He forced Persitz to hold up a photograph of the body parts and explain, in his dispassionate tone, that the ragged slashes in the flesh were the strikes of a hatchet rather than the rips of a saw.

Zachary Persitz had much more to say that afternoon before he was allowed to step down from the witness stand.

He described hiring the staff of the Downtowner Car Wash to clean his trunk. He told of the days that followed the killing, of disbelief, of weeping when Daniel Prozumenshikov came to stay at his house.

When finally excused, Persitz paused for a moment before leaving his perch. Then he began to move—slowly, very carefully, as if afraid of falling. As he shuffled back toward the defense table, hanging his head, he seemed very frail.

Zachary cleared his throat and glanced out at the faces in the spectators' gallery, searching for Julia.

He found her, and for a single moment their eyes met. Then two armed guards rose from their seats and started toward Persitz.

How had it come to this? Briefly, Zachary raised his hand in the direction of the only woman he had ever loved. Julia smiled in return. She could still smile at him, even now. The guards took Persitz by both his arms. Firmly, they led him toward the rear of the courtroom.

When Zachary glanced back over his shoulder, Julia was still smiling.

EPILOGUE

The jury found Zachary Persitz guilty of first-degree murder. After a second, shorter stage of the trial, in which psychiatrists for the state and the defense presented their predictably contradictory interpretations of Zachary's mental health, the jury found Persitz accountable for his actions despite his plea of insanity.

Judge Robert Schiefelbein sentenced him to life in prison. Minnesota law requires Persitz to serve a minimum of thirty years, regardless of his behavior behind bars. He will not be eligible for parole until February 4, 2021—three days before his seventieth birthday.

In July 1993, Zachary entered Stillwater Prison on the St. Croix River, five miles from where he dismembered Michael Prozumenshikov's body. From there he was transferred to Oak Park Heights, a maximum-security prison built into a hillside in rural Minnesota. Authorities use the facility to house the most violent of all criminals and those who are considered escape or suicide risks. All visitors to Oak Park Heights must remove their belts and shoes and pass through two metal detectors before entering.

Julia Persitz lives in a small townhouse in the Minneapolis suburb of Plymouth with her sons, Daniel and Jonathan. She continues to play and teach violin for a living.

Not far away, Ellen Prozumenshikov lives with her boys, Daniel and Ariel, in the house that she and Michael shared. She still works as a dental hygienist.

On the last day of the murder trial, Ellen presented Judge Schiefelbein with a letter, asking that it be entered as part of the official court record. It told of Ellen and Michael's immigration to a new country, their struggle to build a new life, and her husband's love for his family.

"For our family this tragedy never ends," Ellen wrote, "but today we close a chapter. Michael delighted in life and would want us to do the same. This family will heal. We'll move along with our lives now, keeping him close in our hearts, and Michael may rest in peace."

AUTHOR'S NOTE

This book is the product of more than 250 interviews with Michael Prozumenshikov's colleagues, clients and friends, conducted from January 1991 through November 1993. I also used hundreds of documents, including police reports, court and grand jury transcripts, stock trading records, state and U.S. government documents, and Prozumenshikov's academic records, which are on file in St. Petersburg, Russia, once called Leningrad.

Executives of Prudential Securities, Inc., formerly called Prudential-Bache Securities, declined through a spokesman to be interviewed for this book. Jim Tallen, Michael Prozumenshikov's supervisor at Prudential's Wayzata, Minnesota, branch office, also declined repeated requests for an interview. Quotations attributed to Tallen come from police reports and his testimony in court.

William Ahearn, the Prudential Securities spokesman in New York, supplied general information about the firm, such as its profits and losses. But Ahearn declined to respond to a series of questions about Prozumenshikov's business practices, the complaints of his former clients and what Prudential did about them.

Ellen Prozumenshikov, Michael Prozumenshikov's wife, decided not to be interviewed for the book. But she did grant an interview for the *Wall Street Journal* article on which it is based. Quotations and other material attributed to Ellen Prozumenshikov come from this interview and from her grand jury and court testimony and her talks with police officers and prosecutors.

Through his attorneys, Zachary Persitz declined to be interviewed in jail. But he authorized his lawyers and their private investigator to speak freely about the details of his case, which they did, in numerous interviews spanning a period of more than two years. Julia Persitz, Zachary's wife, also granted three in-person interviews and spoke on other occasions over the telephone. I interviewed Alex Shifrin, Zachary's brother, about Zachary's childhood. Material attributed to Persitz comes from these and other conversations, his testimony in court, police reports, and reports prepared by psychiatrists who interviewed him personally.

Direct quotations included in the book come from the speaker, someone who heard the statement or from documents and transcripts. Where possible, I corroborated quotations by checking independently with more than one person who heard the remarks. In a few cases, I used quotations from other publications. In each of those cases, I cited the publication in the text of the book.

INDEX